Voyages in English

Writing and Grammar

Loyola Press

Carolyn Marie Dimick
General Editor

Marie T. McVey
Revision Editor

Carolyn Marie Dimick
Susan Mary Platt
Joan I. Rychalsky
Margaret O'Toole
Midge Stocker
Authors

Editorial

Margaret O'Leary Coyle

Catherine Marcic Joyce

Contributors

Beth Duncan

Elizabeth Cook Fresen

Diane Gonciarz

Karen M. Harrington

Cathy Ann Tell

Patricia Walsh

Richard Weisenseel

Production

Mary Bowers

Genevieve Kelley

Ellie Knepler

Anne Marie Mastandrea

Carla Jean Mayer

Julia Mayer

Molly O'Halloran

Jill Smith

Leslie Uriss

Cover Design

Steve Straus, Think Design

Cover Art

Paul Rendel,
Soaring in the Rockies

 Loyola Press

3441 North Ashland Avenue
Chicago, Illinois 60657
1-800-621-1008

ISBN 0-8294-0996-3

©1988, 1995, 1999 Loyola Press

Printed in the United States of America

01 02   5 4

Table of Contents

Part I *Written and Oral Communication*

Table of Contents

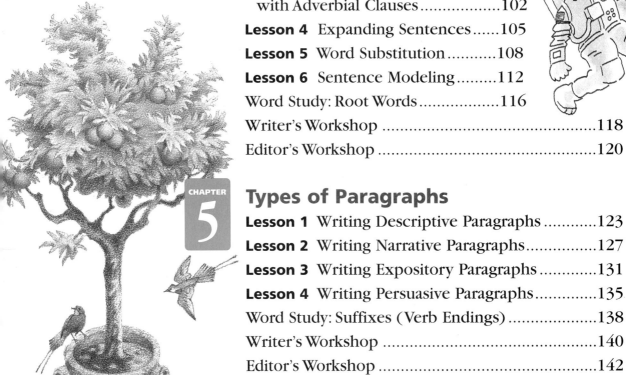

Writing Across the Curriculum

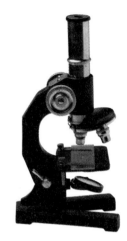

Creative Tools for Writing

Letter Writing

Table of Contents

Part II Grammar, Usage, and Mechanics

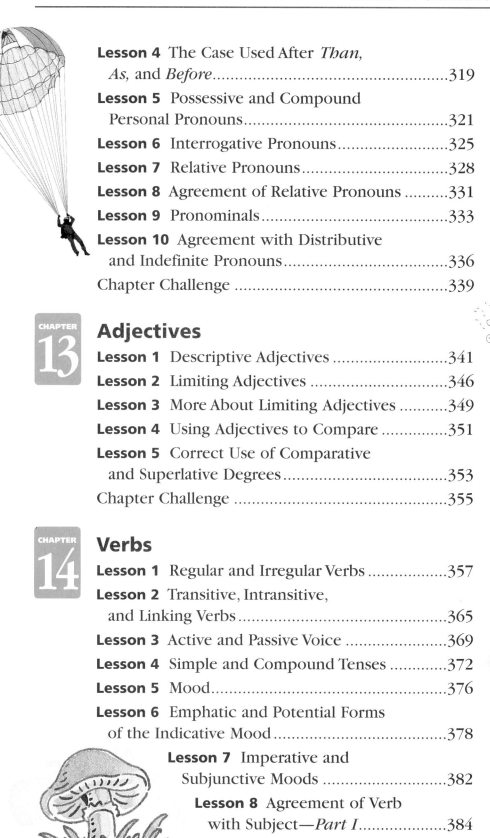

CHAPTER 15 — Verbals: Participles, Gerunds, Infinitives

CHAPTER 16 — Adverbs

CHAPTER 17 — Prepositions, Conjunctions, Interjections

CHAPTER 18 Phrases, Clauses, Sentences

CHAPTER 19 Punctuation and Capitalization

CHAPTER 20 Model Diagrams

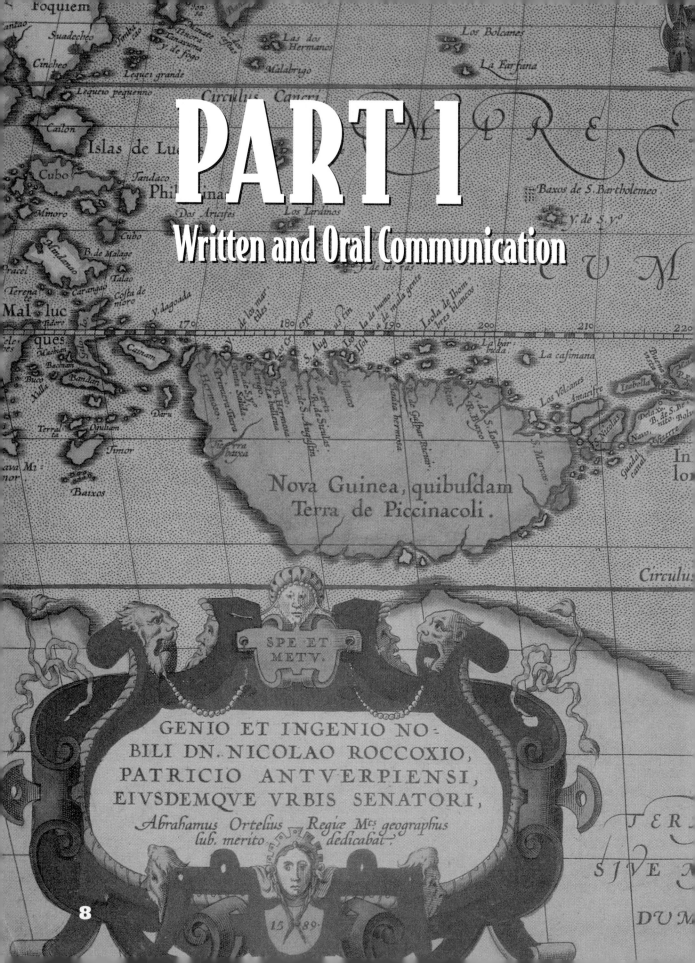

PART 1
Written and Oral Communication

Noua Hispania.

Meſſico.

SI

Iamaica

Circulus Aequinoctialis

Prima ego velivolis ambivi cursibus Orbem,
Magellane novo te duce ducta freto.
Ambivi, meritoǵ vocor VICTORIA, sunt mi
Vela, alæ, precium, gloria, pugna, mare.

Cum privilegijs Imp. & Reg. Maieſtatum,
nec non Cancellariæ Brabantiæ, ad decennium.

CHAPTER 1

Writing a Biographical Sketch

The selection beginning on the next page is an excerpt from the book *Anastasia's Album.* It tells about the life of the Grand Duchess Anastasia, one of the five children of Nicholas II, the last tsar, or king, of Russia.

The book is a biography that uses letters and diary entries to add meaningful details. There are also many personal photographs of the royal Romanovs that show the private life of this very public family.

As you read, pay attention to the facts of Anastasia's life and how the young girl was affected by historical events in Russia. Note that the biographer writes events in chronological order and uses Anastasia's own words and those of other family members to help tell her story. You will want to use some of these same techniques when you write a short biography, or biographical sketch, while following the steps of the writing process.

an excerpt from

Anastasia's Album

by Hugh Brewster

It was spring 1901. Even in the chilly Russian capital of St. Petersburg, the ice had melted on the canals, and the lilacs were in bloom. On days when the wind blew away the fog, the city's magnificent cathedrals and mansions glistened along the broad avenues and canals. All over Russia, people welcomed the end of another long winter.

There were many reasons to be hopeful this year. The entire country awaited the birth of a baby. Tsar Nicholas II and his wife, Alexandra, were expecting their fourth child. The tsar and tsarina already had three beautiful, rosy-cheeked daughters, but in Russia only males could rule. So this time Nicholas and Alexandra wished for a boy, who would be heir to the throne.

On Wednesday, June 18, a healthy child was born in the imperial family's summer villa on the seashore north of St. Petersburg. When Tsar Nicholas heard that the child was a girl, he went for a long walk by himself. Then he put a smile on his face and went in to kiss his wife and newborn baby. Her name was Anastasia, and she was the newest of the Romanovs—the family that ruled the biggest country on earth.

The Romanov's on the deck of the *Standart.*

By the time she was three, Anastasia was a blue-eyed whirlwind, running and playing on the palace grounds. She already had a mind and personality of her own. Noisy and fearless, she rarely cried, even when she hurt herself. She was the baby of the family, adored by her parents and sisters.

(Left) Anastasia swinging while on a family outing; *(Right)* Building a human pyramid with her father and an officer.

But Russia still had no heir to the throne. During the summer of 1904, as Alexandra prepared to give birth to her fifth child, everyone in the household wanted only one thing: a boy who would carry on the mighty Romanov dynasty. On August 12, Alexandra felt pains during lunch and went upstairs to her bedroom. That evening Nicholas wrote in his diary: "A great, never-to-be-forgotten day. . . . At 1:15 this afternoon Alexandra gave birth to a son, whom in prayer we have called Alexei."

In cities and towns throughout the vast land, church bells rang, cannons roared, and there was great rejoicing. But for many Russians the birth of an heir to the throne was not a reason to celebrate. They were becoming impatient with the rule of the tsar and wanted Russia to have a more democratic government. Changes were desperately needed in Russia. But Nicholas said that those who wanted reform were "senseless dreamers." Like all the tsars before him, he believed that God had given him the right to reign. He felt that with the simple goodwill and faith of the people, the Romanovs would continue to rule Russia as they had for almost three hundred years. He was to be proven wrong.

The Romanovs had a warm and intimate family life, but in many ways it was strict, too. The four grand duchesses slept on hard camp cots with no pillows, just as their father had done when he was a boy. Every morning they made their own beds and had a cold bath in a tub made of solid silver.

In those days girls of the upper classes were expected to learn only the skills that would help them pass the time once they were married—how to play the piano, sketch flowers, and do a little needlework. But the girls' mother demanded more. The children studied four languages—Russian, English, French, and German. Alexandra carefully chose books for them to read and supervised their music lessons.

Anastasia knitting.

Every afternoon the whole family gathered for tea. The girls wore fresh ribbons in their hair and clean white dresses with colored sashes. They would wait impatiently for their father's arrival.

Tea was one of the few times during the day that the children saw their father, but they understood why. After all, he was probably one of the most important people in the world.

To the outside world Tsar Nicholas was the ruler of millions, but to his children he was simply their beloved father. He was handsome and gentle, and he never raised his voice. The girls spent hours making drawings and paintings for him and writing little notes, carefully trying to do their best work to please him.

Anastasia spending time with her father.

On August 1, 1914, the tsar arrived home very late for dinner. His face was pale. In a quiet, sad voice he told his wife that Russia was now at war with Germany and Austria. Alexandra burst into tears and ran from the room. Before her marriage to Nicholas, she had been a German princess. Now her home country was an enemy. The First World War had begun.

Alexandra was determined to do all she could to help Russia win the war. She and her two eldest daughters trained as nurses and worked long hours in military hospitals. Anastasia and Marie were too young to become nurses, but they regularly visited wounded soldiers at a small hospital near the Alexander Palace. "I sat today with one of our soldiers and helped him to learn to read," Anastasia wrote to her father. "Two more soldiers died yesterday. We were still with them."

By the autumn of 1916, more and more people were unhappy with the tsar, the tsarina, and the government. Russian soldiers were dying by the millions in the war. At home their families were going hungry. But Nicholas and Alexandra and their children were not aware of the terrible storm that was approaching.

An icy wind howled outside the Alexander Palace on the night of March 13, 1917. Anastasia looked out her window at a huge gun that soldiers guarding the palace had set up in the courtyard. "How astonished Papa will be," she whispered. Her father was expected back from the *stavka* early the next morning. In the distance Anastasia could hear shouting and gunfire. Her mother had told her that the soldiers were just doing military exercises. Alexandra did not want to frighten her children with the truth. She knew that strikes and rioting in St. Petersburg had spread and that angry mobs were threatening to attack the palace. She did not yet know that a revolution had started.

stavka: an old Russian word for an army camp, used to refer to the Russian army headquarters

But it would be over a week before her father returned. And when he did he was no longer the tsar. Members of the *Duma* had formed their own government in St. Petersburg. To prevent further rioting and bloodshed they had asked Nicholas to give up his throne. At the urging of his generals he had agreed. The Romanov family had ruled Russia for over three hundred years. Now Nicholas Romanov was just an ordinary citizen—and a prisoner in his own palace.

Anastasia and her family hoped they would be allowed to live at their beloved palace at Livadia. But instead they learned they were being sent to Siberia. Early on the morning of August 14, the family left the Alexander Palace for the last time.

After a week of travel, the family arrived in the town of Tobolsk. There they lived under guard in a large white house from August 1917 until May 1918. Although the house was cold in the winter and the food was plain, their lives were not unbearable. The girls sewed, embroidered, read, and acted in plays for the family's amusement. Alexei was allowed to play with some local boys, although sickness sometimes kept him in bed. In his diary he often wrote, "Today passed just as yesterday. . . . It is boring!"

In November 1917 the radical Bolshevik party led by Vladimir Ilyich Lenin seized power in St. Petersburg. Lenin hated the tsar. In April 1918, a Bolshevik official arrived at the house and told Nicholas that he had come to take him from Tobolsk. Marie was chosen to go with her parents. The other three girls would stay behind to look after Alexei. The next day at dawn, Anastasia and her sisters watched as their parents and Marie climbed into filthy horse-drawn carts and were escorted away by soldiers. Then they climbed the stairs to their room in tears.

"I want to see you so much it's sad," Anastasia wrote to her parents and sister who were now in Ekaterinburg. "In our thoughts, we are with you all the time." Finally on May 23, 1918, the children were allowed to join their parents. "What great joy it was to see them and embrace them again!" Nicholas wrote in his diary on that day.

The family would live for only two months more. But for now they were together. And that was all that mattered.

Duma: the Russian parliament

Epilogue

All the members of the family, the tsar and tsarina and their five children, were executed by the revolutionists. It is said that the remains of Alexei and Anastasia have never been positively identified. Could one or both of them have escaped somehow?

Anastasia

TALK IT OVER

1. What do you think Alexandra's motives were for raising Anastasia and her sisters in the ways she did?

2. Do you agree that Anastasia was a sensitive girl? Explain your thinking, giving examples from the literature excerpt.

3. Why do you think the revolutionists executed the children as well as the tsar and tsarina?

4. If the Romanovs had stayed in power, what role do you think Anastasia would have played within the family? Publicly?

5. Put yourself in the place of a young member of any royal family. What are some advantages you would have in your life? Some disadvantages?

Biography

In *Anastasia's Album,* the author tells about the short but happy life of Tsar Nicholas II's youngest daughter. He describes Anastasia physically and tells about the kind of person she was. He uses diaries, letters, and other primary resources to reveal Anastasia's thoughts and feelings and those of other members of her family. Although the book is named for Anastasia, it gives biographical information on all the Romanovs—Anastasia's sisters, brother, mother, and father.

The family members' lives were directly affected by their position and the turbulent history of their country. The author skillfully weaves the historical events into his narrative.

A good biography

- focuses on an interesting subject—a person of public importance or a person held in high personal regard by the author.
- contains accurate, factual information.
- presents events in chronological order with dates.
- makes ample use of primary resources—diaries, photos, letters, and so on.
- places the subject's life in a context that helps readers understand his or her actions and motives.

Take a Closer Look

REREAD Reread the excerpt from *Anastasia's Album.* **Then respond to the items below.**

1. Do you think Anastasia Romanov is a suitable subject for a biography? Explain your thinking.
2. Make a character map about Anastasia. Place her name in the center oval of your map. Then in surrounding ovals, record as many adjectives as you can that describe Anastasia. Think about her appearance, her personality, and her behaviors.
3. Based on your completed map, state your overall impression of Anastasia.

DISCUSS Talk over your responses to the items on page 18 with a partner or in a small group. Take a look at the adjectives listed below. How many of them did you include in your character map about Anastasia?

energetic	willful	well-educated
unspoiled	fearless	kind
artistic	loving	adaptable
resourceful	lonely	pretty
beloved	obedient	mannered
caring	dutiful	socially responsible
accepting	good-humored	strong

PRACTICE Read this very brief biography, or biographical sketch. Identify the primary resource materials used to create the sketch. Then say what the most obvious difference is between this biography and the biography about Anastasia.

Grandmother Winslow

My grandmother, Helen Winslow, is an amazing woman. She was born on June 4, 1924. Her date of birth is carefully recorded in the family Bible. When she was only nineteen, she joined the armed services and served in World War II. She recalls that time "as the greatest experience of my life." Later, she raised a family and ran her own business. To this day, my grandmother has sparkling green eyes and is always wearing a smile. Her face is as bright and as warm as it was in those photos taken of her as a new bride and young mother. Next to an album of photos, my family counts among its most prized possessions a journal my grandmother kept as a high-school student. In it she recorded this advice offered to her by her mother: If your heart is healthy and happy, you will not feel age grow on you, nor will you reflect it.

Biographical Sketch

Prewriting
Drafting
Revising
Proofreading
Publishing

Here's a short biography, or biographical sketch, written by Marcie, an eighth grader, for a class assignment. This is her final, published version. Read it carefully. Then take a look on the following pages to see how Marcie developed her biographical sketch by following the steps of the writing process.

John Wesley Powell

Geologist, explorer, and writer John Wesley Powell is one of the West's forgotten heroes. He was born in Mt. Morris, New York, in 1834. His family moved to Illinois where he became involved with the Natural History Society. Powell served in the Civil War in the Union army and lost his right arm at the Battle of Shiloh.

After the war, Powell taught geology in Illinois. He organized an expedition down the Colorado River and through the Grand Canyon. No one had gone all the way down this twisting, rocky river before. It was a risky and dangerous undertaking.

On May 24, 1869, Powell and nine men started down the river in four boats. Months later they entered the Grand Canyon. "We are three-quarters of a mile in the depths of the earth," Powell wrote in his journal, "and the great river shrinks into insignificance, as it dashes its angry waves against the walls and cliffs, that rise to the world above. . . ."

Along the way, four men had deserted. Three of them were later killed by Native Americans. Ninety-nine days after starting out, Powell and the five remaining men returned to civilization.

Powell wrote a book describing the wonders he had seen. He later served as head of the U.S. Geological Survey and was a good friend to Native Americans. He was one of the first white people to study their culture seriously. John Wesley Powell died in 1902, but his memory lives on in the mighty river that he explored.

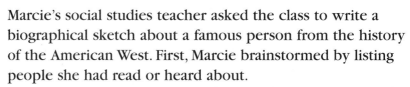

Prewriting
Drafting
Revising
Proofreading
Publishing

STEP 1

Prewriting

Marcie's social studies teacher asked the class to write a biographical sketch about a famous person from the history of the American West. First, Marcie brainstormed by listing people she had read or heard about.

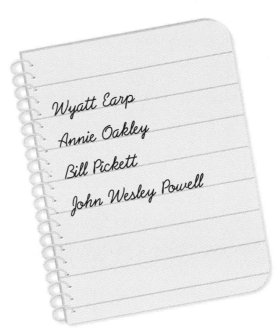

Wyatt Earp

Annie Oakley

Bill Pickett

John Wesley Powell

Marcie went over each name on her list. She decided Wyatt Earp was someone her teacher and classmates would already know something about. Annie Oakley interested her, but on her first visit to the library, she didn't find very much about her. She admired Bill Pickett, the African American rodeo star, but then found out her best friend had already chosen to write about him. John Wesley Powell was courageous, like Bill Pickett and Annie Oakley. But he was also a scientist and writer. Because he wrote a lot, Marcie could use his writings as a primary resource in her sketch. Marcie was confident that Powell would make a great subject for her biographical sketch.

Try It!

▶ About whom would you write a biographical sketch?
Brainstorm a list of possibilities. Then ask yourself:

- Is this person someone who interests me and will interest my audience?
- Did this person achieve something important in his or her life? What obstacles did he or she have to overcome?
- Can I find enough information about this person at the library and through other sources?
- Can I find primary resources about this person, such as diaries, letters, autobiographies, or speeches?

▶ Use your answers to the questions above to help you narrow down your list to the best topic. Mark your choice with a check mark.

Now that Marcie had a person for her sketch, she went to the library and began her research. Some sources she used for information about John Wesley Powell included encyclopedias, a biographical dictionary, books about the West, articles from history magazines, and Powell's own writings.

A	B	C-D	E	F-G	H	I	J-K	L
1	2	3	4	5	6	7	8	9

M	N-O	P	Q-R	S	T-U	V-W	X-Y-Z	Index
10	11	12	13	14	15	16	17	18

Marcie took notes on what she read in her research and organized her notes into the following outline.

John Wesley Powell

I. Early life

A. Born in New York in 1834

B. Fought in Civil War as Union officer

C. Taught geology in Illinois

II. Exploration years

A. Led pioneering expedition

1. First to go length of Colorado River

2. First to go through the Grand Canyon

B. Deserted by four men on team

C. Wrote book about experiences

III. Later life

A. Headed the U.S. Geological Survey

B. Studied and defended Native Americans

C. Died in 1902

Try It!

▶ Look back at the biographical subject you checked off for Try It! on page 23. Do a quick preliminary search of materials you might use if you were writing a short biography. Try to visualize how you would organize your information. Would you use an outline? Or, would you use a word map, a series of lists, or a time line? Talk over your ideas with a partner.

Using Primary Resources to Prewrite

When you are researching information for a biographical sketch, look for primary resources. They can enliven your biography and give unique insights into your subject. Primary resources can include

- letters, diaries, journals, and books written by the person.
- newspaper and magazine articles written at the time of the person's life.
- memoirs, biographies, and autobiographies.
- speeches and interviews in print, on audiotape, or on videotape.

If the person is alive and you know him or her personally, you might be able to conduct a live interview. If the person lives far away, you might conduct your interview on the phone, over the Internet, or in a letter with the questions you would like answered. This personal contact is an invaluable primary resource and will make your biography all the more interesting for your readers.

When using a primary source, you should always

- quote the source directly.
- place quotation marks around the direct quote.
- be sure to credit the primary resource in your writing.

PRACTICE Think about what primary resources you might use to research each of the following people for a biographical sketch.

- a famous writer no longer living
- a contemporary sports figure
- a well-known politician
- your uncle who is a scientist

STEP 2

Drafting

Marcie used the information from her outline and research notes to write the first draft of her short biography. She wrote without pausing because she knew any mistakes could be fixed later. Take a look at Marcie's first draft.

Geolojist John Wesley Powell was born in 1834. His family later moved to Illinois he became invovled with the Natural History Society. Powell served in the civil war in the Union Army and lost his right arm at the battle of Shiloh.

After the war, Powell taught Geology in Illinois. He organized a journey down the colorado river and thru the Grand Canyon. No one had gone all the way down the river before.

On May 24 1869 Powell and nine men started down the river in some boats. months later they entered the Grand Canyon. We are three-quarters of a mile in the depths of the earth, Powell wrote in his journal. and the great river shrinks into insignificance, as it dashes its angry waves against the walls and cliffs, that rise to the world above. . . ."Ninety-9 days after starting out, Powell and the five remaining men returned to civiliqtion.

Powell wrote a book describing the wonders he had seen. Soon, the Grand Canyon would become a national park. He later served as head of the U S Geologikal Survey and was a good friend to Native americans. He was one of the first people to study there culture seriously. John Wesley Powell was a great American.

Marcie looked over her first draft. She saw a number of places where she could improve her biographical sketch. She felt it would help to get some other opinions of her writing. She decided to have a peer group conference.

 ## Peer to Peer

Marcie asked Sally, Calvin, and Donna to read her first draft. Then they all met with Marcie. Here's what each of them had to say.

Sally: I like your biographical sketch. John Wesley Powell sounds like a great person. But your opening is not very exciting. Maybe you could list some of his other accomplishments up front. That would get the reader's interest right away. Also, you need a title.

Calvin: I was really interested in Powell's story, but something bothers me. You write that Powell and nine men started out on the expedition. Then you later say that Powell returned with the remaining five men. What happened to the other four men? I really want to know!

> **Tip #1**
>
> Listen to and consider all suggestions made in a peer conference. You can always reject the ones you don't agree with later.

Donna: I have two things to say. First, I think the sentence about the Grand Canyon becoming a national park is out of place and confusing. I'd drop it or move it to the very end of your sketch. Second, you don't tell us when Powell died. I'd like to know that. By the way, I thought the quote from Powell's journal was great.

Marcie listened to all her friends' suggestions. She was pleased to hear what they liked about her writing. But she listened carefully to what they thought could be improved, too. She took notes on what they said and began work on her next draft. Now she was ready to

- revise her opening.
- fill in important details she had left out.
- take a second look at how she described things.

DISCUSS What changes would you suggest to Marcie that weren't mentioned in the peer conference?

Revising

When you revise something you've written, you improve it. Marcie took her friends' advice and changed several things. Read her revised draft below and compare it to the first draft.

Editor's Marks

∧ Add
⊱ Cut
↫ Move
⟋ Replace
¶ New paragraph

Geolojist John Wesley Powell ⌃explorer, and writer ⌃is one of the West's forgotten heroes. He was born in ⌃1834. His family later moved to Illinois ⌄where he became invoulved with the Natural History ⌃Mt. Morris, New York in Society. Powell served in the civil war in the Union Army and lost his right arm at the battle of Shiloh.

After the war, Powell taught Geology in Illinois. He expedition organized a ~~journey~~ down the colorado river and thru the Grand this twisting, rocky Canyon. No one had gone all the way down ⌃the river before. It was a risky and dangerous undertaking.

On May 24 1869 Powell and nine men started down the four river in ~~some~~ boats. months later they entered the Grand Canyon. We are three-quarters of a mile in the depths of the earth, Powell wrote in his journal. and the great river shrinks into insignificance, as it dashes its angry waves against the walls and cliffs, that rise to the world above. . . ." ¶Along the way, four men had deserted. Three of them were Ninety-9 days after starting out, Powell and later killed by the five remaining men returned to civiliztion. Native Americans.

Powell wrote a book describing the wonders he had seen. ~~Soon, the Grand Canyon would become a national park.~~ He later served as head of the U S Geologikal Survey and was a good friend white to Native americans. He was one of the first ⌃people to study there died in 1902 but his memory lives on in culture seriously. John Wesley Powell ~~was a great American~~ the mighty river that he explored.

Take a Closer Look

Now compare your thoughts about Marcie's revisions with the comments in the chart below.

Marcie's First Draft	Marcie's Revision	Comments
Geolojist John Wesley Powell was born in 1834.	Geolojist, explorer, and writer John Wesley Powell is one of the West's forgotten heroes. He was born in Mt. Morris, New York in 1834.	Marcie came up with a stronger beginning sentence, picking up on Sally's suggestion. She also included the place where Powell was born.
Ninety-9 days after starting out, Powell and the five remaining men returned to civiliztion.	Along the way, four men had deserted. Three of them were later killed by Native Americans. Ninety-9 days after starting out, Powell and the five remaining men returned to civilization.	Marcie added two sentences to explain what had happened to the four men who were no longer with the expedition when it ended.
John Wesley Powell was a great American.	John Wesley Powell died in 1902 but his memory lives on in the mighty river that he explored.	The addition of the date of death brings closure to the chronology of Powell. The ending is strengthened by associating Powell's memory and the enduring river.

WRITE/DISCUSS **Find two more changes Marcie made in her revision. Think of a reason why she made each change. You can make a chart like the one above or discuss the changes with a classmate.**

Note that in her revised draft, Marcie added such colorful, precise adjectives as *twisting, rocky,* and *mighty* to describe the Colorado River. In the Editor's Workshop on page 30, you can learn more about finding the right word when you write.

Tip #2

Always keep your subject at the center of your biographical sketch. Only include other historical events if they relate to your subject.

Using a Thesaurus to Revise

Good writing often consists of finding the right word to use. The more precise and exact the words you choose, the better your writing will be.

A good source for finding the right word is a thesaurus. A thesaurus is a book that lists words that have similar meanings. These words, called synonyms, each give a different shade of meaning. Thesauruses also list antonyms, words with opposite meanings.

When Marcie wrote her first draft, she wrote this sentence:

> He organized a journey down the colorado river and thru the Grand Canyon.

Marcie wanted a better word than *journey* in this sentence. She looked up *journey* in her thesaurus and found these synonyms listed: *trip, excursion, voyage, expedition.*

She decided *trip,* like *journey,* was too general a word. *Excursion* sounded like a vacation, and Powell's journey was anything but that! *Voyage* was a better choice, since the journey Powell took was over water. However, Marcie decided *expedition* was even better, because it sounded more serious and scientific. She felt it best described Powell's purpose.

PRACTICE Read the following paragraph about Powell's expedition. Use a thesaurus to replace the underlined words with more exact ones.

Noteworthy

Some thesauruses are organized by subjects and others are organized alphabetically.

John Wesley Powell enjoyed naming many of the places he saw. At one point on the river, one boat was <u>broken</u> on rocks. Powell named the site "Disaster Falls." Later, he called a <u>part</u> of the Colorado that was thick with mud "Dirty Devil." When things got very <u>bad</u> for the expedition, Powell stopped to pray for <u>help</u> by a <u>pretty</u> stream. He named the stream "Bright Angel."

STEP 4

Proofreading

Next, Marcie proofread and edited her biographical sketch.
When you proofread your writing, you check it for errors in
spelling, punctuation, capitalization, and grammar. You are
editing when you correct the errors.

Prewriting
Drafting
Revising
Proofreading
Publishing

Geolo~~g~~ist ⌃explorer, and writer ,is one of the West's forgotten heroes. He
(John Wesley Powell (was born in ,1834. His family
where   Mt. Morris, New York, in
later moved to Illinois ,he became invo~~l~~ked with the Natural History

Society. Powell served in the civil war in the Union Army and lost

his right arm at the battle of Shiloh.

   After the war, Powell taught Geology in Illinois. He
        an expedition   through
organized ~~a journey~~ down the colorado river and ~~thru~~ the Grand
                                      this twisting, rocky
Canyon. No one had gone all the way down ~~the~~ river before.
It was a risky and dangerous undertaking.
   On May 24, 1869, Powell and nine men started down the
        four
river in ~~some~~ boats. months later they entered the Grand Canyon.

"We are three-quarters of a mile in the depths of the earth," Powell

wrote in his journal,"and the great river shrinks into insignificance,

as it dashes its angry waves against the walls and cliffs, that rise to
                       ¶ Along the way, four men had deserted. Three of them
the world above. . . ." Ninety-9 days after starting out, Powell and were
                          nine   later killed by
the five remaining men returned to civiliztion.   Native Americans.

Editor's Marks

∧	Add
⅄	Cut
⟋	Replace
＝	Capitalize
／	Lowercase
∩	Reverse letters
¶	New paragraph

DISCUSS In what ways is Marcie's short biography better
now that she's revised it? Share your thoughts with a
classmate.

Editor's Marks

∧ Add
↗ Cut
↗ Replace
≡ Capitalize
/ Lowercase
∩ Reverse letters
¶ New paragraph

Take a Closer Look

Look closely at Marcie's newest changes shown in red on page 31.

1. What words did she capitalize in the first paragraph and why?

2. Why did Marcie change *a* to *an* in the second paragraph?

3. Why were commas needed in the first sentence of the third paragraph?

4. What misspelled word did she correct in the new fourth paragraph?

Remember

Abbreviations are usually, but not always, followed by a period.

PRACTICE Here is the final paragraph of Marcie's biographical sketch. Study the editor's marks and then write out the paragraph correctly.

Powell wrote a book describing the wonders he had seen. ~~Soon, the Grand Canyon would become a national park.~~ He later served as head of the U. S. Geologi*c*al Survey and was a good friend to Native americans. He was one of the first ^white^ people to study ~~there~~ ^their^ culture seriously. John Wesley Powell ~~was a great American~~ ^died in 1902, but his memory lives on in^ the mighty river that he explored.

STEP 5

Publishing

The last step in the writing process for Marcie was to publish her biographical sketch. Marcie followed these steps:

1. She copied her sketch in her best handwriting.
2. She checked it carefully as she wrote to see that she omitted nothing.
3. She reread her writing to be certain there were no errors.
4. She prepared her biographical sketch to be part of a class album.

Prewriting

Drafting

Revising

Proofreading

Publishing

One Publishing Plan

Marcie's whole class had written short biographies about men and women of the Wild West. Their teacher suggested that they collect their writing into an album, similar to *Anastasia's Album,* and publish it. They followed these steps:

1. The students found pictures in old magazines and in books of the people they had written about. They cut out the art or made copies.
2. They found more quotes from primary resources (letters, journals, and so on) and wrote or typed them in short columns that could fit in margins.
3. The students pasted their finished biographies to album pages and pasted the pictures and quotes in the margins or at the beginning or end of their writing.
4. They organized the pages into an album with a cover. They called it *Who's Who in the Wild, Wild West.*

DISCUSS **As a class, talk about these questions.**

1. What people might you want to include in a classroom album of the Wild West? Why is each person important?
2. What other historical period would you want to create a class album of biographies about?
3. What other kinds of enhancements could you add to your album besides pictures and additional quotes from primary resources?

Expanding the Publishing Plan

Marcie and her classmates wanted to bring their historical characters from the Wild West to life in a more exciting way. They decided to dramatize and portray each person themselves. To do so, they revised their biographical sketches and turned them into dramatic monologues.

Unlike dialogue, which is a conversation between two people, a monologue is a speech spoken solo by a character. Some plays are all monologue and no dialogue. These are called one-person shows. Marcie's class wanted to create their own series of one-person shows for an audience. They followed these steps:

1. They rewrote the biographies in first person. They added some details and eliminated others. They made their biographies into monologues in which the characters told their life stories to the audience.
2. The students paired off with partners. Each partner performed his or her monologue for the other and then had a peer conference to discuss and improve the performance.
3. The students made costumes, referring to historical photos and illustrations for their designs. They used old clothes and props they could find easily.
4. The students performed one or two monologues each day for the class. Students asked questions at the end of the monologues, and the actors tried to answer in character.

DISCUSS Here are some of the questions the students in Marcie's class asked the characters from the Wild West. What questions might you add?

1. What contribution did you make to the West?
2. If you were alive today, what would you be doing?
3. How would you compare the West in your day to the way it is today?

Tips for Group Discussions

Group discussions are opportunities to share your opinions and hear the opinions of others. Frequently in school you will be asked to be part of a group discussion, not just in peer conferences. Here are some helpful tips on listening and speaking in a group discussion.

Listening

- Listen politely to others in the group. If you disagree with something said, jot it down so you can remember to mention it later.
- Take notes on what others say. Write down key words, not whole sentences. What others say may help you organize your own ideas.
- Listen carefully to opinions. Don't let yourself be distracted by what you are going to say next. Pay attention to who is speaking. Look at the person.
- If you find people are talking too long or straying from the topic, suggest the group set a time limit on how long each group member can speak.

Speaking

- Wait your turn patiently. Don't interrupt someone else who is speaking, unless you are asked to respond.
- Speak clearly and directly. Make sure you can be heard by everyone and understood. Keep eye contact with members of the group.
- Be constructive. If you are criticizing another person's writing or performance, tell what you liked as well as what you didn't like. If you disagree with someone, state your opinion in a friendly manner.
- Stay on the topic. Don't stray and don't talk too long. If you do, people will grow bored and tune you out, even if you have good points to make.
- Don't repeat what someone else has already said. If they have already addressed a point you were going to make, think of something else to say.

PRACTICE Make a note of the behaviors in the Listening and Speaking lists that you need to work on. Next time you have a group discussion, make a conscious effort to follow the appropriate tips.

ON-LINE—Using the Internet for Research

When doing research for a biography or other nonfiction report, you don't have to confine yourself to books or other paper sources. Why not log on to the Internet?

What Is the Internet?

The Internet is a huge network of computers worldwide that "talk" to one another, sending all kinds of information in the form of words, pictures, sounds, and moving images. Here are some originating sources of information you will find on the Internet:

- TV programs
- universities
- films
- product advertisers
- newspapers
- museums and libraries
- magazines
- other organizations

The World Wide Web is a graphical form of the Internet. Individuals and organizations can display information on their personal Web sites.

On-line servers organize Internet resources into helpful categories that make your research easier. Here are some categories that may interest you:

- news, weather, and sports
- travel information and information about different countries
- archival photos and sound bites
- original documents and primary resources

Here are some helpful tips for using the Internet to do research.

- Check your source. Some of the Web sites you'll find on the Internet may be created by individuals who are not experts. Learn to separate opinions from facts. If you think that the information you find may be inaccurate, look elsewhere on the Internet or in other sources.
- Check the Web site at a later time. Resources on the Internet are often being updated. By checking back later, you can get the most up-to-date information for your report.
- Keep your focus. It's easy to get sidetracked on the Internet. Going from one site to another is fun when you have the time. When you're doing research for an assignment, focus on the subject or topic and stick with it.

Putting It All Together

Marcie followed the steps in the writing process to guide her writing of a biographical sketch. Here's a handy visual to help you recall the process when you write.

STEP 1 **Prewriting**
- Select a subject.
- Decide on your audience.
- Collect details.

STEP 2 **Drafting**
- Get all your ideas on paper.
- Don't worry about mistakes.

STEP 3 **Revising**
- Read and review your draft.
- Share your draft with someone.
- Make changes to improve your writing.

STEP 4 **Proofreading**
- Check your spelling, capital letters, punctuation, and grammar.
- Write a neat final copy.
- Check one last time for errors.

STEP 5 **Publishing**
- Share your writing.

Writer's Corner

▶ Now it's your turn. Write a biographical sketch. It could be about almost anyone, from a famous athlete to your neighbor down the street. You might choose the person you selected in Try It! on page 23, or choose another person. Do your research. Use an outline, character map, or other organizer for your notes. Follow the steps of the writing process to complete your biographical sketch.

Building the
Paragraph

LESSON

1

Selecting a Topic

A topic is the idea about which a composition is written.

Did you ever wonder where authors get their ideas? They get them from the same place you will get your ideas for writing: the experiences of life. Every person's life is filled with joyful, sorrowful, and ordinary events. These events provide subject matter that can be developed into your writing.

Thinking about or discussing the following questions can help you begin to explore some of your life experiences.

- Was there ever a time when you were lost? Try to remember all the details, especially how you felt.
- Did you do something during vacation that was exciting, frightening, or funny?
- Were you ever in a hospital? Were you a patient or a visitor? How did you feel?
- Did you ever see a blazing sunset, a tree covered with snow, or a butterfly landing on a flower? Try to remember exactly how it looked and describe it.
- Did you ever try to convince your parents or teacher to let you do something or go somewhere? What arguments did you use? Did you win or lose?
- What kinds of books do you like to read? Why do you enjoy them?

◄ About the Photograph

This student is breezing through an essay test. You can too if you know how to build paragraphs!

- Did you ever travel in a plane? How did you feel the first time? Why did you feel this way?
- Do you have a secret fear? Are you afraid of the dark, of heights, or of failing in school? What events in your life may have caused these fears?
- What kinds of things make you angry? Did you ever want to tell your side of the story?
- What kind of music do you like? To what kind of music do you listen when you are in a bad mood? A good mood? Why?
- How do you feel when you wake up on Saturday morning and it is raining outside? What do you do all day?
- What sports or games do you know a great deal about or play well?
- Did you ever have a day when everything went wrong?
- Has school ever been canceled because of bad weather? How did you feel when you heard the news? What did you do all day?

The answer to one of these questions could be a good topic for you to develop and write about. Remember, authors write from their own experiences.

Sometimes in school, topics are assigned to you, or you are given several topics from which to choose. Before you choose a topic, ask yourself these questions:

- Do I know something about this topic from experience or reading?
- Does this topic interest me enough to find out something about it?

If the answer to either of these questions is yes, then you will probably enjoy the writing experience and produce a better composition.

Activity **A**

Now explore some interests you may have. Below is a list of topics. On a separate sheet of paper, copy each topic. If you have firsthand experience of the topic, write *experience* next to it. If the topic is something you've read about, put *read* next to it. If you know nothing about the topic, write *nothing* next to it.

1. Making a cake
2. A personal computer
3. Taking care of a pet
4. Playing on a team
5. Photography
6. Working parents
7. Tennis
8. Vampire bats
9. Niagara Falls
10. A snowball fight

Writer's Corner

▶ Listed in pairs are some topics that could be assigned in social studies, science, or math class. If you had to choose one topic from each pair, which would you choose and why? Write your answers on a sheet of paper.

1. The Great Depression or The New Deal
2. Earthquakes or Volcanoes
3. World War I or World War II
4. The Emancipation Proclamation or Women's suffrage
5. How a computer works or How to write a computer program
6. United Nations or The League of Nations
7. Job programs for youth or Job programs for those with disabilities
8. Poverty in our cities or Entertainment in our cities
9. Environmental protection or Urban development
10. Nuclear power plants or Solar energy

Narrowing the Topic

A topic must be narrowed to a specific idea.

Once you have found a topic that interests you and with which you feel comfortable, the next step is to limit your topic to a specific idea. How do you begin to narrow down your topic? Suppose you chose the subject food. Innumerable things could be written about food, so you must first brainstorm for ideas related to the topic. Your brainstorming might look something like this:

restaurant   stores   food   pizza
popcorn   junk food   hamburgers
snacks   deli   desserts   chicken

Read over the ideas you have written down and decide which appeals to you the most. Suppose you choose desserts. Since this is still a large topic, you might ask yourself: What kind of desserts? You find yourself thinking of ice-cream cones, sundaes, and chocolate-covered ice cream on a stick, so your answer is ice-cream desserts. That's still too much to write about in a short space, so you ask yourself: What kind of ice-cream desserts? You decide sundaes are your favorite ice-cream desserts.

Now ask yourself one last question: What can I say about sundaes? Well, you know you don't like just any sundae; for you, there is a perfect kind of sundae. Therefore, you might decide to write about what makes the perfect sundae. You have put the topic food through a strainer and come up with one specific idea about which to write. In chart form, your thinking process would look like this:

Food	
Desserts	
Ice-cream desserts	
Sundaes	
What makes the perfect sundae	

Activity A

On a separate sheet of paper, draw two blank charts like the one in the food example above. Narrow down the ideas listed for the following two topics. In each chart the broadest topic should be on the first line and the narrowest on the last line.

1.
Books
    Library books
    The Pigman
    Fiction
    How John and Lorraine
        take advantage of
        Mr. Pignati

2.
Trees
    Deciduous trees
    Blights that affect
        maple trees
    Maple trees
    Trees in the United States

Activity B

The broadest and narrowest topics are given on these thinking process charts. On a separate sheet of paper, complete each chart by putting in three more items that show the narrowing down process.

1.

Electronic devices
The advantages of having a classroom computer

2.

Famous people
Washington's military strategy at Valley Forge

Writer's Corner

▶ Draw four thinking process charts on a sheet of paper. Choose any four of the six topics listed below, brainstorm for ideas, and then narrow them in four or five steps to one specific idea. Share your results with the class.

A. Sports   **D.** Animals
B. Dancing   **E.** Cars
C. Money   **F.** Clothes

Writing Topic and Beginning Sentences

LESSON 3

Topic Sentences

A topic sentence states the main idea of a paragraph.

Why is a topic sentence so important? A topic sentence tells the reader where you, the writer, are headed. It is a general statement giving the reader an overview of the paragraph. If you were asked to summarize a paragraph or tell its main idea in one sentence, you would be giving the topic sentence.

A topic sentence should include the topic as well as the narrowed topic, for example:

- Down into the cool depths of tropical waters go dauntless swimmers whose dangerous occupation is pearl diving.

What is the topic?	Pearl diving
What is the narrowed topic?	Pearl diving is a dangerous occupation.

- Family members arrive from all parts of the country, each contributing some delicious surprise to the Thanksgiving dinner.

What is the topic?	Thanksgiving dinner
What is the narrowed topic?	How each family member contributes to the dinner

Activity

Here is some practice in writing topic sentences. The topic and narrowed topic are provided. On a sheet of paper, write a topic sentence for each example that expresses both ideas.

1. Topic: A deserted mansion
   Narrowed topic: The mystery surrounding the deserted mansion
   Topic sentence:

2. Topic: Climate
   Narrowed topic: How climate affects people's lives
   Topic sentence:

3. Topic: Stringed musical instruments
   Narrowed topic: The harp has the largest range in the orchestra.
   Topic sentence:

4. Topic: A curious cat
   Narrowed topic: How the cat fell into the swimming pool
   Topic sentence:

5. Topic: Sports
   Narrowed topic: Gymnastics requires balance and skill.
   Topic sentence:

Activity B

A topic sentence may come at the beginning of a paragraph, stating the main idea, or it may come at the end of a paragraph, summarizing the ideas. In the paragraphs below, the topic sentences have been omitted. On a separate sheet of paper, write an original topic sentence for each.

1 _____

_____ . After he overthrew his father, Jupiter divided the world between his brothers, Pluto and Neptune. Pluto dominated the underworld, and Neptune, the seas. For himself, Jupiter kept the heavens and controlled the actions of both gods and humans.

Decide: What is the topic?
What is the narrowed topic?

2   Gingerly, I walked out to the end of the diving board. The instructor carefully stepped behind me and gently bent my body at the waist, encouraging me to almost touch my toes with my fingertips. With a light nudge he pushed me over, and miraculously I landed headfirst in the water. _____

_____ .

Decide: What is the topic?
What is the narrowed topic?

Beginning Sentences

A beginning sentence may be, but is not always, a topic sentence.

Sometimes the beginning and topic sentences are one and the same, and sometimes they are two separate sentences. A good beginning sentence will

- attract the reader's attention.
- arouse the reader's curiosity.
- encourage the reader to read on.

You can incorporate these qualities in several ways. Your beginning sentence can be

- a descriptive sentence: The engine sputtered and spat a few empty syllables, dying a slow death.

- an interrogative sentence: Does the abominable snowman really exist?

- a direct quote: "Are you sure there's a social studies test today?" inquired the pale-looking student.

Activity C

Listed below are topics and narrowed topics. On a separate sheet of paper, write three different beginning sentences for each one. Remember: The beginning sentence does not have to be the topic sentence.

1. Topic: Rock stars
   Narrowed topic: Why _____ is the most popular rock star today
   Beginning sentences:
   Descriptive: _____
   Interrogative: _____
   Direct quote: _____

2. Topic: School
   Narrowed topic: Some of my best moments in school
   Beginning sentences:
   Descriptive: _____
   Interrogative: _____
   Direct quote:_____

Activity D

Below are five topic sentences. Write three more interesting beginning sentences—one descriptive sentence, one interrogative sentence, and one direct quote—for each one.

1. The desert can be a very dangerous place.
2. Every year a new fad comes into existence.
3. The principal sent for me at 9:00 A.M.
4. _____ is one of the best books I've ever read.
5. The pioneers faced many difficulties as they traveled west.

Writer's Corner

▶ Below are three topic sentences. Write one beginning sentence for each. Next are three beginning sentences. Write one topic sentence for each.

Topic Sentences
1. I found out that wearing the proper shoes can make all the difference in the world.
2. Riding on the back of an elephant is truly a unique experience.
3. Winning the science competition was the most exciting moment of my life.

Beginning Sentences
4. Our new family member caused us a few surprises.
5. Have you ever gone around in circles?
6. "Only thirty seconds left!" shouted Kim.

Collecting Supporting Details for Middle Sentences

The details of a composition are those ideas that support the topic.

Once you have narrowed your topic to one idea, you are ready to continue with the next step in writing: gathering the details that support your topic. Suppose you chose the topic computers and narrowed the topic to how computers work. You are now ready to list the things that are related to your narrowed topic. There are several ways to list supporting details. The example below uses a method called word mapping.

1. Write your narrowed topic and draw an oval around it.

2. Around the oval, name ideas that are related to your narrowed topic. These ideas are called subtopics. Draw lines connecting each subtopic to the topic in the center.

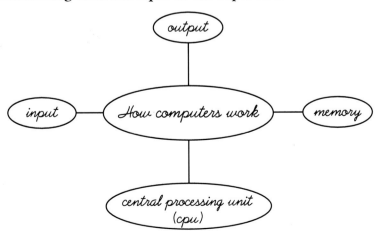

3. Around each subtopic, write any details relating to that particular subtopic. These details may be things you already know, or you may need to discover them through research.

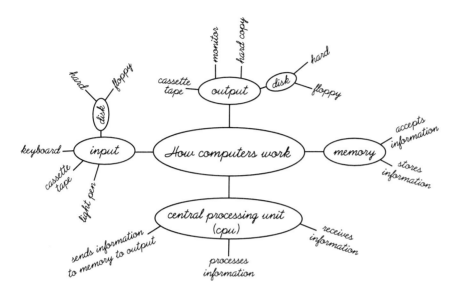

4. Examine your word map and decide if you have too much information for one paragraph. If so, eliminate some of the least important details about your subtopics.

Before you begin writing your paragraph, examine the relationship between your subtopics and your topic. Is there any particular order or arrangement that the subtopics should have? For the topic of how computers work, there is a definite process involved: the input comes first, the memory and cpu interact next, and the output comes last. Remember: It is important to write about the subtopics in the same order in which they naturally occur.

In the preceding lesson, you learned how to develop a good topic/beginning sentence. Now you will write sentences about your subtopics. These will be your middle sentences.

How computers work ──►	The working of a modern computer is a complex operation.
Input ──────────►	Material, referred to as input, enters the computer by means of a keyboard, light pen, disk, or cassette.
Memory ─────────►	The information enters the memory, where it is either stored or transmitted to the central processing unit (cpu) to be processed.
CPU ───────────►	The cpu performs the required function and returns the information to the memory for storage or for retrieval by the operator.
Output ─────────►	The processed information can be saved as hard copy (printout) or stored on a disk or cassette.

The sentences you have written will not automatically form a good paragraph. Some words will have to be changed and others added in order for the sentences to flow smoothly from one to another. Watch particularly for words that are repeated, and use synonyms to replace them. After several revisions and peer/teacher consultation, your paragraph might resemble the one on page 53.

Title

<u>The working of a modern computer is a complex operation.</u> Material, referred to as input, is entered into the computer by a trained operator using a device such as a keyboard, light pen, cassette tape, or floppy or hard disk. Once it is entered, the information passes to the memory function of the computer, where it is either temporarily stored or transmitted to the central processing unit, or cpu, to be processed. The cpu performs the required function and returns the processed information to the memory for temporary storage, or to the operator for immediate retrieval. This finished copy, or output, may appear in several ways: on a monitor, as hard copy (using a printer), or on a disk or cassette tape. _____

_____

TOPIC SENTENCE

MIDDLE SENTENCES CONTAINING SUPPORTING DETAILS

ENDING SENTENCE

Activity A

Make a word map for each of the following topics. Use a textbook or an encyclopedia to help you.

1. Wind instruments in the orchestra

2. The parts of a flower

3. The branches of the federal government

4. Types of clouds

5. Olympic Games

6. Number systems (e.g., whole, rational, irrational, integers, etc.)

Writer's Corner

▶ Select any one of the topics above and compose a paragraph using the details in your word map.

Writing the Ending Sentence

The ending sentence draws the paragraph to a close.

After the topic, beginning, and middle sentences have been completed, it is necessary to draw all that you've written to a close. This is called the ending sentence. There are different ways of writing an ending sentence. It can express an emotion or a feeling about what you have written.

> When the class bell rang, Cathy uttered a sigh of relief, knowing she was safe for another day.

> Next time I'll think twice before examining a beehive.

The ending sentence can summarize what you have written and restate in other words what the topic sentence has already expressed.

> It is no wonder that Edgar Allan Poe's short stories have become a favorite of teenagers everywhere.

> The entire process takes less than a second, but it involves the complicated interaction of highly sophisticated electronic equipment.

Activity A

Choose the ending sentence that would best complete each idea expressed. Discuss your answers in class.

1. Martina had always feared traveling by plane. After her first flight, she wrote a paragraph telling how she lost her fear of flying. Select the best ending sentence.

    a. Now I am anticipating my next opportunity to see Wichita from the air.

    b. I was terrified as the attendant said, "Fasten your seat belts; we're about to take off."

    c. Wichita looked like a toy village from the air.

2. Ben is writing about why he likes football. Which is the best ending sentence for Ben's topic?

    a. Football is a very invigorating sport.

    b. Is it any wonder, then, that every autumn finds me practicing football, my favorite sport?

    c. Everyone likes the fast-moving action and the exhilaration of a Saturday afternoon football game, and I am no exception.

Activity B

On a separate sheet of paper, write original endings for the following paragraphs. For one paragraph, try to express an emotion; for the other, restate the topic.

1

A Jack of All Trades

Our school janitor, Claus Jansen, is a very special person. Because he takes pride in his work, our sidewalks are always cleanly shoveled and our corridors shine. He unjams stubborn locker doors and repairs broken desks with skill and good humor. As if these qualities weren't enough, Claus also shows an uncommon creativity. He designed and built a fascinating wooden playground structure for the younger children, and he has guided the construction of imaginative sets for our school plays. He is willing to share his talents and workshop space any time we need help, whether it is with a science project or with something as minor (but embarrassing) as the day the heel came off my shoe. _____

_____

2

The Mighty Peanut

You may have enjoyed eating the crisp, brown delight known as a peanut at a baseball or hockey game. However, you may not be familiar with the importance of this delicious tidbit. In the United States, the peanut is chiefly used for peanut butter. But, around the world, two-thirds of the peanut crop is crushed for peanut oil. The leftover shell and other bits are made into animal feed products. _____

_____

Activity C

Below are four narrowed topics for possible paragraphs. On a separate sheet of paper, write an ending sentence for each and tell whether you have expressed an emotion or a feeling or have restated the topic.

1. Narrowed topic: Why reading books is a worthwhile pastime
   Ending sentence: _____

2. Narrowed topic: Why driving is important to a sixteen-year-old
   Ending sentence: _____

3. Narrowed topic: Why students need a longer lunch break
   Ending sentence: _____

4. Narrowed topic: Humorous antics of my pet
   Ending sentence: _____

Writer's Corner

▶ Write ending sentences that would express each of the following emotions: anger, fear, joy, surprise, confusion.

Creating a Title

The title of a written work is usually a short, creative expression of the composition's main idea.

A title that is cleverly worded will catch a potential reader's eye and draw him or her into the work. Sometimes clever titles come to an author's mind as a flash of creative insight. At other times, titles must be written, revised, and refined until the author is satisfied.

Some professional writers employ figures of speech in creating their titles. Alliteration is used by Edgar Allan Poe in his title "The Tell-Tale Heart"; Lenore Kendel uses a play on words in her poem "Wonder Wander"; allusion to a child's story is apparent in A. A. Milne's "The Ugly Duckling," a play about a princess; and Vachel Lindsay uses personification in the poem title "The Potatoes' Dance."

Besides being short and creative, the title should reflect the main idea of the work. The title can

- name the person, place, thing, or event around which the main idea takes place.
- indicate the theme or underlying message of a work.

"Top Man," by James Ramsey Ullman, is a story that revolves around a mountain-climbing expedition. The underlying message is suggested by asking: Who is the "Top Man"?

Begin creating your titles by brainstorming all the ways you can use different figures of speech or clever words to state your main idea. Remember to follow these guidelines whether you are writing a title for a novel, short story, or even a paragraph:

- Keep your title short.
- Be creative.
- Focus on the main idea.

Activity A

Read each paragraph topic and choose the title you think would be better. Tell why.

1. A serious bike accident
   a. The Day I Got Hit by a Car
   b. Almost Fatal!
2. A large raccoon raiding a campsite at night
   a. Raccoon Raider
   b. A Beastly Fright in the Night
3. A personal experience about a girl's first attempt at skiing
   a. Downhill Daredevil
   b. Gliding down the Slopes
4. Catching a home-run ball
   a. Prize Possession
   b. The Best Baseball Game Ever
5. Being lost in a cave
   a. Trapped Inside the Earth
   b. The Lost Boy

Activity B

Below are several paragraphs that need titles. Read each and write a title that would arouse a reader's interest.

1 _____

Writing can be a challenging experience. Sometimes when I sit down to write, I can't think of anything to say. When that happens I have several options. I can stay in my chair, twiddle my pen, and look out the window. Or, I might pick up a book and read for a while to stimulate my thinking. The best thing for me to do, however, is put on my shorts, T-shirt, and running shoes and head out the door. Once I am outside, I relax. I think better. Still, I often have to run a long while before I can go back to my desk and put thoughts on paper.

2 _____

The first morning of my summer vacation found me speeding to a frightening seaside experience. After a short run down the beach, I felt the cool water cover my ankles and the misty spray of foam fan my face. I plunged delightedly into the water for my first swim of the season. My enjoyment soon faded, however, when I spied a shark dangerously near. Land seemed miles away. Suddenly a giant wave thrust me to the bottom, and I came up gurgling and choking. Gripped by fear, I struck out for the shore. Surely, I thought, the shark must be near enough to capture me with its sharp teeth. Just then another wave engulfed me. When my blurred vision cleared, I found myself on the beach with my pursuer lying close beside me. To my surprise and relief, I discovered that it was nothing more than a piece of driftwood.

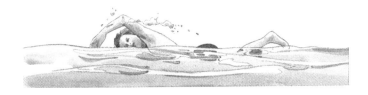

3

_____

As I reached the high rocky shelf, I paused and turned for a better view of the beautiful valley through which I had come. Far below, a little creek pushed insistently past its banks. Wild ducks moved swiftly through the clear water, their blue-green plumage gleaming with an almost metallic brightness. Warm sunlight shining through the trees cast lacy patterns of light and shadow on the ground. The trees themselves stood proud and tall, conscious of their riotous coloring, and paid to every passing breeze a gracious tribute of drifting leaves. As I gazed down upon this lovely valley, I was filled with a deep sense of gratitude for this beautiful country of ours.

4

_____

What is personality? It is certainly something that everyone has. In fact, personality is what distinguishes one person from another. It is a combination of social, physical, intellectual, and emotional characteristics. Although personalities are not fixed, but grow and develop, experts seem to agree that people are born with certain traits. This can be seen most clearly in a set of twins who grow up in exactly the same environment. It can even be seen in animals. Anyone who has watched a litter of kittens develop, for instance, will have noticed how one kitten might be daring, another timid, and yet another very affectionate. Of course, the most interesting aspect of all about personality is that each one is unique.

Writer's Corner

▶ Create a title for a paragraph on each of the following topics.

1. The day the smoke alarm went off
2. The year your team won the championship
3. Taking a huge dog for a walk
4. The time your friends gave you a surprise party
5. Catching a prize-winning fish

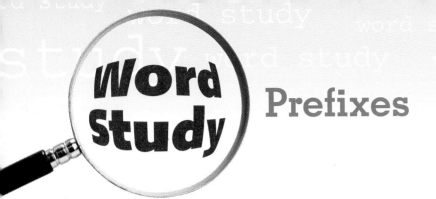

Prefixes

A prefix, a syllable or syllables added to the beginning of a root or a word, changes the meaning of the word.

Many of our prefixes come from other languages, such as Latin and Greek.

Activity A

Using your dictionary, discover whether the prefixes are derived from Latin or Greek. Write your answers on a sheet of paper.

PREFIX	MEANING	LANGUAGE
1. pan-	all	_____
2. semi-	half	_____
3. mono-	single	_____
4. intro-, intra-	inside of	_____
5. multi-	many	_____
6. poly-	many	_____

Activity B

Copy the following chart. Using your dictionary, give two new words for each prefix and write the meaning next to each new word. Make certain that the meaning uses the definition of the prefix. The first one is done for you.

PREFIX	NEW WORDS	MEANINGS
1. pan-	panacea	cure for all difficulties
2. semi-	_____	_____
	_____	_____

3. mono- _____ _____

4. intro-, intra- _____ _____
_____ _____

5. multi- _____ _____
_____ _____

6. poly- _____ _____
_____ _____

Activity C

Think of a word that would best complete each of the following sentences. The prefix of the word is given for you. If you need to, use the dictionary.

1. My birthday gift was a mono_____ sweater.
2. In the play, the main character read a mono_____ .
3. I would like you to intro_____ me to that girl.
4. Intra_____ sports are popular at our school.
5. Everyone said that John was an intro_____ because he was so shy.
6. The multi_____ banner attracted our attention.
7. A multi_____ of people gathered outside the theater.
8. Sometimes a semi_____ is used to divide a compound sentence.
9. The basketball team made it to the semi_____ .
10. His pants were made of poly_____ and cotton.
11. A poly_____ is commonly called a lie detector.
12. On weekends, we always have eggs and pan_____ for breakfast.
13. Pan_____ broke out when the lead singer threw his hat into the crowd.
14. The cinematographer is filming with pan_____ film.

WRITER'S WORKSHOP

Writing for a Reason

Do you groan when you see an essay question on a big test or as part of an assignment? Don't panic! Essay answers are just paragraphs, and you write those every day. Make up an essay question you might find on a test or an assignment in any subject. Write your answer and include it in a class book of essay-writing tips.

 Prewriting

Think about all the things you've already learned this year. Make a list of topics you could use for your essay question and answer.

Ask yourself questions like these to help you choose a topic.

- What subject is my favorite this year?

- What stories have I read in English class?

- What concepts have I learned in social studies?

- What science principles can I explain?

- What steps do I use as I solve math problems?

Choose a topic and write a question. Word your question carefully. Will you compare and contrast, explain, or describe? Write a question that cannot be answered with just one sentence. Make sure you know the answer so you can concentrate on organizing your thoughts.

Then get ready to write your answer. Make a word map to record the ideas and facts you recall. You may use class notes or a textbook if you wish.

Interpreting Essay Questions

1. Read the question quickly to get its general idea.

2. Reread to find out what you are being asked to do. Underline words that give directions, like *explain* or *compare*.

3. Reread the question to make sure you understand its content. Circle key terms like *World War II* or *gravity*.

Drafting

An essay answer begins with a topic sentence. Always use the question's key words in your topic sentence. Imagine that your reader has not seen the question.

This is not a good topic sentence:

> That was because they felt that the British government was unfair.

This is a good topic sentence:

> The American colonists declared their independence because they felt that the British government was unfair.

The details in the body of your essay are the most important part of your answer. They prove that your topic statement is true, and the number and quality of your details show that you understand what you learned. Use ideas from your word map to write the body of your essay.

Complete your essay answer with a sentence that restates the idea in your topic sentence and sums up your ideas.

Guidelines for Writing Your Draft

1. Write quickly and fluently.

2. Write your draft while all your prewriting ideas are fresh in your mind.

3. Keep your prewriting notes in front of you.

4. Don't worry about correct spelling or punctuation at this point.

5. Don't be afraid to add things to your draft that are not in your notes. You can always take them out later.

6. Remember, your draft should not be perfect. The purpose of a draft is to get all your ideas down on paper quickly.

7. After writing your draft, have a peer conference to get feedback from another writer. (See page 35 for conferencing tips.)

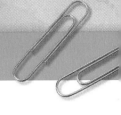

Revising, Proofreading, and Publishing

Revising

Time to Take Another Look

Before you write your final copy, reread your draft to find ways to make your essay answer clearer and more complete.

Ask yourself these questions to help you revise your essay answer.

❑ Does my paragraph begin with a topic sentence?

❑ Does my beginning sentence include key words from the question?

❑ Do I need to add any details to support my topic sentence?

❑ Do I need to take out any extra details that don't really answer the question?

❑ Do I need to rewrite anything that is not clear?

❑ Do I need to reorganize details to make my answer more logical?

❑ Does my final sentence restate the idea in my beginning sentence and sum up my ideas?

Remember, you are writing to show what you know. Make sure your essay answer expresses your ideas exactly.

Revise your paragraph, using a colored pencil to make your changes stand out.

Use Signal Words

Signal words like *because, while, however, then,* and *finally* help show the relationship between sentences and ideas. As you revise, look for ways to clarify your ideas with signal words.

 **Proofreading**

Time to Look at Capitalization, Punctuation, and Spelling

Mechanical writing errors can be distracting. They make it difficult for your reader to concentrate on your ideas. After you revise your draft, proofread it to check your capitalization, punctuation, spelling, and grammar.

Use the checklist below to edit and proofread your essay answer.

- ❏ Did I indent the first word of my paragraph?

- ❏ Did I capitalize proper nouns correctly?

- ❏ Did I use the correct mark of punctuation at the end of each sentence?

- ❏ Did I spell each word correctly?

One Line at a Time

To help focus your attention, place a blank sheet of paper under the top line of your essay so you cannot see the other lines. Proofread the line you see, and then move down to the next one.

 Publishing

Time to Share

Publish your essay question and answer to share helpful, essay-writing tips.

To publish, follow these steps:

1. Copy your revised draft in your neatest handwriting, or use a computer to produce a printed copy.

2. After you finish, proofread your final copy one more time.

3. Check your final copy against your revised draft to make sure you have not left out any important details.

Make the class Essay-Writing Tips Handbook.

1. Work together to make a short list of tips for answering essay questions. Have one writer record them.

2. Collect your essay answers and organize them by subject.

3. Make a cover and bind the pages together, beginning with the tips page.

4. Place your book in the classroom reference center and refer to it before you take an essay test.

5. At the end of the year, leave your book behind to help next year's eighth graders get off to a good start.

Unity

A paragraph has unity when all the sentences relate to the topic, or main idea.

Sentences that do not relate to the topic, or main idea, are called misfit sentences. When you read the paragraph below, look for the topic sentence, the related middle sentences, and the misfit, or unrelated, sentence.

> Among the world's greatest treasures are the exquisite diamonds owned by governments, royalty, and museums. The United States proudly displays the Hope diamond in the Smithsonian Institution. In the Louvre Museum in France is the beautiful Regent diamond, while the Koh-i-noor remains secure in the possession of Great Britain. Some diamonds can even be produced by artificial means under the right conditions. Russia's prize, the Orloff diamond, was supposedly stolen from the eye of a Hindu idol. Such rare gems are surely the earth's gift to humankind.

- Which is the topic sentence?
- What is the general topic?
- What is the narrowed topic?
- Is the topic sentence the beginning sentence?
- Which are the supporting middle sentences?
- Which sentence is not related to the topic?

About the Photograph

Many people find it much easier to write using a computer than writing with pencil and paper. Do you like to write using a computer?

- Why doesn't this sentence relate to the topic?
- Which is the ending sentence?
- Does the ending sentence express a feeling or restate the topic?

Now read the same paragraph, omitting the misfit, or unrelated, sentence. When all middle sentences relate to the topic, this is called unity. Since all the sentences in the paragraph now tell about the great diamonds of the world, the paragraph has the quality of unity.

Activity A

Read the following paragraph. Look for the topic sentence, the related middle sentences, and the misfit, or unrelated, sentence.

The students' voices soar as they try to squeeze in a quick word with their friends. One girl's voice rises above the others as she reminds participants about the bicycle ride to support the zoo, and two boys can be heard desperately trying to discover who made this year's football squad. Teachers, chatting loudly, race to the faculty room to rescue forgotten test papers or grab a quick sip of coffee. The coffee was brewed early in the day. Needless to say, at the change of classes, the noise level is at a feverish pitch.

Write answers to the following on a sheet of paper:

1. The topic sentence
2. The general topic
3. The narrowed topic
4. The sentence that is not related to the topic
5. A sentence of your own that would relate to the other middle sentences and take the place of the misfit sentence

Activity B

Read the following paragraph and, using the questions on pages 69 and 70, discuss the qualities that give the paragraph unity.

Rocking Chair Saga

Household furnishings often occupy a prominent place in the memories of an individual. Many of the recollections of my early years are built around a comfortable wooden rocking chair that stood in the corner of our big kitchen. What opportunities it offered for three imaginative children! Disguised by a blanket and turned on end, it became a smugglers' cave inhabited by buccaneers who were a constant menace to the pantry shelf. Without the covering, a patient steed groaned under the weight of three sturdy riders. If other pieces of furniture could be pressed into service, the rocker was transformed into a locomotive hauling a train of startling appearance. The chair in its natural position, however, holds the dearest memories of all. Then it became the place where Mother soothed her tired children and rocked away the cares of a weary day. Pirates' cave to haven of comfort and love—could anything but a sturdy pine rocker have stood the strain?

Writer's Corner

▶ Choose one narrowed topic from the list below. Write four or five supporting details, including one misfit sentence. Then write a topic sentence and an effective ending sentence. Give your sentences to a partner and ask him or her to identify the misfit sentence.

A. The first time I tried to ski (skate, water-ski, in-line skate, etc.)

B. How my sister (brother) and I managed to ruin dinner

C. Music that makes me want to dance

D. Why _____ makes me laugh (supply your own idea)

E. Where I go when I need to think things over

Coherence

A paragraph has coherence when it is in logical and natural order. Coherence means "sticking together."

A paragraph will have coherence if it flows naturally from one idea to the next. In other words, there must be a sense of order in the paragraph. Order can be sequential (time, order of importance, directions) or spatial (space).

Sequential Order

When a paragraph is written in sequential order, the sentences follow a logical pattern. Most often the pattern is according to time (chronological order) or order of importance. Many "how-to" compositions (how to plan a trip, how to use a VCR, etc.) are written according to sequential order. Read the following paragraph and note the words that signal sequence.

> Almost all things in nature can be recycled. The leaf is a perfect example of nature's recycling process. First, the leaf must fall to the ground to allow the autumn rains to soften it. Next, bacteria break down the materials that make up the leaf. Then rainwater dissolves the matter and slowly washes it back to earth. All this decayed substance adds food to the soil and, finally, improves the ground's fertility for the new plants that will grow there. Recycling is just one of nature's many phenomena.

- Name all the words that indicate sequential order.
- Read the paragraph again, reversing the third and fourth sentences. What happens to the coherence in the paragraph?
- What transition word signals the conclusion of the process?

If you put sentences together point by point, the result will be a paragraph with short, choppy sentences. To make a paragraph smooth and coherent, it is necessary to use transition words. Listed below are some of the most commonly used transition, or signal, words for sequential order.

after	in conclusion	now
afterward	later	soon
as soon as	meantime	then
finally	meanwhile	to begin with
first, second, etc.	next	

Activity

Below are supporting details that are not in sequential order. First, study the process of setting up a terrarium. Then, on a separate sheet of paper, show the correct sequence of the various steps by numbering them in the order in which they should occur.

TOPIC: A terrarium

NARROWED TOPIC: How to arrange a terrarium

_____ Place pebbles on the bottom of the bowl.
_____ Place plants in the soil.
_____ Purchase a glass bowl with a cover.
_____ Add soil composed of loam, sand, and peat moss.
_____ Moisten the soil thoroughly.
_____ Place the terrarium in the light.

Activity

Use transition words to connect the instructions for building a terrarium in Activity A. Write a topic sentence, put the middle sentences in sequential order, and then write a concluding sentence. Don't be afraid to add extra words or phrases to make the paragraph more interesting.

Spatial Order

Sometimes a paragraph needs a special kind of ordering called spatial order. Spatial order is arranging details from left to right, down to up, or near to far. The arrangement that is decided upon should be used consistently throughout the paragraph. As you read the paragraph below, look for the words that signal spatial order.

Every year Mom plants a garden that is picture perfect. The earthen plot is thirty feet wide by twenty feet long. The ground is carefully divided into three equal sections. Beginning with the left section, she plants carrots in the front, beets behind the carrots, spinach behind the beets, and, finally, a row of tomatoes. In the middle section, she plants radishes first, celery second, lettuce third, and corn last. The plot to the right contains cabbage, onions, peas, and parsley in the same order. What a summer's worth of good eating is rooted in that soil!

- Name all the words that indicate spatial order.
- What specific type of spatial order is used?
- Are there any transition, or signal, words that can be used for both sequential and spatial order?

Even when ideas are put in spatial order, they will not automatically form a well-worded paragraph. You may find some short, choppy sentences, just as you did with sequential order. Certain transition words can tie these sentences together and give a clearer sense of the order of ideas. Listed below are some of the most commonly used transition, or signal, words for spatial order.

above	farther	to the left
across	here	to the right
before	in front of	under
behind	next to	underneath
below	opposite of	

Activity C

Use the transition words on page 74 to connect the ideas in your own paragraph using spatial order about a room in your house, apartment, or another place you know well. Write a topic sentence, put the middle sentences in spatial order, and then write a concluding thought. Use extra words and ideas to make the paragraph more interesting.

Activity D

Below are twelve topics for paragraphs. Decide if the ideas for each should be organized by sequential or spatial order. Indicate your choices on a separate sheet of paper by writing the number of each topic and the word *sequential* or *spatial.*

1. To explain how to get to your home from school
2. To explain the arrangement of the furniture in your bedroom
3. To describe the design of a flag
4. To trace the history of the automobile
5. To explain how to make a banana split
6. To outline the steps in the writing process
7. To explain what makes a volcano erupt
8. To describe the clothes on a model
9. To explain how a computer works
10. To explain how to set a table
11. To show how you have matured from first to eighth grade
12. To trace your roots back to your great-grandparents

Writer's Corner

▶ To reinforce your skills in writing coherently, choose one of the topics in Activity D or a topic of your own and write a brief paragraph about it.

Comparison

Many of your high school writing assignments will involve comparing and contrasting. You might be asked to compare and contrast such things as poems, historical periods, or the results of experiments. To help you get started in writing of this kind, let us first look at what we mean by comparison.

Comparison is a method of writing that shows the similarities among persons, places, or things.

In order to organize your thoughts and ideas, it is helpful to map the similarities among the objects being compared on a piece of paper. Here is an example. In the large oval are two objects being compared: a station wagon and a van. The smaller ovals coming from the large oval show the many ways in which the two are similar.

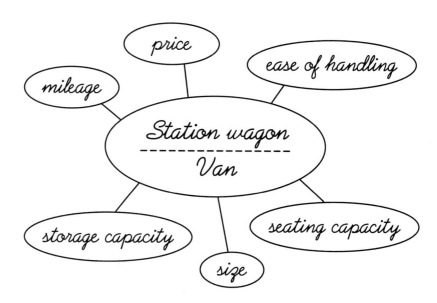

Once you have your ideas mapped out, you can put them into paragraph form.

Here is a list of useful transition words for comparison writing.

also	just as	resembles
furthermore	like	similarly
in the same way	likewise	so

Activity A

Here is a paragraph someone wrote about the similarities between a station wagon and a van. As you read the paragraph, look for the things mentioned in numbers 1–4 following the paragraph.

Decisions! Decisions!

Like many adventurous Americans, the Wilders decided to try camping for recreation. Knowing that a new form of transportation would be required, the family faced a dilemma: Should it be a van or a station wagon? They compared the two vehicles. The van was roomier than their present car, but compact and easy to handle on the highway. So was the station wagon. The station wagon had the capacity to transport all the family members and their camping gear, just as the van did. In the same way, the highway mileage of both vehicles was comparable. Furthermore, the van and the wagon had almost identical sticker prices. The family realized they were going to have to find more factors on which to base their decision.

Write answers to the following on a sheet of paper:

1. The first four words of the topic sentence
2. The first three words of the beginning sentence
3. The transition words that signal points of comparison
4. How many points of comparison were made

Activity B

The four sets of topics below and on page 79 are ready for comparison. On a sheet of paper, draw each oval, write in the topics to be compared, and then in smaller ovals coming from the large oval, write in all the similarities you can think of.

Swimming pool

Lake

Football

Hockey

Winter break

Summer break

Your school

Nearby school

Writer's Corner

▶ Choose one of the topics from Activity B, or create an
original set, and write a short paragraph showing
comparison. Use transition words to keep the paragraph
unified and coherent.

Contrast

Contrast is a method of writing that shows the differences among persons, places, or things.

Showing the differences among topics is a more difficult task than showing the similarities, but it can be a very rewarding way of writing. In order to point out differences, the subjects must be alike. This sounds like a contradiction, but it is really a very logical statement. Things cannot be contrasted unless they have similar natures. You can contrast a daffodil with a tulip, but you cannot logically contrast a daffodil with a butterfly. You can contrast a lobster with a crab because they are both shellfish, but a lobster and a cat have no mutual points on which they can be contrasted.

Here are some transition, or signal, words you can use in contrast writing.

| but | in contrast | unlike |
| however | on the other hand | whereas |

Activity A

Copy the following ten topics onto a sheet of paper. Next to each topic, write the name of something that can be sensibly contrasted with it.

1. ballet
2. lizard
3. cheddar cheese
4. computer
5. candle

6. dictionary
7. pencil
8. toothbrush
9. collie
10. piano

Activity B

As you read the following paragraph, look for the things mentioned in numbers 1–4 below.

All the Better to See You With

Without a doubt, contact lenses are a vast improvement over glasses. Lenses can correct every visual defect that glasses can and, because lenses are worn directly on the eye, can correct some defects that glasses cannot. Lenses move with the eye, so they give better peripheral (side) vision. They can never slide down one's nose or make a mark on it. Neither do they fog over in cold or damp weather. Where sports are concerned, contact lenses definitely show their superiority: They can be worn with almost no fear of breakage. Glasses, on the other hand, cannot solve as many visual problems. Because their position is fixed, they also give poorer peripheral vision. More often than not, they are at the end of one's nose, leaving a little red mark at the top. In cold or damp weather, the lenses on glasses quickly steam up, impairing vision. Furthermore, glasses are very easily broken during active play. It's no wonder contact lenses have become so popular.

Write answers to the following on a sheet of paper:

1. The topic sentence
2. The two topics being contrasted
3. The points of difference discussed
4. The transition phrase used to show contrast

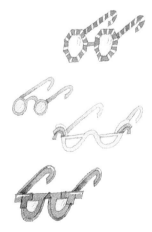

Activity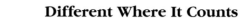

As you read the following paragraph, look for the things mentioned in numbers 1–5 below.

Different Where It Counts

Although the Thoroughbred and the Clydesdale are about the same height, there are striking differences between these two breeds of horses. The Thoroughbred is lighter with longer legs, enabling it to be one of the swiftest creatures in existence. The Clydesdale, on the other hand, is a heavier and stronger animal, able to pull hefty loads. While the Thoroughbred is considered to have a nervous temperament, the Clydesdale, in contrast, is known for its good disposition. The unique features of these two horses have been bred into them over the years so that they could serve humans in different ways. The Thoroughbred developed from the Arabian horse and has always been a saddle animal, whereas the Clydesdale is a descendant of the early workhorses of central Europe. These handsome creatures are just two of the many interesting breeds of horses found all over the world.

Write answers to the following on a sheet of paper:

1. The topic sentence
2. The word in the topic sentence that signals a contrast
3. The two topics being contrasted
4. The points of difference discussed
5. The transition words used to show contrast

Now look at the writing plans on the next page. Choose the plan that best fits the paragraph you just read and tell why you made the choice.

PLAN A

Thoroughbred
- body build
- temperament
- origin

Clydesdale
- body build
- temperament
- origin

PLAN B

Thoroughbred—body build
Clydesdale—body build

Thoroughbred—temperament
Clydesdale—temperament

Thoroughbred—origin
Clydesdale—origin

You can see that either plan is effective and both can be formed into well-organized paragraphs. Which plan is more like the paragraph you just read? Both plans use transition words, but one plan uses more transition words than the other. Which plan does that?

Writer's Corner

▶ Listed below are some possible topics for contrast. First determine what they have in common, and then determine the differences. On a piece of paper, write one point of comparison and three points of contrast for each set of topics.

1. Movies at the theater
Movies on a VCR

2. Motorcycle
Automobile

3. Cello
Violin

4. Table
Desk

5. Elevator
Escalator

6. Digital watch
Traditional watch

▶ Next, choose a set of topics from the list above or create an original set, and compose a short paragraph stressing contrast. Use transition words from the list on page 80 to keep the paragraph unified and coherent. Make sure you choose the plan that works best for you.

LESSON 5

Practicing Revision

Revision means "the act of seeing again." To revise a piece of writing means to take a second look at it and decide whether you should <u>C</u>hange sentences around, <u>A</u>dd or <u>R</u>emove words, or <u>S</u>ubstitute new ones (CARS).

All writers revise their work. When they first put their ideas down on paper, they end up with what is called a first draft. They then read over the first draft and see how they can improve it. There will sometimes be several drafts before the final version.

As a writer, your goal is to create paragraphs that will express your ideas in a clear and interesting fashion. It is important to revise your writing until it reads exactly the way you want it to. When you read over your first draft, you should check for unity, coherence, appropriate word choices, and effective transitions. It is also helpful to ask yourself the following questions:

To whom am I writing?
- myself
- my teacher
- other students
- the local community

What is the subject of my writing?

Why am I writing?
- to describe
- to inform
- to tell a story
- to persuade

The following paragraph needs to be revised. Read it over and decide what changes you would make. Discuss these ideas with your teacher or with other students. Use the Checkpoints for Revision at the end of the paragraph to help you focus on revision.

First Draft Paragraph

My cat, whose name is Ariel, misses me when I am not at home. When I go to school, she tries to follow me. If she gets out the door, I have to get her back in the house. Then she sleeps in the sun and looks out the window and plays with her toys. I have some friends who let their cats follow them to school. Ariel gets particularly upset when my family and I go away for a weekend, even though I leave her food and water. She likes my company. I know how she feels. I get lonely when I'm by myself too much, too.

Checkpoints for Revision

- ❏ Is there a topic sentence that clearly states the main idea of the paragraph?
- ❏ Are there enough supporting details?
- ❏ Do all of the details fit the topic?
- ❏ Are the details in the correct order?
- ❏ Are effective transitions used?
- ❏ Are there different kinds of sentences?
- ❏ Are the words precise and accurate?
- ❏ Is there a strong ending sentence?

Now read the revised version of the paragraph about the cat on page 86. What did the writer do to improve the paragraph? What is changed around, added, or removed?

Revised Paragraph

My cat, Ariel, misses me when I am not at home. As I leave for school in the morning, she tries to follow me. Sometimes she squeezes out the door, and I have to chase her back in the house. She is particularly upset if my family and I go away for a whole weekend, even though I make sure she has plenty of dry food and water. When I am gone, Ariel passes the time by sleeping in the sun, looking out the window, or playing with her toys. She likes all those things, but seems to enjoy my company most of all. I know how she feels, because I also get lonely when I'm by myself too much.

Activity A

Combine the following sentences to create a paragraph. Then revise and rewrite the paragraph by adding or deleting words, moving sentences around, or substituting new words. Use the Checkpoints for Revision on page 85 to help you discover where improvements are needed.

TOPIC SENTENCE	People have different approaches to doing homework; some approaches are more effective than others.
SUPPORTING DETAILS	● Andrew refuses ever to do homework.
	● Cynthia does everything that is assigned, as soon as it is assigned.
	● Jon reads the beginning and the end of every assigned reading and glances at the middle.
	● Nicole takes good notes in class and studies those for tests but never reads anything else.
	● Tod tries to decide what is most important and does that.
ENDING SENTENCE	Tod and Cynthia get the best grades. Do you think their grades are related to how they study?

Activity B

Consider how the following paragraph might be revised, and then rewrite it on a separate sheet of paper.

> Building a house requires many different kinds of workers. An architect creates a plan for the house. Cement workers pour the foundation. Roofers climb around on the nearly completed outer structure to put on shingles. Carpenters put up studs and beams to compose the frame. A contractor hires workers of many kinds. An electrician puts in the wiring. Painters are needed for both the inside and the outside of many houses. Other times a stonemason or bricklayer puts finishing touches on the outside.

Writer's Corner

▶ Look over the paragraphs you have written in past lessons and choose one that you feel could be improved. Exchange paragraphs with another student and practice the revision process on each other's work. Afterward, discuss why you made the changes you did.

Practicing Proofreading

Proofreading is the last step in the writing process. Use the following when you make a final check:

- Punctuation: periods, commas, colons, semicolons, apostrophes, hyphens, question marks, exclamation points.
- Capitalization: first word of each sentence, first word of direct quotation, proper nouns, proper adjectives.
- Spelling: start at the last word and work backward; consult a dictionary for problem words.
- Correct usage: subject-verb agreement, consistent verb tenses.
- Smoothness: copy all words correctly from last revision; read composition aloud, give work to another person to read.
- Appearance: handwriting neat and legible, appropriate margins on paper, name on your work.

Here are some symbols that a proofreader uses when going over a paper for the last time.

SYMBOL	MEANING	EXAMPLE
¶	begin a new paragraph	over. ¶Begin a new
⌒	close up space	close u⌒p space
∧	insert	students∧think *should*
⤶	delete, omit	that the the book
/	lowercase letter	/Mathematics
∼	letters are reversed	letters are reve∼rsed
≡	capital letter	≡washington

Activity A

Proofread the following paragraph. On a separate sheet of paper, note each error by writing down the two words preceding it and the two words following it. With a different color pen, use proofreaders' symbols to indicate the corrections needed. HINT: There are fifteen errors in the paragraph.

Nowadays I sail every chance I can get, but I didn't always feel that way abut the sprot. My first sailing lesson did not go well from the very beginning. After my Instructor, Mike, introduced himself, he told me to toss my canvas bag into the dinghy. I tossed a little too enthusiastically, and mike had to row out to save my bag from certain death by drowning Things didn't improve wh en we finally got out to the sailboat. I caught my pantleg on a on a hook and literally fell into the boat. After Mike carefully showed me how to put the small sail on correctly, I puttt it on upside down. I also managed to dip hafl the mainsail in the water, bang my shin on the anchor, and flip an ore over the side. (They float!) I began to regard the Boat as an enemy and was sure it felt the same way about me. Mike managed to get us ready sail despite me but I felt no real pleasure as we moved away from our mooring. Instead I looked mournfully back at familiar landmarks I was sure i would never sea again.

Writer's Corner

▶ Take a paragraph you have written that is in its final form and rewrite it, inserting seven errors. They should be the kinds of mistakes that can be corrected by the proofreaders' symbols you have just learned. Trade paragraphs with another student and see if you can find each other's deliberate errors. Use the proofreaders' symbols to indicate corrections that need to be made. Return the paragraphs and check that all errors were found and that you both used the symbols correctly.

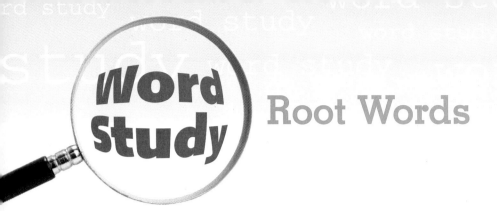

Root Words

A root word is a base word from which other words are built.

Root words have their own meanings. Some can stand alone as words; others add a prefix or suffix in order to form a word. Many root words come from the Latin and Greek languages.

Activity A

Listed below are five root words. Using a dictionary, determine whether they are derived from [<] the Latin or Greek language. Write your answers on a sheet of paper.

ROOT	MEANING		LANGUAGE
1. ped	foot	<	_____
2. meter	measure	<	_____
3. chrono	time	<	_____
4. duct	lead	<	_____
5. scribe	write	<	_____

Activity B

Copy the following chart. Using your dictionary, write three new words from each root word listed in Activity A, and then write the meanings of the new words.

ROOT	NEW WORDS	MEANINGS
1. ped	_____	_____
2. meter	_____	_____
3. chrono	_____	_____
4. duct	_____	_____
5. scribe	_____	_____

Activity C

Complete each of the following sentences by using a word based on the root word shown in parentheses.

1. The little boy (scribe) all over the painted wall.
2. The secretary (scribe) the letter perfectly.
3. Please arrange everything in (chrono) order.
4. In (chrono) swimming, team members perform challenging routines together in the water in time to music.
5. If your toenails hurt, you may need a (ped).
6. All (ped) are to cross the street at the corner.
7. If you wish to know what the temperature is, check a (meter).
8. A (meter) is one-tenth of a meter.
9. Water is an excellent (duct) of electricity.
10. The (duct) in Rome carried water throughout the city.

Describing a Place

How do you paint a picture? You could use a paintbrush, or you could use a pencil to paint a picture with words. Write a word picture of a place you know well. Read your paragraph aloud and challenge your classmates to draw the place you described.

 Prewriting

Make a list of familiar places that could be described in one paragraph.

Questions like these will help you think of a topic.

- Where do I go when I want to spend time alone?

- Where do my best friend and I go to spend time?

- Where would I take a person who is visiting our town for the first time?

- What is my favorite room in our home?

- What is my favorite outdoor place?

- What place that I've visited would I like to visit again?

- What is the most interesting room I've ever seen?

Choose one place to describe. Close your eyes and think about it for a few minutes. Try to remember every detail. Then freewrite for five minutes, writing down every detail you can think of as quickly as you can. Write phrases, not sentences, and leave a line between each detail.

Narrow Your Topic

If you decide that your favorite place is too large to write about in one paragraph, don't give up. You can still write about the topic you chose. Just narrow it down. Imagine that you are a photographer looking through a zoom lens. Focus in on the most important part of your favorite place. Keep focusing until you have zeroed in on a topic you can manage.

Drafting

As you write your draft, remember to put down your ideas as quickly as you can. Don't worry about spelling, punctuation, or grammar. You'll have a chance to check those things later.

Start right in with a sentence that lets your readers know what place you are writing about. For your draft, work on setting the scene. You can revise your beginning sentence to make it more interesting in the next stage. Once you've written your first sentence on the page, the rest will be easier.

Read the box below to review a method of organizing your ideas that will help you write a coherent paragraph. Then cut your prewriting notes apart so each detail is on its own scrap of paper. Put your details in order, and expand your notes into sentences to write the body of your paragraph.

Complete your descriptive paragraph with a sentence that sums up your feelings about the place you've described.

Writing with Coherence

Your paragraph will have coherence if your ideas flow naturally from one to the next. But having coherence takes some planning. The order in which you relate your ideas makes a difference.

When you write to describe a place, you will most often use spatial order. That is, you will choose a beginning point and move around the space in order from one point to another. Imagine that you are standing in one place as you write and are recording what you see as you move your head. Arrange the details in your paragraph so they flow in one direction—from left to right, down to up, or near to far. Don't change your point of view as you write.

Help your reader see what you see by using transition words for spatial order, such as *on the right, across from, behind, in front of, under,* and *above.* Write as if your reader were using your paragraph to draw a map. Imagine that the transition words you use are arrows pointing the way.

EDITOR'S WORKSHOP

Revising, Proofreading, and Publishing

Revising

Time to Take Another Look

As you reread your paragraph, check to make sure your reader will be able to picture the place you described. Then look for ways to make your descriptive paragraph sound more interesting.

Ask yourself these questions to help you revise:

❏ Does my first sentence let my reader know what place my paragraph is about?

❏ Does the first sentence sound interesting enough to capture my reader's attention?

❏ Do I need to add any details to make my word picture clearer?

❏ Do I need to rearrange the order of any details to make my paragraph flow more smoothly or logically?

❏ Do I need to add transition, or signal, words so my reader will know just where everything is?

❏ Does my last sentence bring my paragraph to a close and let my reader know how I feel about the place I described?

Make the changes you think will make your paragraph clear and interesting. Use a colored pen or pencil to make your revisions stand out. Talk over your changes with a partner if you like.

CARS Can Help You Remember

Use the letters of the word CARS to help you remember what to do when you revise.

Change a word or sentence to make your writing flow smoothly.

Add important information that you left out.

Remove unnecessary words by combining two short sentences.

Substitute more precise words for weak, overused verbs and adjectives.

Proofreading

Time to Look at Capitalization, Punctuation, and Spelling

When you are satisfied that your paragraph paints a clear word picture, check your capitalization, punctuation, spelling, and grammar. The checklist below will help you.

❏ Did I indent the first word of my descriptive paragraph?

❏ Did I begin each sentence, proper noun, and proper adjective with a capital letter?

❏ Did I use the correct mark of punctuation at the end of each sentence?

❏ Did I spell each word correctly?

Check Spelling by Computer

If you typed your final draft on a computer, run the spelling program before you print. Remember, though, that many spelling programs will not catch words that are spelled correctly but used incorrectly. The computer might accept a sentence like *They're are too pictures oven the bed.* So don't rely on the computer to find everything. The human brain is still the best proofreader.

 Publishing

Time to Share

Publish by reading your descriptive paragraph aloud to a small group of classmates.

To publish, follow these steps:

1. Copy your revised draft in your neatest handwriting or type it on a computer.
2. Proofread your final copy one last time.
3. Reread your final copy against your draft to make sure you did not leave anything out.

Challenge your friends to draw the place you described.

1. Find two or three classmates who have never seen the place you described in your paragraph.
2. Read your paragraph aloud slowly, as your classmates listen and draw a sketch. Your friends may ask you to slow down or to repeat a line, but they may not ask any questions.
3. If the sketches are similar to the place you described, then you described the important details accurately.

CHAPTER 4

Refining Your Writing Skills

Combining Independent Clauses

In a compound sentence, the combined independent clauses vary sentence length and make paragraphs more interesting.

If a paragraph contains too many short sentences, it will not read smoothly. When two short sentences are closely related in thought, they can be combined to form one longer sentence. The longer sentence is called a compound sentence because it contains two simple sentences, or independent clauses, properly connected. Most independent clauses are connected by coordinate conjunctions, each of which varies slightly in meaning and changes the thought of the sentence.

CONJUNCTION	FUNCTION	EXAMPLE
and	suggests ideas that are of equal importance	The safe was open and the money was gone.
but/yet	suggests opposite or contrasting ideas	Dan often travels by plane, yet he is afraid of flying.
or	suggests options or alternatives	I could paint the walls, or I could put up wallpaper.
nor	suggests no possible option or alternative	My sunglasses weren't in the house, nor were they in the car.

About the Photograph

When it comes to improving our writing, we all can use a little help. Who or what has helped you become a better writer?

Activity A

On a sheet of paper, combine the following simple sentences to form compound sentences by inserting an appropriate conjunction. Tell the function of the coordinate conjunction.

1. Jeanne could take a course in early American history. She could take a course in modern poetry.

2. The mechanic used all his skills. Nothing corrected the engine problem.

3. Suddenly the wind started blowing strongly. It began to rain.

4. Jack does not walk to school. He does not ride a bus.

5. The tomato is treated like a vegetable. It is really a fruit.

6. Peter could pitch in tomorrow's game. He could pitch next Saturday instead.

Activity B

Write five original compound sentences showing the proper use of *and, but, yet, or,* and *nor.* Draw on information from your science, math, or social studies classes. Be able to identify the function of each coordinate conjunction.

Writer's Corner

▶ Write a short paragraph about an event that happened at school or at home. Include at least three compound sentences using different coordinate conjunctions.

Sentence Combining with Adjectival Clauses

In a complex sentence, the principal clause is the more important idea expressed. The dependent clause is the less important idea. An adjectival clause is a dependent clause.

You have learned that you can use a coordinate conjunction to combine two simple sentences to form one compound sentence. When this is done, each sentence remains an independent clause. Another way of combining sentences is to make one of the sentences an independent clause and the other sentence a dependent clause. When you combine an independent clause and a dependent clause, you create a complex sentence.

An adjectival clause is one kind of dependent clause. It can be added to a principal clause by means of a relative pronoun. The principal clause, or independent clause, always contains the main idea. The adjectival clause, or dependent clause, expresses the idea of lesser importance. Look at the following sample sentence.

> Florida, which is a favorite destination for tourists, is located in the southeastern part of the United States.

The writer wishes to stress the location of Florida. The main idea of the sentence is: Florida is located in the southeastern part of the United States. The adjectival clause, beginning with the relative pronoun *which*, states an idea of lesser importance: Florida is a favorite destination for tourists.

Suppose the writer wants to stress that Florida is a favorite destination for tourists. The writer would then subordinate the idea that Florida is located in the southeastern part of the United States. An appropriate relative pronoun would introduce this statement. The complex sentence would read:

> Florida, which is located in the southeastern part of the United States, is a favorite destination for tourists.

Now compare the two sentences.

Activity A

Following are five complex sentences. Each contains an independent clause and a dependent clause. Read each sentence and then write its main idea on a sheet of paper.

1. The Parthenon, which stands on the Acropolis, overlooks the city of Athens.
2. The earliest type of armor, which was made of animal skins, protected the body.
3. Ferdinand Foch, who was a French military leader, was one of the greatest Allied generals of World War I.
4. The flounder has a flat body that blends in with its surroundings.
5. Castles, which are fortified dwellings, played a prominent role during the Middle Ages.

Activity B

For each sentence, locate the clause containing the less important idea and copy it onto a sheet of paper.

1. The Sears Tower, which is located in Chicago, is 110 stories high.
2. The name *Florida,* which in Spanish means "full of flowers," was given by Ponce de León.
3. Fog is a low cloud that rests near the ground or a body of water.
4. Animals that live in the polar regions are usually hairy with thick hides.
5. The centaur was a mythological creature that was half man and half horse.

Activity C

On a sheet of paper, rewrite the sentences in Activities A and B so that the clauses are reversed. This means that the importance of the ideas will also be reversed. What was formerly the main idea will become the less important idea, and what was less important will become the main idea.

Example:

<u>The Parthenon</u>, [which overlooks the city of Athens,] <u>stands on the Acropolis.</u> ⟶ **main idea**

adjectival clause

Activity D

Combine each pair of sentences, making the sentence in italics the principal clause. Connect the dependent clause to the principal clause with an appropriate relative pronoun: *who, whom, which, what,* or *that.* Some words will be omitted when the sentences are combined.

1. *Atlantis was a mythical island in the Atlantic Ocean.* Atlantis was destroyed by earthquakes and floods.
2. John Adams was the second president of the United States. *John Adams was the first president to live in the White House.*
3. *Students should know about the encyclopedia.* The encyclopedia contains many interesting facts.
4. Babe Didrikson Zaharias was a great athlete. *Babe Didrikson Zaharias won two gold medals for track and field in the 1932 Olympic Games.*
5. A dingo is a wild dog of Australia. *The dingo may have been brought to Australia by prehistoric settlers.*

Writer's Corner

▶ Write five original complex sentences. The principal and the dependent clauses should be joined by a relative pronoun. Use information from your other subject areas to write your sentences.

Sentence Combining with Adverbial Clauses

In a complex sentence, the principal clause is the more important idea expressed. The dependent clause is the less important idea. An adverbial clause is a dependent clause.

An adverbial clause is a type of dependent clause. It can be added to a principal clause by means of a subordinate conjunction. The subordinate conjunction, or subordinator, establishes the relationship between the two clauses. Look at the sentences below and note the different types of relationships. The adverbial clauses are italicized.

Cause and effect: Carlos has an extensive vocabulary *because he is an avid reader.*

Time: *As soon as I pack my suitcase,* I'll be ready.

Comparison: An Olympic athlete performs better *than an amateur college athlete does.*

Manner: Sandra works *as though there will be no tomorrow.*

Conditional: *Although Monica wanted to be a great gymnast,* she was unwilling to practice every day.

Changing the subordinator can change the meaning of a sentence. Read the sentence below, using a different subordinator each time. Discuss the shades of meaning.

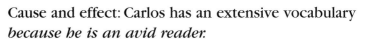

Rose went home–before–she swam the twenty laps.

The entire subordinate clause, which includes the subordinate conjunction, may be placed before or after the principal clause. Using different placements provides sentence variety. Look at the following example.

The old, weathered prospector built a fire [because the temperature dropped to thirty degrees.]

[Because the temperature dropped to thirty degrees,] the old, weathered prospector built a fire.

Activity A

The relationship between the sentences in each set is given in parentheses. Show this relationship by using the proper subordinate conjunction to combine the two sentences.

1. Paper was scarce and expensive in the Middle Ages. It had to be used sparingly. (cause and effect)

2. Little children went to school. The children were given a hornbook. (time)

3. The hornbook was a flat board with a hole in its handle. The hornbook could be worn around the neck. (cause and effect)

4. The hornbook was used in England and the United States. Printed books became cheaper. (time)

5. Some hornbooks were made of gingerbread. Children could eat the letter of the alphabet they had mastered. (cause and effect)

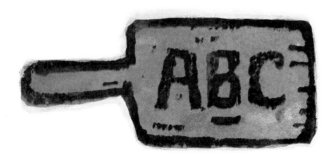

Activity B

Combine each pair of sentences by making the italicized words into an adverbial clause. Introduce the clause with an appropriate subordinator from the list below, and tell what relationship is established.

although	for	since	then
after	if	so	unless
because	provided	than	when
before			

1. Chess is a difficult game to learn. *Checkers is not a difficult game to learn.*
2. *Mark Twain is a noted novelist.* He also has written many outstanding short stories.
3. *Caesar had a cruel manner.* He was greatly disliked.
4. Ann discovered the gasoline tank was leaking. *We had traveled many hours.*
5. Two bears arrived on the scene. *We cleared the picnic area.*

Activity C

Reverse the position of the adverbial clause in each sentence of Activity B. If the clause was introductory, make it final; if final, make it introductory.

Writer's Corner

▶ Write original complex sentences showing the following relationships: cause and effect, comparison, time, manner, and condition. Vary the positions of the adverbial clauses to create variety.

Expanding Sentences

Expanding sentences involves adding extra words, phrases, or clauses in order to make the sentences more interesting.

One way to make a sentence more interesting is to add extra information to it, or to expand it. This can be done by inserting words, phrases, or clauses in appropriate places in the sentence.

This added information can tell

where	why
when	how

It can also describe

nouns	adjectives
verbs	adverbs

Notice the following sentence. The arrows indicate several places where information can be added to expand the sentence.

The ∧woman walked∧to the∧store.

One possible expansion could be:

The *tired, old* woman walked *slowly up the block* to the *corner* store.

If other words were used to expand the sentence, an entirely different picture might emerge.

The *tall, dark-haired* woman walked *briskly across the mall* to the *discount clothing* store.

Activity A

Expand the following sentences by adding words, phrases, or clauses where the arrows indicate.

1. Karen ∧ decorated for the ∧ party ∧.

2. ∧ John ∧ finished his ∧ homework.

3. The ∧ TV broke ∧.

4. ∧ The ∧ bell ∧ rang to begin ∧ class.

5. ∧ The ∧ train ∧ screeched to a ∧ stop.

Activity B

Expand the following sentences by adding words, phrases, or clauses where you think they would fit.

1. The doctor examined the patient.

2. The beach chair collapsed.

3. The rock broke the window.

4. Katy's bike was stolen.

5. Nicole received a stereo.

6. The fire burned the house.

7. The bus moved along.

8. The pioneers traveled west.

9. Charles Dickens wrote novels.

10. The women made the quilt.

Activity C

Use words, phrases, and clauses to expand each of the following sentences, and then combine the sentences to make an interesting, creative paragraph.

1. The room was wallpapered.

2. There was a rug on the floor.

3. There was furniture scattered about.

4. White curtains framed the windows.

Writer's Corner

▶ The paragraph below needs revision. Use the skills you have learned for expanding and combining sentences to make the paragraph more interesting. Rewrite the paragraph on a sheet of paper and give it a title.

We went hiking on the trail. The sun was shining. The air was cool. It felt good. The leaves were already changing. Many had fallen. They smelled wonderful. We tramped through them. We saw squirrels foraging for nuts. A flock of geese flew over. Fall was here. The signs were everywhere. Winter was around the corner.

Word Substitution

Word substitution involves the choosing of vivid, colorful vocabulary to convey your message in an interesting manner.

Look at the sentence below and note the colorless way in which it is written. Then look at all the possible substitutions that can be made to enliven the sentence. The important thing is not just to tell your reader what happened, but to let your reader experience the event.

> Feeling quite scared, I sat in the colorful roller coaster waiting for it to go up the first hill.

- How did you feel?

  soaring spirits   fear and trepidation
  wildly pounding heart   excitement
  mounting terror

- How did you sit?

crouch	tremble	stiffen	cling
huddle	slide	cringe	jerk
slouch	grasp	squirm	shudder

- How can you describe the roller coaster?

  gaudily painted   riotously colored
  brightly hued   silver-toned
  gleaming

- What else can you call a roller coaster?

  chariot   rocket car
  coach   express train
  Thunderbolt

- What can a roller coaster do?

swoop	soar	glide	crawl
careen	zip	plunge	lurch

● What was the ride like?

    downward plunge   crawling ascent

    mad rush through time   perilous curves

    and space

Your new sentence might look like this:

(Feeling quite scared)

With a wildly pounding heart, I huddled in the silver-toned chariot, anxiously awaiting its crawl up the mountain, for the initial downward plunge.

(I sat in the colorful roller coaster)

(waiting for it to go up the first hill)

What does a paragraph look like when vivid, colorful vocabulary replaces worn-out, drab words?

Eventful Journey

Mingled emotions of fear and regret clashed within me as I settled myself in the Thunderbolt that July afternoon. The strident shouts of the operator cut across the air as the screeching of released brakes noisily announced the initial ascent. With a racing heart I stiffened myself against the back of the brightly gleaming car. For one thrill-packed second I was conscious of being unwillingly poised on a gigantic hill. Then down, down I plunged at breathtaking speed. Before I had even a slim chance of retrieving my composure, this mad rush was repeated with terrifying rapidity. Desperately I clung to the steel bar of the chariot as it careened and whizzed around each perilous curve. Suddenly, as I shuddered and cringed in my place, the rocket car gave a wild, uncontrolled lurch, then with an asthmatic cough wheezed to a full stop. Head reeling, I staggered out of the coach, relieved and grateful for the feeling of solid ground under my feet. I am sure that even a trip around the world would not be so thrilling as that five-minute ride on the roller coaster.

How do you come up with a phrase that paints a picture? One way is to use words that describe as accurately as possible the experiences of your senses: sight, hearing, taste, smell, and touch. To say, for instance, that music came from the speakers might not describe your experience of the sound as accurately as saying that music blasted from the speakers.

Activity A

SIGHT is the sense through which we collect the most images. Think of five words that could be substituted for each word in italics in order to make the action come alive.

1. People *walk*.
2. Animals *walk*.
3. Leaves *drop*.
4. Waves *fall*.
5. Lights *shine*.

HEARING is the second most common way in which we gather experiences. List five words that could be substituted for each word in italics.

6. Voices *talk*.
7. Water *flows*.

8. Birds *sing*.
9. Bells *ring*.

Many images come through TASTE. Give five words for how

10. food tastes.
11. beverages taste.

Other images come to us through the sense of SMELL. Give five words that describe how

12. flowers smell.
13. forests smell.

14. air smells.

The last way you receive impressions or images is through TOUCH. Give five words to describe how

15. water feels.
16. cloth feels.

17. fruit feels.
18. wind feels.

Activity B

Find substitutes for the words in italics and rewrite each sentence using your substitutions. Use your imagination and expand your ideas wherever you can.

1. The car *went* down the road.
2. Amy made a *beverage* that *tasted good.*
3. Her perfume *smelled good.*
4. The *cat walked* through the tall grass.
5. Hamburgers *were frying in the pan.*
6. The water *in the shower* was *hot and relaxing.*
7. The *horse trotted* along.

Writer's Corner

▶ How many words can you substitute for the word *nice?* Read the following paragraph and provide more specific adjectives. On a sheet of paper, write the more precise adjective and the word that follows it. After you have finished this exercise, reread the paragraph to make certain that every substitute for *nice* is as exact as possible.

Ringing in the New Year

The school added a *nice* affair to the social calendar this year: the New Year's Eve dance. The dance committee aroused our interest by planning a *nice* theme and hiring a *nice* band. With its colored lights, swinging silver bells, and plump snowmen, the gym presented a *nice* sight. The Satellites, a local group, played *nice* dance music. Best of all, the brightly decorated table offered a tempting variety of *nice* food, donated by *nice* sponsors. As the striking clock ushered in the New Year, everyone agreed that the dance had brought the holidays to a very *nice* close.

Sentence Modeling

Modeling is the imitation of a given pattern.

When you read good books, you will notice that authors use a variety of sentence patterns and combinations of patterns. This adds interest to the writing and forms part of what is called an author's style. As you discover different ways of structuring sentences, you will want to try them out in your own writing. Such experimentation will help you grow as a writer, and eventually you will develop a writing style of your own.
A good way to learn a new sentence pattern is to analyze the structure of the sentence and then use the model and analysis to write a sentence of your own. Here are some examples of sentence modeling.

MODEL	He is the player who led the team to victory.
ANALYSIS	**adjectival clause** He is the player ⌐who led the team to victory.⌐
NEW SENTENCE	Joan is the runner who won the women's marathon.

MODEL	We saw them when we were in San Francisco.
ANALYSIS	**adverbial clause** We saw them ⌐when we were in San Francisco.⌐
NEW SENTENCE	I will give you the money when you need it.

MODEL	That the earthquake was severe was noted on the seismograph.
ANALYSIS	**noun clause (subject)** ⌐That the earthquake was severe⌐was noted on the seismograph.
NEW SENTENCE	That you are determined to go is obvious to me.

MODEL	Learning a new word every day increases one's vocabulary.

gerund phrase (subject)

ANALYSIS	Learning a new word every day	increases one's vocabulary.

NEW SENTENCE	Controlling your weight requires willpower.

MODEL	My father's chief delight is to read mystery novels.

infinitive phrase (subj. comp.)

ANALYSIS	My father's chief delight is	to read mystery novels.

NEW SENTENCE	The duty of the governor is to enforce the laws of the state.

MODEL	They watched the boat sailing down the river.

participial phrase

ANALYSIS	They watched the boat	sailing down the river.

NEW SENTENCE	The lifeguard watched the children swimming in the pool.

Activity A

Label the pattern in each sentence below. Compose an original sentence using that pattern. Refer to the model examples on pages 112 and 113 for help.

1. Did you hear the children singing in the street?

2. Solving crossword puzzles is fun for me.

3. That Michelangelo painted the Sistine Chapel is well known.

4. Darlene learned the value of exercise when she lived in the mountains.

5. Leonardo da Vinci, who was a great painter, was also an accomplished architect.

6. Your best plan is to go by airplane.

Activity B

The next six sentences are variations of the patterns in the examples on pages 112 and 113. Identify and label these patterns, and compose original sentences using them.

1. Paula related what happened yesterday on the trip.

2. We should try to reach camp before dark.

3. Lucia did not know when the check would arrive.

4. Having tried liver before, Sara refused to eat it.

5. His job was grooming horses.

6. Since I had my tonsils removed, I have been free of sore throats.

Writer's Corner

▶ **Model an original sentence after each sentence given below. Change the topic, but keep the basic parts of speech.**

1. When the moment arrived, I stood frozen in my tracks, but something inside me urged me to approach this awesome, horrifying creature.

2. Trudging and stomping along, the youth finally reached his destination.

3. Excited? Me? Never!

4. I wonder—although I think I know the answer—why the coach never puts me in the game.

5. Apparently he didn't notice the new building. Why would he?

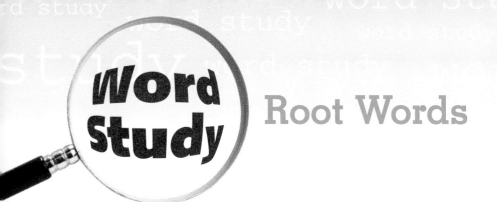

Root Words

A root word is a base word from which other words are built.

As you learned in the Word Study in Chapter 3, root words have their own meanings and may either stand alone or be part of a word. Many root words are derived from either the Latin or Greek language.

Activity A

Here is a new list of five root words that will help you write other related words. Copy the chart onto a sheet of paper and look up each root word in your dictionary. Write the meaning of the root and its origin, Latin or Greek.

ROOT	MEANING		LANGUAGE
1. cosmo	_____	<	_____
2. vert	_____	<	_____
3. scope	_____	<	_____
4. astro	_____	<	_____
5. audio	_____	<	_____

Activity B

Consult your dictionary and find one word based on each root. Write the meaning of each new word.

ROOT	NEW WORD	MEANING
1. cosmo	_____	_____
2. vert	_____	_____
3. scope	_____	_____
4. astro	_____	_____
5. audio	_____	_____

Activity C

Complete each of the following sentences by using a word based on the root shown in parentheses.

1. The nurse used an (audio) to test our hearing.
2. Because there was so much noise outside, the directions were barely (audio).
3. All submarines are equipped with a (scope).
4. The beat of the heart can be heard through a (scope).
5. Because Seth was an (vert), he really looked forward to meeting new people.
6. The work was so intense, I took a walk just for a (vert).
7. (cosmo) rays penetrate the earth's atmosphere.
8. A Russian space traveler is called a (cosmo).
9. The (astro) used her telescope to track the path of the comet.
10. Sally Ride was the first American female (astro).

WRITER'S WORKSHOP

Class News

What do you tell family members when they ask, "What did you do in school today?" Do you ever get tired of repeating the same stories over and over? Here's the solution. Write a news article about a major class activity or event. Publish it in a class news magazine and take home a copy for your family members to read.

 Prewriting

Make a list of current class activities and events that would make interesting topics for a news article.

Ask yourself questions like these to help you get started.

- What new things am I learning this year?
- Has my class taken any trips?
- Does my class participate in projects that help others?

- Am I rehearsing for any special performances, such as concerts or plays?
- Has my class held any fund-raising events?
- How are my sports teams doing?
- Have I or any of my classmates won any special honors or awards?

News articles answer five questions, called "the five W's."

> <u>W</u>ho?
> <u>W</u>hat?
> <u>W</u>hen?
> <u>W</u>here?
> <u>W</u>hy?

Before you begin your draft, use a chart like the one below to gather all the information you need to answer the five questions.

First, fill in the basic details. Add other details under the appropriate heading.

Who?	What?	When?	Where?	Why?
our academic varsity team: Shari, Dan, Theo, Mai adviser is Mr. Loomis	Academic Super Bowl quiz-type competition among all our city's schools	next Tuesday at 4:00 currently practicing every day after school	city-hall auditorium	to show our school pride

Drafting

Begin your draft with an opening sentence, called the lead, that summarizes the answers to the five W's.

WHEN	Next Tuesday at 4:00,
WHO	our academic varsity team
WHY	will show their school pride
WHAT	by competing in the Academic Super Bowl
WHERE	at the city-hall auditorium.

In the body of your story, expand on the ideas in your lead by adding interesting details from your prewriting and interview notes.

In your final sentence, summarize the article or suggest an action your readers might take.

> Win or lose, we are proud of the dedication our classmates have shown.

> Let's all be in the audience next Tuesday to cheer on our team.

Finish by writing a short, attention-getting headline.

Conducting an Interview

Follow these guidelines when you conduct an interview.

1. Arrange an appointment in advance.
2. Ask permission if you plan to tape-record the interview.
3. Prepare a list of questions to ask.
4. On the day of your interview, be on time.
5. Greet your interviewee politely before asking your first question.
6. Listen carefully and take notes as quickly as possible.
7. Ask your interviewee to repeat any details you miss.
8. Ask your interviewee to spell names of people and places.
9. Invite your interviewee to add information that was not covered by your list of questions.
10. Review your notes while the interview is still fresh in your mind and fill in any missing details.
11. After your interview, thank the person you interviewed. If the person is not a classmate, write a thank-you letter and offer to show the interviewee a copy of the completed article.

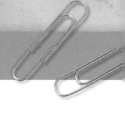

EDITOR'S WORKSHOP

Revising, Proofreading, and Publishing

Revising

Time to Take Another Look

After you've written your draft, revise your article to make it clearer and more interesting.

Reread your article carefully and ask yourself these questions:

❑ Do I need to make my headline more interesting to capture my reader's attention?

❑ Does my lead sentence answer the questions who, what, when, where, and why?

❑ Do I need to rewrite parts of the article that are confusing or unclear?

❑ Do I need to add important information that I left out?

❑ Do I need to cut out any unnecessary words, phrases, or sentences?

❑ Do I need to rearrange details that seem out of place?

❑ Do I need to recheck any of my facts?

Use a colored pencil to revise your draft. Concentrate on making your article say exactly what you want it to say.

Add a Quotation
A quotation is a person's exact words enclosed in quotation marks. Give your article credibility by adding a quotation from a participant in the event or activity in your article. Use your interview notes or your tape-recorded interview to find interesting material to quote.

 ## Proofreading

Time to Look at Capitalization, Punctuation, and Spelling

A reporter for a news magazine would now send his or her story to the copy editor, who would check capitalization, punctuation, spelling, and grammar.

For this article, you will be your own copy editor. Use the checklist below to edit and proofread your news article.

❑ Did I begin each sentence and proper noun with a capital letter?

❑ Did I use correct punctuation for quotations?

❑ Did I use the correct mark of punctuation at the end of each sentence?

❑ Did I spell the names of people and places correctly?

Double-Check Proper Nouns

Most people enjoy seeing their name in print, but they hate seeing their name spelled incorrectly. Double-check the names of the people, places, and events in your article.

 ## Publishing

Time to Share

Share your news by publishing your article in a class news magazine.

To publish, follow these steps:

1. Copy your revised draft in your neatest handwriting or type it on a computer.

2. Check to make sure you haven't left anything out.

3. Reread your final copy to be sure there are no errors.

4. Add an illustration if you wish.

Make the class news magazine.

1. Collect everyone's final article.

2. Decide together on a title for your magazine.

3. Assemble the articles into a magazine.

4. Make copies of your magazine for each writer, or place the magazine in the class library so everyone can borrow it to share with family members.

Types of Paragraphs

Writing Descriptive Paragraphs

A descriptive paragraph uses words to vividly portray a person, place, or thing.

In descriptive writing, vivid, colorful language and sensory images are used to present a picture. A writer chooses words that will appeal to the reader's senses: sight, hearing, taste, touch, and smell. Often a writer will use figures of speech, such as simile, metaphor, or personification, to better communicate the image he or she has in mind. Read the paragraph below and then answer the questions on the next page.

Twilight of Evening

Big flakes of wet snow are whirling lazily about the street lamps. . . . Iona Potapov, the sledge-driver, is all white like a ghost. He sits on the box without stirring, bent as double as the living body can be bent. If a regular snowdrift fell on him, it seems as though even then he would not think it necessary to shake it off. . . . His little mare is white and motionless too. Her stillness, the angularity of her lines, and the sticklike straightness of her legs make her look like a halfpenny gingerbread horse. She is probably lost in thought. Anyone who has been torn away from the plough, from the familiar gray landscapes, and cast into this slough, full of monstrous lights, of unceasing uproar and hurrying people, is bound to think.

About the Photograph

When painting a picture with words, a writer employs sensory images. When you look at this photograph, what descriptive words come to mind?

1. This paragraph is a description of
   a. a snow scene in the country.
   b. a snow scene in a town.
   c. a snow scene on the road between the country
      and a town.

2. The description of this place leads us to believe that it is
   a. quiet.   b. noisy.   c. lonely.

3. The sense which the author appeals to the most is
   a. sight.   b. hearing.   c. taste.   d. touch.   e. smell.

4. Find as many words as you can that tell about people, places,
   or things with which you are not familiar. Look up these
   words in the dictionary and define them.

5. Find two similes in the paragraph. What do they compare?
   Do you think that it is better to use a simile than to use other
   descriptive words?

6. Can you find any words in the paragraph that refer to the
   sense of touch?

7. If you were an artist and wanted to paint this picture, would
   you have enough information? Describe your picture. What
   colors would you use?

Now that you have investigated how writers use description,
you can begin to develop your own descriptive writing skills.

Activity **A**

List the vivid words in each sentence.

1. Nervously, the young man entered the bustling office for his job interview.
2. The deep blue sky was dotted with fleecy cotton clouds.
3. Hanging from an invisible thread, the spider labored to spin its majestic web.
4. As we descended the ancient cellar stairs, a damp, musty odor enveloped us.
5. Weather-beaten and dirty, the old homeless woman shuffled toward the park bench.
6. She had a joyous, free kind of laugh that was impossible to resist.
7. The blazing sun beat down mercilessly on the exhausted hiker.
8. The aroma of sizzling bacon filled the house and tickled the nostrils of the groggy sleepers.
9. White-capped waves glistened in the sun as they surged toward the shore.
10. As the misguided hammer smashed his unprotected thumb, the boy gasped with pain.

Activity **B**

Improve the sentences by substituting vivid words for plain ones.

1. We were surprised that the building was so large.
2. The happy child ran to his mother.
3. The ruler gave nice gifts to her loyal servants.
4. In the distance stood a dark mountain, plainly outlined against the sky.
5. The horse ran quietly along the curved path.
6. All day, we worked in the small office.
7. I could not do a difficult puzzle like that.
8. Seagulls flew back and forth as the waves flowed onto the beach.
9. The eagle flew down from the high cliff.
10. Our friend told us about funny happenings at school.

Activity C

List ten details that could describe each of the scenes below. Be sure to appeal to as many of the senses as you can, and include your own feelings.

1. a stray dog that wandered up to your house
2. a deserted street late at night
3. the kitchen at your house just before dinner
4. a large concert hall where a rock star is performing
5. being awakened at night by the sound of a siren
6. an abandoned car in a junkyard
7. a pair of old sneakers in the school gym

Writer's Corner

▶ Choose one idea to develop into a descriptive paragraph of your own.

A. You saw the crime. At the police station, you give your detailed description of the criminal to the composite artist. Write your detailed description of the criminal. When your paragraph is finished, ask a friend to draw a picture from your description.

B. You have just received a brand new CD player for your birthday. You call your friend on the phone and describe its appearance and all of its features.

C. The party has ended. Your last friend just went home. Now you have to clean up. The place looks like a disaster area! Describe it.

D. You lost your shoes during gym class. They were really different from anyone else's in school. Write a description of them for the Lost and Found bulletin board.

E. You are a creature from another planet. Your spacecraft just landed at a busy intersection in a big city. This is your first encounter with human beings. When you write your entry in your travel log, this is how you describe them.

F. You gave two million dollars to a contractor to build your mansion. Your limousine pulls up in the driveway, and you see your magnificent new home for the first time. You had no idea it would look like this! Describe it.

Writing Narrative Paragraphs

A narrative paragraph tells a story.

Narrative writing tells a story. The writer must relate the events in the order in which they happen, name the characters, tell where the events happen, and give the story an ending. There are different types of narrative writing.

TYPES OF NARRATIVE WRITING

PERSONAL EXPERIENCE	A short piece of writing that tells a single incident in the life of the author
BIOGRAPHY	The life of a person written by someone else
AUTOBIOGRAPHY	A personally written account of one's life
LOG	A written record of daily progress; usually of a voyage
JOURNAL	A regularly kept record of experiences, ideas, or reflections for private use
DIARY	A record of events or observations kept daily or at frequent intervals, usually intended for private use; similar to a journal
LEGEND	A story that comes from the past and is thought to be historical, although it cannot be verified
FANTASY	A fictional story that often contains strange settings and unusual characters
MYTH	A story that uses fantasy to explain people's beliefs or some phenomenon in nature
FABLE	A fictitious story intended to stress a useful truth, often by giving animals the power of speech
NEWS STORY	The report of an incident told in the order in which the events occurred; contains the *who, what, where,* and *when* of the event, and sometimes the *why*

Many narrative paragraphs contain transition words to help the readers understand the order of events. Some of these words are *first, then, later, before, during, while, next, finally, after, at last, when,* and *at once.*

Read the paragraph below and answer the questions that follow.

One evening my mother told me that I was old enough to help with the grocery shopping. She took me to the corner store to show me the way. I was proud; I felt like a grown-up. The next afternoon, I looped the basket over my arm and went down the pavement toward the store. When I reached the corner, a group of boys snatched the basket, took the money, and sent me running home in a panic. That evening I told my mother what had happened, but she made no comment; instead she sat me down at once, wrote another note, gave me more money, and sent me to the grocery store again. I crept down the steps and saw the same group of boys playing down the street. I ran back into the house.

1. Where does this story take place? What words indicate this?
   a. farm   **b.** town   **c.** mountains
2. Recount three events from the story in the order in which they happen.
3. List any transition words the author uses in the paragraph.
4. In what span of time do you think the story takes place? What words show this?
5. Would you call this paragraph
   a. a biography.   **b.** a personal experience.   **c.** a diary.
   Why?

Two things are important in narrative writing: relating the events in the order in which they take place and having each event flow smoothly into the next.

Activity **A**

Below are two personal experiences. The events were listed out of order of occurrence. On a sheet of paper, write the first two words of each event in a column, and then number them in the order in which they would have occurred. Finally, rewrite them as an entire paragraph.

The Giant Fish

_____ Although it looked as if a storm was heading our way, we stayed another hour.

_____ Finally, my father got a bite!

_____ The wind was getting stronger, and the water was becoming choppy.

_____ I waited with the net while my brother and uncle stood by to see if they should bring in the fish or cut the line.

_____ The tug-of-war rocked the boat furiously, and Dad almost fell overboard.

_____ By now, the wind had picked up speed, but Dad continued to struggle.

_____ Looking over the side of the boat, I began to laugh.

_____ Just as Dad pulled in the line, we all noticed that he had hooked the boat's anchor.

Changing Times

_____ After all these years, my old school was being torn down.

_____ I wondered what had happened to the friends with whom I had lost touch.

_____ I stood in the doorway of Room 335 and felt a wave of sadness.

_____ Then I remembered Mr. Jenkins, my biology teacher in sophomore year.

_____ As I gazed down at its scarred surface, the room suddenly became filled with sounds and faces.

_____ This was a great place, and it will always live in my memories.

_____ Looking around, I spotted my old desk and carefully crossed the torn-up floor to stand beside it.

_____ I had never studied so hard for a class as I did for his, and that was the year I developed my love of science.

Activity B

Choose one of the following topics and imagine what might have happened. List specific details for the event. Then, using the list as a guide, write a narrative paragraph.

A. You have fallen asleep. Your dream begins. It is the most unusual dream you have ever had.

B. All that you and your friends were doing was clowning around in an old museum. How were you supposed to know that the Time Machine actually worked?

C. An accident occurred one evening and you were the only witness. You are now giving your story to the police.

D. You are at a costume party, and everyone is dressed up. When you see this creature, though, something tells you that it is not a party guest in costume.

E. You are on the Ferris wheel at an amusement park. Seated next to you is a total stranger about your own age. When your car reaches the top of the wheel, the ride breaks down. You then begin to realize that choosing this ride was the biggest mistake you ever made.

Writer's Corner

▶ Write a narrative paragraph about a personal experience. Select some event or special day in your life: an unexpected school holiday, something you did on vacation or on a school trip, an accident or other misfortune you had, or an ordinary Saturday you would like to share. Make a list of the events as they happened to use as a guide when you write your first draft. Revise and proofread your paragraph.

Writing Expository Paragraphs

An expository paragraph explains something or informs the reader.

Expository writing must be clear and simple, with details in a logical order. This kind of writing can be used to explain information, directions, or definitions.

Writing Informative Paragraphs

An informative paragraph communicates knowledge to the reader. It should be written in a clear and interesting manner, with an effective topic and beginning, middle, and ending sentences. All middle sentences should relate to the narrowed topic, and any terms the reader is not likely to recognize should be explained.

Activity A

Read the paragraph below and answer the questions that follow.

> All poisonous snakes are dangerous, but the king cobra, or hamadryad, is especially lethal. Whereas a common cobra is rarely more than five feet long, a king cobra may reach a length of sixteen feet. It has enough venom in its poison glands to kill five hundred human beings. That isn't all. The hamadryad is the only snake known to attack without any provocation. These fearful creatures have been reported to trail a man through the jungle for the express purpose of biting him. They are so aggressive that they have closed roads in India by driving away all traffic. This is probably because hamadryads, unlike other snakes, guard their eggs and young, and if a pair sets up housekeeping in a district, every other living thing must get out—including elephants. When a king cobra rears up, it stands higher than the head of a kneeling man. It is unquestionably the most dangerous animal in the world today.

1. The general topic of this paragraph is

   a. snakes.   **b.** cobras.   **c.** king cobras.

2. The specific topic of this paragraph is

   a. how king cobras care for their young.

   b. that king cobras are the most dangerous animals in the world.

   c. how king cobras are different from other snakes.

3. What is the topic sentence in this paragraph?

4. Make a list of all the words the author uses as a substitute for *king cobra.*

5. List all the facts about the king cobra that you find in this paragraph.

6. In what ways is the king cobra unlike other snakes?

132

Writing Directions

Besides providing information, the expository paragraph can be used to give directions or recipes. In all expository writing, it is important to list the details or steps in the proper order. For directions and recipes, the order is that which will produce the desired results in the most efficient way.

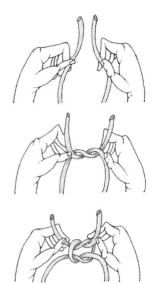

Directions for tying a square knot would be:

1. Take two ends of cord and hold one in each hand.

2. Take the cord in the right hand and place it over and under the cord in the left hand. Pull both ends slightly.

3. Take the cord that is now in the left hand and place it over and under the cord in the right hand.

4. Pull both ends to tighten into a square knot.

Activity B

Write a paragraph giving directions for three of the following topics. Don't forget to make a list of the steps involved before you begin to write your first draft.

Explain how to

A. make French toast   **H.** iron a shirt

B. brush one's teeth   **I.** make your favorite sandwich

C. tie a shoe   **J.** wash a load of laundry

D. make a milkshake   **K.** plan a party

E. braid something   **L.** fly a kite

F. wash and wax a car   **M.** carve a pumpkin

G. make popcorn   **N.** your own idea

Writing Definitions

Writing definitions is similar to writing directions. You must first make a list of all the details in the proper order. For definitions the order proceeds from the general characteristics of the object or term to the specific characteristics.

If you had to write a composition explaining what an orange is to someone who had never seen one, here is how you could begin.

Orange:
1. citrus fruit
2. grown in a tropical climate
3. grown on a tree
4. round
5. about the size of a baseball
6. red-yellow color
7. juicy
8. sweet-tangy taste
9. juice is a common breakfast drink

Activity C

Using the list of details above, write a paragraph defining an orange.

Writer's Corner

▶ **Below is a list of topics for expository writing. Choose one and develop it into a well-organized paragraph.**

A. I'm new in this country. What exactly is this food called "pizza"?

B. You are a computer whiz kid. You are being paid a million dollars to invent a new game. Design it and write a composition explaining how it works.

C. You have hidden a treasure in a secret place in school. In case you don't return, you want to leave a note explaining where to find it.

Writing Persuasive Paragraphs

A persuasive paragraph states an opinion and supports it in a convincing way.

Persuasive writing attempts to convince the reader that the point of view expressed is the right one. This is done by logically presenting evidence to support the ideas. In some cases, references to the work or statements of well-known authorities on the subject are included.

The area of persuasive writing is broad. It includes such things as advertisements and commercials, letters to the editor and editorials, and campaign speeches.

Read the paragraph below; then discuss or write the answers to the questions on the top of page 136.

> If everyone eligible to vote in the United States actually cast a ballot on election day, then we would have a representative government. As it stands now, when the turnout for a national election is over 50 percent, news reports comment on the high percentage of participation. And that's only half of the registered voters! What about all those people who never registered? Who are they, where are they, and why don't they vote? Many people have been discouraged from voting and encouraged to believe they are powerless. As long as they don't vote, the truth is they are powerless. They are invisible. If we want to be governed fairly, we have to make ourselves visible—every one of us.

1. According to the author, the United States
   a. has a fair system of government as it now operates.
   b. has the potential to have a fair system of government.
   c. needs to change its system of government completely.
2. What does the author think people should do?
   a. vote only when they are sure people they will vote for will win
   b. accept the fact that they are unimportant
   c. vote in every election and encourage others to do so
3. What is the general tone of the paragraph? (Is the author angry, sad, hopeless, hopeful?) What makes you think that?
4. Discuss those sections of the paragraph that try to convince the reader through logic or reasoning. Discuss those sections intended to appeal mainly to emotions.

Read this paragraph orally in class. Use your voice to convey the meaning you think the author intends.

Persuasive writing must sound convincing. Your arguments should be presented in a way that stresses your point of view, and any facts you include should clearly support your arguments. You can strengthen your position by using statements that appeal to reason or emotion or both.

Activity A

Below are some topics about which people have different opinions. Make a list of all the reasons you can think of *for* and *against* each of the topics.

1. capital punishment
2. United States involvement in the political affairs of underdeveloped countries
3. nuclear power

Activity B

Select any topic below and decide your point of view. Make a list of supporting statements and write a paragraph to explain how you feel about the issue.

A. attending school year-round, with December, April, and August off
B. taking a competency test before graduating from high school
C. raising the driving age to eighteen
D. earning your own spending money
E. attending school only in the morning

Activity C

Write a commercial or design an advertisement to sell the items listed below.

1. tickets to a rock concert
2. submarine sandwiches for a team's fund-raising campaign
3. tickets for a neighborhood car wash

Writer's Corner

▶ Below are topics for persuasive writing. Choose one and develop it into a well-organized paragraph using the guidelines presented in this lesson.

A. You are applying for a part-time job as a baby-sitter. Write a paragraph giving all your qualifications and stating why you would be good for the job.
B. You are the editor of the school newspaper. Write an editorial giving the reasons there should be school only four days a week.
C. Do you think that professional athletes are overpaid? Write a convincing paragraph to defend your point of view.

Word Study

Suffixes (Verb Endings)

A suffix is a syllable added to the end of a word to make a new word.

A suffix often changes the part of speech of a word, as in the case of the suffixes in Activity A. These suffixes change the words to verbs.

Activity A

Add the suffix to the word in order to create a verb. In some cases you will have to drop the original ending of the word and use the suffix in its place.

WORD	SUFFIX	VERB
1. legal	-ize	_____
2. hesitant	-ate	_____
3. identity	-ify	_____
4. failure	-s, -ing, -ed	_____
5. deep	-en	_____

Activity B

Change each word below to a verb by using one of the suffixes listed in Activity A.

1. departure
2. mortification
3. personal
4. sharp
5. commentator
6. dedication
7. height
8. analysis
9. captive
10. terror
11. crystal
12. considerable

Activity C

Choose an appropriate verb from Activity B to complete each of the following sentences.

1. Campers should _____ all their clothing by sewing on name tags.
2. The roving band of thieves _____ the countryside.
3. If you want to be a poet, you must _____ your senses to the world around you.
4. The owner is _____ opening a new store in this area.
5. The mayor _____ the statue in honor of the war veterans.
6. When fudge is put in the refrigerator, it tends to

   _____ .
7. I was _____ when I realized what I'd said.
8. The teacher _____ on the upcoming humanities fair.
9. The novel was so good, I was _____ for the whole day.
10. My anxiety _____ when I discovered that the report was due a week earlier than I'd thought.
11. The train is _____ at 8:58 A.M.
12. The chemist tried to _____ the mixture.

WRITER'S WORKSHOP

Writing to Persuade

Have you ever heard the expression "The pen is mightier than the sword"? It means that using words to persuade others is more effective than using force. Use your mighty pen to write two persuasive paragraphs about two sides of an issue. Publish your paragraphs in a pro and con pamphlet.

 Prewriting

Make a list of possible topics for your persuasive paragraphs. Think of school, community, or political issues about which people have differing opinions.

Choose one of the issues below or use the list as a springboard for your own ideas.

- All students should wear school uniforms.
- Students should be assigned at least two hours of homework every night.
- Every community should have a recreation center with teen activity programs.
- The United States government should spend more money on the space program.

Choose a statement from your list. Think of arguments for and against the issue. Record your ideas on a pro and con chart like the one below.

STATEMENT: Our community should have a recreation center with teen activity programs.

PROS	CONS
help community members get to know each other	cost taxpayers money
keep teenagers busy and out of trouble	plenty to do in our community
kids whose parents work have a place to go after school	teens already too busy with chores, schoolwork, lessons, and extracurricular activities

Drafting

You probably have strong feelings about the issue you chose to write about. To see both sides of the issue, you will be writing two paragraphs, one that agrees with your issue statement and one that argues against it. Imagine a person who feels differently about the issue. Write one paragraph from that person's point of view.

The beginning sentence of each paragraph will be a variation of your issue statement. The *pro* paragraph will probably have the word *should* or *needs*. Often, the *con* paragraph will have negative words such as *should not* or *does not need*.

Use notes from your chart to write the body of each paragraph. Support your opinions with reasons. Use facts or statistics if they are available.

End with a statement that sums up your feelings about the issue or asks your reader to take an action for or against the issue.

PRO

Our community needs a recreation center. People from neighboring cities that have rec centers say the rec center has built community spirit by helping townspeople get to know each other better. Both parents and children are happier. They know that teenagers who have nothing to do often find ways to get in trouble. Teenagers whose parents work enjoy the center the most. They no longer have to go home to an empty house and watch boring TV shows after school. Now our community has a chance to build its own rec center. For healthier, happier citizens, vote yes for the rec center.

CON

The last thing our town needs is a community recreation center. Rec centers cost money, and taxpayers in our town already pay too much. Besides, there are plenty of things to do here. We have a mall, a movie theater, and a library. The rec center sponsors say our town needs more things for teenagers to do, but teenagers are already far too busy. They have chores and homework. Many of them take music or dance lessons. The school provides sports and other extracurricular activities. Let's save our money for the things we really need, like roads, firefighters, and police. On Tuesday, vote against the rec center.

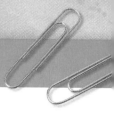

Revising, Proofreading, and Publishing

Revising

Time to Take Another Look

Before you write your final copy, reread your draft to make sure both paragraphs have convincing arguments.

Ask yourself these questions to help you revise your persuasive paragraphs.

- ❏ Does each beginning sentence make my feelings about the issue clear?

- ❏ Do I need to add arguments to support either opinion?

- ❏ Do I need to delete details that don't support my opinion?

- ❏ Do I need to rewrite anything that is not clear?

- ❏ Do I need to replace vague words with more powerful words?

- ❏ Does each paragraph end with a sentence that sums up my arguments or asks the reader to take action?

Use a colored pencil to make revisions that will make your arguments more logical and persuasive.

Use a Thesaurus

What you say is important, but how you say it is important, too. Use powerful, precise words to present a strong argument. A thesaurus is one tool that can help you. Read your draft and circle vague, overused, and weak words. Then use the thesaurus to find synonyms that say exactly what you mean.

Proofreading

Time to Look at Capitalization, Punctuation, and Spelling

When you're satisfied that both your paragraphs present strong, persuasive arguments, proofread your draft to check capitalization, punctuation, spelling, and grammar.

Use the checklist below to edit and proofread your paragraphs.

- ❑ Did I indent the first word of each paragraph?
- ❑ Did I capitalize proper nouns correctly?
- ❑ Did I use the correct mark of punctuation at the end of each sentence?
- ❑ Did I spell each word correctly?

Check Punctuation by Reading Aloud

Read your paragraphs aloud. As you come to each punctuation mark, exaggerate it. Pause at each comma. Stop for each period. Emphasize sentences that end with exclamation points. Concentrating on each punctuation mark will help you find extra commas or incorrect ending punctuation.

 ## Publishing

Time to Share

Publish your persuasive paragraphs in a pro and con pamphlet. See which argument persuades your classmates.

To publish, follow these steps:

1. Copy your revised draft in your neatest handwriting or type it on a computer.

2. After you finish, proofread your final copy one more time.

3. Check each paragraph to make sure you included all your supporting arguments.

Make a pro and con pamphlet.

1. Fold a large sheet of construction paper in half so it looks like a card.

2. Open the fold, and staple one paragraph on the left and the other on the right.

3. Write your issue statement on the outside front cover.

4. Staple a blank comment sheet on the outside back cover.

5. Ask classmates to read your paragraphs and write comments on the back cover to tell which paragraph they find the most persuasive.

CHAPTER 6

Writing Across the Curriculum

Answering Essay Questions

Essay questions must be answered in paragraph form.

Essay questions require you to really think about the material you have been studying, and they are often the best evaluation of how well you understand it. This is why teachers put them on tests. Answers to essay questions are always written in paragraph form, so you must give more than a one-word answer. Sometimes an essay question will ask for facts; other times it will ask for your interpretation of facts. The key to knowing exactly what type of answer you should give is to look at the verb used in the question.

Below are some verbs commonly used in essay questions.

- Compare: Show how two things are alike.
- Contrast: Show how two things are different.
- Discuss: Give the facts and tell how they relate to one another.
- Define: Give the meaning of a term.
- Explain: Tell how or why something is done.
- Describe: Give a word picture of something.
- Trace: Give all the events in sequential order and tell how they are related.
- Prove: Give evidence to show that something is true.

It is important to analyze each essay question that you are given in order to determine what kind of information is being asked of you. Study the example question on the next page.

About the Photograph

This student is pouring a liquid for an experiment. Afterward, she'll answer an essay question about her experiment and write a lab report.

Question: Give three major concepts presented in Abraham Lincoln's Gettysburg Address, and explain why these ideas are particularly relevant to our society today.

The two key words in this question are *give* and *explain. Give* is a sign that factual information is being requested. *Explain* indicates that a personal interpretation is also required.

Facts: three concepts in Abraham Lincoln's Gettysburg Address

Interpretation: How are the concepts relevant today?

Once you have analyzed your question, you are ready to compose the answer by writing a well-constructed paragraph. One way to provide a topic sentence for your answer is to restate the question. For example:

Question: Explain why so many Europeans came to America between 1607 and 1733.

Topic sentence: Between 1607 and 1733, many Europeans came to America in search of religious freedom, economic opportunities, and land ownership.

When answering an essay question, remember to

1. study the question to find out what it asks you to do.
2. decide if the answer is factual, interpretive, or both.
3. map or outline your answer, making sure all information is related to the question.
4. restate what is asked in the question and make it the topic sentence, which is often the opening sentence.
5. give your information in a well-constructed paragraph with appropriate transitions.
6. reread your paragraph to make sure you have given the information that the question requires.

Activity A

Listed below are some essay questions that require only factual information and some that ask for facts plus interpretation. Divide a sheet of paper in half from top to bottom. On one side, write "Facts," on the other "Interpretation." Analyze the questions and place the appropriate part of each sentence in the correct column.

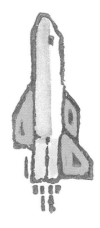

1. In John Steinbeck's novel *The Red Pony,* Jody admires the hired hand Billy Buck. Give two reasons why Jody likes Billy, and what effect this has on Jody's life.
2. Give the effects of a volcanic eruption upon the atmosphere.
3. Compare the Sahara with the Mojave Desert.
4. In your opinion, what are the benefits of the space shuttle as a form of modern transportation?

Activity B

Below are four topic sentences. They belong to the four questions in Activity A. On a separate sheet of paper, write each question from Activity A and, under it, the topic sentence that belongs to it.

1. The space shuttle has many possibilities as a modern-day means of transportation.
2. In John Steinbeck's novel *The Red Pony,* Jody admires the hired hand Billy Buck for two specific reasons, and their relationship has a strong impact on Jody's development.
3. Although the Sahara and the Mojave Desert are on different continents, they have many points in common.
4. A volcanic eruption can have varied effects upon the atmosphere.

Activity C

Analyze the following essay questions from various subject areas. Tell what kind of answer the verb indicates and whether the answer will be factual, interpretive, or both. Then write topic sentences for any five of the essay questions.

1. Discuss the relationship between poverty and crime.
2. Explain the stages of the water cycle.
3. Prove that Franklin Delano Roosevelt increased the power of the presidency during his administration.
4. Describe the characteristics of the Ice Age.
5. Explain why the piano is considered both a string instrument and a percussion instrument.
6. Define the commutative property of multiplication.
7. Trace the civil rights movement from the time of the Emancipation Proclamation to the present.
8. Define sedimentary rock.
9. Contrast the orchestra with the band.
10. Compare the Atlantic Ocean with the Pacific Ocean.
11. Contrast the foreign policy of Franklin Delano Roosevelt with the foreign policy of John Fitzgerald Kennedy.
12. Discuss the impact the Russian satellite *Sputnik I* had on educational priorities in the United States.
13. Compare the oboe with the clarinet.
14. Define the baroque period. How did music and art reflect the trends of that time?
15. Discuss the effects of the Industrial Revolution on small businesses, child labor, and the national economy.

Writer's Corner

▶ Use the questions provided in any of your textbooks to perform the following activities:

1. Locate and copy
   a. five questions that ask for factual information.
   b. five questions that ask for your interpretation.
   c. five questions that ask for facts and interpretation.
2. Select one question from each of the three groups above and write a topic sentence by rewording the question.
3. Select any one question from the above and write a complete answer in paragraph form.

Outlining and Writing a Report

An outline is an organized plan for a report, an essay, or a term paper.

If a report or an essay is going to be two, three, or more paragraphs in length, it is worthwhile making an outline, or plan, to give direction to your writing. An outline has a specific format.

I. Paragraph topic
  A. Subtopic
    1. Detail
    2. Detail
    3. Detail
  B. Subtopic
    1. Detail
    2. Detail
    3. Detail
II. Paragraph topic

Answer the following questions about this outline format:

1. What indicates a paragraph topic?
2. How many subtopics does the first paragraph have?
3. What indicates a subtopic?
4. How many details support each subtopic?
5. How is a detail indicated?
6. Why is capital letter B under capital letter A?
7. What happens in the design of the outline every time it changes from a numeral to a letter?

Suppose you have been assigned to write a paper about deserts. The narrowed topic is "how the desert can support life." After going to the library to use the encyclopedia and other sources, you might draw a map of your ideas like this:

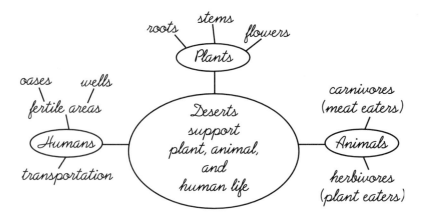

The ideas can easily be put into outline form.

Subject: Desert life

Narrowed topic: How plant, animal, and human life can exist in the desert

  I. Introductory paragraph

 II. Plant life

    A. Roots

    B. Stems

    C. Flowers

III. Animal life

    A. Carnivores (meat eaters)

    B. Herbivores (plant eaters)

 IV. Human life

    A. Fertile areas

       1. Oases

       2. Wells

    B. Transportation

       1. Automobile

       2. Train

       3. Airplane

  V. Concluding paragraph

Once the outline is completed, you can begin the writing stage of the process. A first draft and revisions, along with peer and teacher conferences, will be necessary. Below is a final draft of the report on desert life, showing how the elements of the outline were incorporated.

The first paragraph includes the narrowed topic, expressed either in the same words or in a different way. This paragraph tells the reader what will be in the report.

> **1**   The desert has a unique terrain. Because it tends to appear dry and flat, many people conclude that there is no life at all on its shifting sands. Contrary to popular belief, however, a desert is rarely barren, but instead supports a substantial amount of plant, animal, and human life.

The second paragraph includes the expanded ideas contained under Roman numeral II of the outline. The first sentence should state the topic of the paragraph.

> **2**   Plants are the most obvious form of life in the desert. Although this vegetation may be sparse, what does exist is both hardy and colorful. Succulents, such as the cactus plant, have shallow roots that absorb water quickly from light rainfalls and flash floods. The water is then stored for long periods of time in the plants' thick, waxy stems and leaves and used as needed. In addition to being rugged survivors, desert plants bring beauty to their surroundings by producing brilliant orange, red, and violet flowers.

The third and fourth paragraphs on page 152 include expanded ideas contained under Roman numerals III and IV. Again, the first sentence for each paragraph should state the topic. Note that each topic sentence begins with a transition word.

3 Besides plants, many animals have adapted well to the desert environment. Some obtain their needed moisture from the meat of the animals they prey upon. Others get their water from the juicy leaves and stems of succulents. Certain animals, such as the camel and the burro, which have long accompanied humans through the desert, sustain life both from what the desert has to offer and from what people can supply.

4 Finally, humankind has now come to inhabit this vast territory. Because of islandlike areas in the desert, called oases, people can survive the brutal heat and dryness. Some oases are natural, developing from the desert's own underground springs, and others have been created by the rerouting of rivers and streams or by other artificial means. Highways and railroads have made travel to oases easier, and many former watering holes have blossomed into larger cities. Today, visitors can even travel by air to areas that were once inaccessible to all but the most adventurous.

The concluding paragraph pulls together in one or two sentences all the ideas from the preceding paragraphs. It often contains a personal observation on what has been written and should reflect the comments made in the first paragraph.

5 All forms of life, then, flourish in the desert. No longer must people fear this formerly inhospitable area. We are free to share its richness with the plants and animals, as long as we are careful not to destroy its wonders in the process.

Activity A

Use the words on the right to complete the outline on the left.

Subject: Bread

Narrowed topic: Some kinds of bread, their food value, and the process involved in making bread

I. Kinds

    A. _____

        1. White

        2. _____

        3. Rye

        4. _____

    B. Special

        1. _____

        2. Zucchini

        3. _____

II. _____

    A. _____

    B. _____

    C. Thiamine

III. _____

    A. Mix flour

    B. Add water, yeast, minerals

    C. _____

    D. Cut dough

    E. _____

Dough begins to rise
Raisin and nut
Iron
Whole wheat
Process
Common
Place in pans to bake
Protein
Pumpernickel
Applesauce
Food value

Activity B

Put the following information in outline form. The subject, narrowed topic, and two paragraph topics are indicated. All others are subtopics and details.

Subject: Poems

Narrowed topic: How to appreciate a poem

Paragraph topics:

  I. Careful oral reading

  II. Careful listening

Subtopics and details:

Watch punctuation	Notice rhyme scheme
Personification	Metaphor
Pronounce words carefully	Feel the rhythm
Listen for figures of speech	Alliteration
Simile	Read slowly
Onomatopoeia	Listen for sound devices

Writer's Corner

▶ From the list below, choose two topics to outline. Then choose one of the two outlines and develop it into a written report, following the guidelines given in the lesson.

  A. Define the three types of rocks and explain how they are formed.

  B. Contrast plane and solid geometric figures.

  C. Compare the violin, cello, and bass.

  D. Discuss how cloud formations help in the prediction of weather.

  E. Name and explain the elements of art.

  F. Discuss the causes of the Great Depression.

  G. Explain the value of two current TV shows.

  H. Explain the uses of three different types of aircraft.

Writing a Lab Report

Scientific writing is the type of writing used to communicate scientific information.

There is a special form of writing called scientific writing. Its main purpose is to explain scientific information. For this reason, the facts, directions, and descriptions are stated in a straightforward manner. Concise words are chosen, and any picturesque language, imagery, or personal opinions are avoided. This type of language is used in most science books, scientific magazine articles, science fair projects, and lab reports.

The Lab Report

A lab report gives information about a scientific experiment that has been done. Ordinarily it is organized into five parts:

1. Purpose: This section tells why the experiment was done. Often the purpose of an experiment is to test a scientific hypothesis, or theory. Sometimes it is simply to measure or observe something. A well-designed experiment should have a clear and specific purpose.

   Examples:
   A. to observe the crystal structure of table salt
   B. to measure the melting point of an unknown liquid

2. Materials: This is a complete list of the supplies and equipment used in the experiment.

   Examples:
   A. light microscope
      glass microscope slide
      NaCl (table salt)

B. 75 ml of the unknown liquid
   100-ml beaker
   1000-ml beaker
   mercury thermometer (−40° to +45° Celsius range)
   stopwatch
   dry ice

3. Procedures: This section gives the steps used in the experiment. The procedures should be clearly explained so that another person could repeat the experiment exactly as it was done originally. It is important to explain just how the materials were used and to describe any special techniques that were employed.

Examples:
A. 1. NaCl crystals were spread in a sparse, single layer on a microscope slide.
   2. The crystals were observed under the light microscope with a magnification of 100 times normal.
B. 1. A dry-ice bath was prepared by filling a 1000-ml beaker two-thirds full with crushed dry ice.
   2. 75 ml of the unknown liquid at room temperature was placed in a 100-ml beaker.
   3. The 100-ml beaker containing the sample was placed in the dry-ice bath with a mercury thermometer submersed in the liquid.
   4. The temperature of the sample was recorded every 60 seconds until the sample was completely frozen.

4. Results: This section presents all the measurements and observations taken during the experiment. No interpretations are given at this point. Note that there are two types of data: qualitative observations describe what happened; quantitative observations describe what happened by giving numerical measurements. Results should be clearly presented, using tables and graphs where possible.

Examples:

A. At 100X, the crystals appeared large enough for easy viewing. They varied in size by approximately a factor of two. They all had smooth definite faces. Most of them appeared to be perfect cubes.

B.

Time (sec.)	Temp. (°C)	Time (sec.)	Temp. (°C)
0	+30	241	−18
61	+10	301	−18
122	−10	359	−18
178	−18	425	−25

At time equal to 160 seconds, the first crystals of solid appeared. At time equal to 380 seconds, the sample appeared completely frozen.

5. Conclusions: This is the section in which the results are interpreted. The conclusions should always be supported with facts from the data, and they should be written without the use of personal pronouns.

Examples:

A. The crystal structure of NaCl (table salt), as evidenced by observation under a microscope, is cubic.

B. The melting point can be defined as the temperature at which a liquid and its solid coexist. In this experiment the sample was present in both its liquid and solid form from an elapsed time of 160 sec. to 380 sec. Within this range, four temperature readings of −18°C were taken. The melting point of the unknown liquid is therefore −18°C.

On page 158 is an example of a completed lab report.

Model: Lab Report

Purpose:
>
> To test the hypothesis that water expands when it freezes

Materials:
>
> 75-ml beaker
> freezer (not self-defrosting) set at 0° Celsius
> wax pencil
> 50 ml distilled water
> ruler (with mm markings)

Procedures:

1. 50 ml of distilled water was placed in the 75-ml beaker.
2. The beaker was placed in the freezer until ice just began to form.
3. The beaker was allowed to stand outside the freezer until the newly formed ice just melted. (Careful stirring was used to speed this process.)
4. The level of the liquid was marked on the outside of the beaker with the wax pencil. An *l* (liquid) was placed next to this mark.
5. The beaker was returned to the freezer, and the water was allowed to freeze completely (5 hours).
6. The level of the solid water was marked on the outside of the beaker with the wax pencil. An *s* (solid) was placed by this mark.
7. The difference in mm between the two levels was measured.

Results:
>
> The solid mark was 4.5 mm above the liquid mark.

Conclusions:
>
> The hypothesis that water expands when it freezes is supported by the results of this experiment.

Activity A

Here is an account of a scientific experiment. It contains all the information needed, but it is not written in formal, scientific language. Rewrite it in the format of a lab report.

My cousin and I were interested in performing an experiment to see if sunlight really is necessary for plant growth. We found two plants exactly alike in type and size and decided that we would check the color and number of leaves on each plant at the beginning and end of our experiment. First, we examined the plants. Plant #1 had 30 green leaves; plant #2 had 28 green leaves. Then we fed each plant 200 ml of a standard plant nutrient solution. Next, we placed plant #1 on a windowsill in a room with southern exposure. We placed plant #2 in a room with no windows or lights. The following week, we fed each plant again with 200 ml of nutrient solution.

After two weeks, both plants were brought to another room and the number of leaves and color were again compared. Plant #1 had 33 green leaves; plant #2 had 6 leaves, which were yellow. Our experiment had proven that plants require sunlight in order to remain healthy and to grow.

Writer's Corner

▶ Write a lab report for an experiment you have conducted recently in science class.

Writing About Books

Books and the interesting characters they bring to life can stir deep emotions and have a tremendous influence on you. To discover the many values hidden within the pages of a book, you must be ready to exert yourself in the treasure hunt. That means you must choose your books wisely and read them intelligently. In the company of great books, you will experience a rewarding and an exciting life.

Book Advertisements

A book advertisement is meant to arouse your interest in a particular novel or factual work. You can find advertisements in newspapers, magazines, or bookstore catalogs. Some newspapers and magazines have regular columns in which they mention a number of books they think might be of interest to their readers. Libraries advertise books, too, by making up booklists that describe recommended books in certain categories, such as mysteries or cookbooks. Since a book advertisement is meant to capture a reader's attention, it is usually short, lively, and to the point. It reveals just enough of the book's contents to promote the sale or reading of the book.

Here is a sample book advertisement.

Model: A Book Advertisement

What was it like to be a black person in the South in the late 1950s? John Griffin, a white man, decided to find out. How he changed the color of his skin, shaved his head, and posed as an educated black man makes a moving and dramatic story. Discover the hardships of life for blacks under the Jim Crow rules; see from an inside-outside view the unity of the Southern black community. Read *Black Like Me* by John Griffin.

Activity A

Read the following book advertisement and then answer the questions.

The White House Gang was the terror of every Washington official. Led by Quentin, President Roosevelt's son, the gang managed to make life exciting for themselves and for everyone they encountered. Needless to say, they were brought to justice more than once. The presiding officer at the court was none other than Theodore Roosevelt. Kindly and understanding, he dealt with the boys in a manner that won their everlasting admiration. Earle Looker reveals many daring adventures in *White House Gang,* for he was once a member. This is a book that demands a place on the bookshelf.

1. What type of book would one expect *White House Gang* to be?

2. Does this advertisement make you want to read it? Why or why not?

Activity B

Try writing your own book advertisement. The book you have enjoyed the most will probably be the best and the easiest to write about.

Book Reports

A book report summarizes a book, gives a personal reaction to it, and usually follows a set format.

Book reports are longer than book advertisements and contain more information. They give the contents in greater detail, name the principal characters, and tell how the reader felt about the book. Often they are requested as class assignments to show what books a student has read and to provide practice in thinking about books. Writing a summary of a book and your reaction to it can lead to a better understanding of the author's message. It is also a way to keep a record of the books you have read so that you can refresh your memory as to what the book was about or to share your thoughts on the book with a friend.

When preparing a book report, there is a specific format you can follow to make sure you include the essential information.

1. Title (underlined, or italicized if using a word processor)
2. Author
3. Type of book (novel, science fiction, historical fiction, fantasy, nonfiction, biography, play, etc.)
4. Principal characters
5. Brief summary
6. Personal reaction

Read the following book report and note how it follows the format.

Model: A Book Report

TITLE: *The Member of the Wedding*
AUTHOR: Carson McCullers
TYPE: Novel
CHARACTERS: Frankie Addams, Berenice Sadie Brown, John Henry West, Royal Quincy Addams (Frankie's father), Jarvis Addams, Janice Evans, Honey Brown, T. T. Williams, the redheaded soldier, the monkey man, Aunt Pet, Uncle Charles, Mary Littlejohn

SUMMARY: *The Member of the Wedding* is the story of one summer in the life of F. Jasmine "Frankie" Addams, who is going on thirteen. The summer is long and hot, the impossible Southern kind. It is a summer when Frankie feels "unjoined." Her best friend has moved away, and she spends her time with her five-year-old cousin John Henry and the family cook, Berenice. But Berenice has friends of her own: her brother Honey and her boyfriend T. T. Williams. Frankie feels alone and bored. She has a strong need to find her place in the world but doesn't know how. Finally she decides the answer to her problems lies in the upcoming marriage of her brother Jarvis to Janice Evans. She will join them as a "member of the wedding," and the three of them will go off and live together forever.

MY REACTION: This story shows the loneliness felt by many people in our society. The particular awkwardness Frankie feels is part of being a teenager—no longer a child and not yet an adult. Carson McCullers makes it clear that this is just one kind of isolation.

Activity **C**

Prepare a book report for your class, following the format of the model book report.

Book Reviews

A book review is a critical evaluation of a book.

A book review tells in detail what the reviewer liked and disliked about the book, and whether or not it is recommended to other readers. A book report is a summary of a book, whereas a book review is an evaluation. Many newspapers and magazines contain reviews of new books along with book advertisements.

Reviews differ from advertisements in that they are longer, more thorough, and not necessarily favorable. A book advertisement is always a very positive recommendation of a book and mentions only the book's good points, while a review might tell what is wrong with a book as well. Also, in a book review the reviewer has to tell why he or she liked or did not like the book. It is always good when reading an unfavorable review to remember that the reviewer is giving a personal impression.

The format of a review is not as structured as that of a report, but it usually contains a few standard items. The introductory paragraph gives the reader a general impression of how the reviewer responded to the book and an idea of what the book is about. The concluding paragraph contains a summary of the reviewer's evaluation and tells whether or not he or she recommends the book.

In the middle paragraphs, the reviewer discusses the plot, setting, and characters of the book. The number of middle paragraphs depends on how much the reviewer has to say and how much space he or she has. Often there is only one middle paragraph containing brief comments on each of the three elements.

Here are some questions to consider when evaluating a fiction book:

- Plot: Do the events seem to follow in logical order? Does the author make the story believable? Is there enough suspense to make you want to read to the end? Do you feel satisfied with the way the story ends?

- Setting: Is the setting well described? Can you picture it in your mind? Should the author have given more details? Why or why not? If there are illustrations, are they good representations of the characters and setting?

- Characters: Are the characters interesting? Can you relate to how they think or feel? Are you able to picture how they look? Is each character's behavior consistent with the type of personality he or she has been given? Do the characters grow or learn through their experiences?

Following is a review of *The Incredible Journey* by Sheila Burnford. As you read it, look for the elements discussed above.

Model: A Book Review

Sheila Burnford's *The Incredible Journey* is an exciting, heartwarming story of three heroic animals· who must cross the Canadian wilderness in order to be reunited with the people they love. Although the two dogs and a cat never speak or in any other way behave like humans, their characters are so beautifully drawn that they are inspiring and unforgettable in their own way.

It is the young Labrador retriever, with his excellent sense of direction, who initiates the journey and starts off first. He is quickly joined by the gentle old bull terrier, and then, with some hesitation, by the Siamese cat. The cat turns out to be the most resourceful of the group and pulls them out of several rough spots. Yet it is obvious that not one of the three could have made the journey alone, and their reliance on one another is one of the most inspiring parts of the book.

There is constant tension as the travelers face the problems of finding food and shelter in the vast wilderness and of fending off wild animals. In describing the rugged country through which they travel and the natural obstacles they encounter, the author never wastes a word; yet, she manages to fully convey how each scene looks, feels, and smells.

This is not a story for animal lovers alone, but for anyone who enjoys an exciting tale of determination and courage. It is highly recommended to readers young and old.

Activity D

Write a review of a novel or play that you have read recently.

Writer's Corner

▶ Take the book report you wrote earlier and rewrite it as a book review.

Suffixes (Noun Endings)

Besides changing words to verbs, suffixes can also change words to nouns.

In seventh grade you studied the following noun-forming suffixes: *-ity, -ion, -ment, -ship,* and *-ness.* Now you will learn six new suffixes.

Activity A

On a sheet of paper, write the nouns that are formed when the suffixes in the second column are added to the words in the first column. The endings of some words will have to change before the suffixes can be added.

WORD	SUFFIX	NOUN
1. criticize	-ism	_____
2. act	-or	_____
3. teach	-er	_____
4. attend	-ance	_____
5. motherly	-hood	_____
6. responsible	-ility	_____

Activity B

Use a suffix from Activity A to change each word to a noun.

1. irritable
2. speak
3. guide
4. childish
5. profess
6. terrorize
7. invent
8. patriotic
9. drive
10. reliable
11. perform
12. neighborly

Activity C

Choose an appropriate noun from Activity B to complete each sentence.

1. Because of Pauline's _____ , I always trust her to feed my cat when I'm away.
2. Carlos spent his _____ in Ecuador.
3. Even though she was suffering from the flu, the actor gave an excellent _____ .
4. When my brother is facing a deadline, his _____ keeps everyone away from him.
5. Acts of _____ result in the loss of many innocent lives.
6. Guglielmo Marconi was the _____ of the radio.
7. On the Fourth of July, Americans show their _____ by displaying the flag.
8. I received _____ from my dance instructor on how to stay loose for the performance.
9. Most of the people in our _____ live in apartment buildings.
10. Tonight's guest _____ is a professional basketball player.
11. The bus _____ made sure the little girl got off at the right stop.
12. My mother is a college _____ .

WRITER'S WORKSHOP

Writing for All Subjects

Even though your school day may be divided into several different class periods, everything you learn is really connected. Combine what you've learned in science, English, and social studies to write a report about a constellation. Create a class planetarium to present your report.

 Prewriting

The ancient Greeks devised constellations as a way to remember and identify stars in the vast sky. They named constellations after mythological characters.

Some familiar constellations are listed below. Which other constellations do you know? Choose one that you want to know more about to research.

- Ursa Major (The Great Bear)
- Orion (The Hunter)
- Gemini (The Twins)
- Sagittarius (The Archer)
- Taurus (The Bull)
- Pegasus (The Winged Horse)
- Leo (The Lion)
- Cassiopeia (The Queen)

Your report will have two parts—the scientific part and the literature and social studies part. In the first part, you will describe the constellation. In the second part, you will learn more about ancient cultures by relating the myth behind the constellation's name.

Research your constellation and take notes on individual note cards.

Sources of Information

Look first in the encyclopedia for general information. You may find a picture of the constellation in the encyclopedia.

Check books about astronomy for more detailed information.

Books of Greek and Roman mythology will introduce you to the characters for whom the constellations were named.

Drafting

Group your note cards and use them to make an outline for your report. Preparing your outline will help you see whether you missed any important details as you did your research. If necessary, do further research to fill in any gaps.

Expand your outline to write your report. Each Roman numeral of your outline will begin a separate paragraph.

Use the subtopics that follow capital letters in your outline to write the main-idea sentences of your paragraphs. Use the details that follow Arabic numerals to write the detail sentences that support your main ideas.

I. Facts about the constellation Ursa Major
   A. Ursa Major, Latin for "Great Bear"
   B. Can only be seen in the Northern Hemisphere
      1. Includes the Big Dipper
      2. Appears every night of the year
II. Story behind Ursa Major's name
   A. Callisto lived happily with her son
      1. Hera, queen of the gods, became jealous
      2. Hera turned Callisto into bear
   B. Bear Callisto tried to hug human son
      1. Son didn't know bear was his mother; he was going to shoot bear
      2. Zeus, king of gods, saved them by turning them into constellations

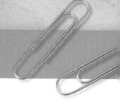

EDITOR'S WORKSHOP

Revising, Proofreading, and Publishing

 ### Revising

Time to Take Another Look

Reread your report carefully and look for ways to improve it. As you reread, ask yourself these questions.

❑ Does my report have two separate paragraphs?

❑ Does each paragraph have its own topic sentence?

❑ Do the details in each paragraph support the topic sentence?

❑ Do the details in both parts flow in logical order?

❑ Do I need to add more scientific information to the first part?

❑ Do I need to add details I left out of the story in the second part?

❑ Do I need to substitute more interesting words to make the story more exciting?

Make your revisions with a colored pencil so they will be easy to see. Then discuss your revisions with a partner or with your teacher.

Vary Sentence Order

Do all your sentences begin with the subject? You can make your report sound more interesting by writing different kinds of sentences. Try turning a few sentences around so the subject comes last or a dependent clause begins the sentence.

Change this:

Callisto hid when she heard a human approaching. She peered out through the bushes and saw her son. She leaped toward him with her arms opened wide.

to this:

When she heard a human approaching, Callisto hid. Peering out through the bushes, she saw her son. With her arms opened wide, she leaped toward him.

Proofreading

Time to Look at Capitalization, Punctuation, and Spelling

When your revisions are complete, proofread your report for capitalization, punctuation, spelling, and grammar.

Use the checklist below to edit and proofread your report.

- ❑ Did I begin each sentence and proper noun with a capital letter?
- ❑ Did I indent the first word of each paragraph?
- ❑ Did I use the correct mark of punctuation at the end of each sentence?
- ❑ Did I spell names and scientific terms correctly?

Ask a Partner to Proofread

Sometimes it can be difficult to proofread a piece of writing you've been working on for a long time. A fresh pair of eyes can catch mistakes the writer misses. Ask a partner to proofread your report while you proofread his or hers.

 # Publishing

Time to Share

Create a class planetarium to show your constellation as you read your published report.

To publish, follow these steps:

1. Copy your revised draft in your neatest handwriting or type it on a computer.

2. Proofread your final copy once more.

3. Illustrate your report by drawing your constellation on a sheet of black construction paper and, with your pencil, punching holes where the stars are.

Present your constellation report.

1. Rehearse reading your report aloud several times before presenting it to the class.

2. Tape your construction paper illustration to a window so the light shines through the holes.

3. Stand near your illustration as you read your report.

4. Read your report slowly in a firm, clear voice.

Creative Tools
for Writing

Simile

A simile is a figure of speech that compares two unlike things. It usually contains the word *like* or *as.*

William Wordsworth, who recognized the greatness of John Milton as a man and a poet, wrote this simile about him in "London, 1802":

> Thy soul was like a Star, and dwelt apart;
> Thou hadst a voice whose sound was like the sea.

1. How many similes are used in these two lines?

2. To what does Wordsworth compare Milton's soul?

3. When Wordsworth writes, "and dwelt apart," do you think he is speaking of Milton as a man, a poet, or both? Why?

4. To what is Wordsworth referring when he uses the word *voice?*

5. To what does Wordsworth compare Milton's voice? Why does he use this comparison?

You probably use similes in your speech more often than you realize. A simile helps to convey an idea by giving your listeners "double vision." They can see in their minds both the actual object and the one to which it is being compared. With their double vision, they gain a clear understanding of what you are trying to express. Writers use similes for the same reason.

About the Photograph

Your writing is like the green plants being planted in this photograph. Both writing and plants need extra care in order to thrive.

Activity **A**

In each sentence, there are two objects being compared.

First, name the two objects that are being compared.

Second, note what specific quality or idea about these objects is being compared (point of comparison).

Third, list as many ideas as possible that are similar about these two objects.

Fourth, set up a diagram like the example for each sentence.

Example:

My sister's brain works like a computer.

Brain is compared to a *computer.*

works

(point of comparison)

memory	memory (same)
calculates	calculates (same)
creative	programmed (different)
generates output	generates output (same)
works quickly	works quickly (same)

1. The tree shook its branches as a girl shakes her rain-drenched hair.

2. The barbell fell from Jeff's hands like a sack of potatoes.

3. Upon hearing the news, the man turned as pale as a ghost.

4. Seeing the dog, the thief darted like a streak of lightning.

5. Having completed her performance, the ballerina collapsed like a wilting flower.

Activity B

Read the following poem and notice the many similes the poet uses to describe a face without a smile.

Smile

Like a bread without the spreadin',
    Like a puddin' without sauce,
Like a mattress without beddin'
    Like a cart without a hoss
Like a door without a latchstring,
    Like a fence without a stile,
Like a dry an' barren creek bed—
    Is the face without a smile.

Like a house without a dooryard,
    Like a yard without a flower,
Like a clock without a mainspring,
    That will never tell the hour;
A thing that sort o' makes yo' feel
    A hunger all the while—
Oh, the saddest sight that ever was
    Is a face without a smile!

Answer the following questions.

1. To how many objects is a face compared?

2. To how many objects is a smile compared?

3. Explain some of the comparisons; for example, why is the face without a smile like "bread without the spreadin'"? What does a smile do for a face that a flower might do for a yard?

Writer's Corner

▶ Create two original similes for each of the qualities listed below. One has been done for you.

Example:

Height

The mountain peaks loomed above us like skyscrapers in the sky.

The basketball players were like giants stomping across the court.

1. Fear
2. Beauty
3. Loneliness
4. Nervousness
5. Speed
6. Courage
7. Friendship
8. Pride
9. Spring

Metaphor

A metaphor is an implied comparison between two things. It is almost like a simile except that *like* and *as* are not used.

Read the following poem.

Dreams

Hold fast to dreams
For if dreams die
Life is a broken-winged bird
That cannot fly.
Hold fast to dreams
For when dreams go
Life is a barren field
Frozen with snow.

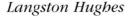

Langston Hughes

1. Find two lines that give examples of metaphors.

2. How are these two lines different from a simile?

3. What are the two things being compared in both lines?

4. Why is life a broken-winged bird if dreams die?

5. Why is life a barren field if dreams leave?

6. How do the metaphors of broken-winged bird and barren field help you "picture" life?

Read the next two examples of metaphors and answer the questions that follow.

All the world's a stage.
And all the men and women merely players:
They have their exits and their entrances;
And one man in his time plays many parts . . .

> William Shakespeare,
> *As You Like It,*
> Act ii, sc. 7, l. 139

1. Which line has the metaphor?

2. What do you think Shakespeare meant when he implied that the world is a stage?

3. What is the metaphor in the following line?

> . . . we are caterpillars born to form
> the angelic butterfly.

> Dante Alighieri,
> *Purgatory,* Canto X

4. What do you think Dante means?

In a simile, you see the two objects, but in a metaphor you see only one object. It's as if the two have merged into one. The world is really a stage, and we are genuinely caterpillars.

Activity A

Following are eight similes. Change each one to a metaphor by making the two objects become one.

1. The supple trees swayed like graceful dancers.
2. His tongue was as sharp as a knife.
3. The fan swirled the air like a small tornado.
4. The old man rambled on like a babbling brook.
5. Having no sense of direction is like being in a ship without a rudder.
6. The track star ran like a gazelle in the forest.
7. Like the parched earth, the little boy longed for a drink.
8. The aged lady's face was like a delicate etching.

Implied and Extended Metaphors

Read the following poem.

Southbound on the Freeway

A tourist came in from Orbitville,
parked in the air, and said:

The creatures of this star
are made of metal and glass.

Through the transparent parts
you can see their guts.

Their feet are round and roll
on diagrams or long

measuring tapes, dark
with white lines.

They have four eyes.
The two in back are red.

Sometimes you can see a five-eyed
one, with a red eye turning

on the top of his head.
He must be special—

the others respect him
and go slow

when he passes, winding
among them from behind.

They all hiss as they glide,
like inches, down the marked

tapes. Those soft shapes,
shadowy inside

the hard bodies—are they
their guts or their brains?

May Swenson

The poem "Southbound on the Freeway" on page 179 contains two types of metaphors, implied and extended. From the description given, the poet expects the reader to be able to identify the second half of the metaphor. This is why it is called an implied metaphor.

You already know that the basic metaphor is that the intelligent inhabitants of earth are automobiles. Because the poet uses so many comparisons based on the original metaphor and extends the comparison from beginning to end, it is called an extended metaphor.

Activity B

Reread the poem on page 179 and answer the following questions.

1. What are the two objects being compared?

2. Which of the two objects is actually stated by the poet?

3. The second object is described but never stated. What is the implied object?

Now divide a sheet of paper into two columns. In the first column, list all the parts in the poem that belong under human being. In the second column, list all the parts of the automobile that are compared to a part of a human being.

Activity C

Listed below are eight nouns. Write each one as a metaphor and underline the two objects being compared.

Example:

Hair: On a windy day, <u>Jan's hair</u> is a <u>knotted mass of string</u>.

1. bee   **3.** turtle   **5.** moon   **7.** waves
2. ship   **4.** clouds   **6.** book   **8.** face

Writer's Corner

▶ Follow the pattern below to create your own poem using a metaphor. An example is provided for each line.

Begin by thinking of a metaphor:

Example: The sun is a fiery chariot.

Line 1: **Use the second object in the metaphor as the first line in the poem.**

The fiery chariot

Line 2: **Add a verb (action word).**

descends

Lines 3, 4, and 5: **Add three adverbs of manner.**

gradually

gracefully

gently

Line 6: **Add an adverbial phrase.**

into the placid glass.

Line 7: **Name the first part of the metaphor (sun) in a creative way.**

Earthbound traveler.

LESSON 3   Personification

Personification is a figure of speech that allows an idea, inanimate object, or animal to take on the qualities of a person.

The Sea-Gull

Hark to the whimper of the sea-gull
He weeps because he's not an ea-gull.
Suppose you were, you silly sea-gull,
Could you explain it to your she-gull?

Ogden Nash

1. What is being personified in the poem by Ogden Nash?
2. What words give it the quality of a person?
3. Which line reveals an attitude?
4. Do you agree with this attitude? Why or why not?

Because the seagull is behaving like a person, it is being personified.

Activity A

Discuss what lifelike qualities you see and hear in each of the following two poems. Tell what is being personified.

A silver-scaled Dragon with jaws flaming red
Sits at my elbow and toasts my bread.
I hand him fat slices, and then, one by one,
He hands them back when he sees they are done.

William Jay Smith

In the gray evening
I see a long green serpent
with its tail in the dahlias.

It lies in loops across the grass
And drinks softly at the faucet.

I can hear it swallow.

Beatrice Janosco

Activity B

Read the two sentences. Tell what is being personified in each and what specific words give it human qualities.

1. Summer, brightly dressed, danced throughout
   the town.
2. The arms of the ocean opened wide for all the
   summer residents.

Activity C

Complete each sentence by supplying one or more words to personify the nouns in italics.

1. The discarded *toy* _____ as it was thrown into the
   trash heap.
2. When it was batted into the outfield, the *baseball* _____ .
3. My *school desk* _____ out, "_____."
4. The *daffodils* _____ the breeze.
5. *Poverty* _____ millions of people.
6. The *car's engine* _____ as it came to a sudden stop.
7. The rickety *elevator* _____ its way to the eleventh
   floor.
8. The *wind* _____ a _____ .

Activity D

Listed below are six nouns that can be personified. Write a creative sentence for each, showing your ability to use personification effectively.

1. time   **3.** happiness   **5.** bulldozer
2. moon   **4.** morning   **6.** mirror

Writer's Corner

▶ Television commercials often use personification to get an audience's attention, and there are often personified objects in children's stories. What trains, animals, houses, and even decks of cards can you think of that have been given human qualities? Draw an object and write a description of it using personification.

Hyperbole

Hyperbole is a figure of speech that exaggerates. It usually exaggerates the truth about something in order to emphasize an idea.

The following line is taken from "Concord Hymn" by Ralph Waldo Emerson:

> . . . And fired the shot heard round the world.

Emerson refers to the battles of Lexington and Concord, where the first shot of the American Revolution was fired on April 19, 1775.

1. Was the shot really heard around the world?

2. What does Emerson mean when he says the shot was heard around the world?

The following line is taken from *Ars Amatoria* by Ovid:

> Tears too are useful; with tears you can melt iron.
> Bk. i, l. 659

1. Can tears really melt iron?

2. What does the writer mean?

3. What is meant by "tears too are useful"?

Sometimes exaggerations are humorous. Read the following poem by Shel Silverstein for many examples of hyperbole.

Hungry Mungry

Hungry Mungry sat at supper,
Took his knife and spoon and fork,
Ate a bowl of mushroom soup,
Ate a slice of roasted pork,
Ate a dozen stewed tomatoes, twenty-seven deviled eggs.
Fifteen shrimps, nine baked potatoes,
Thirty-two fried chicken legs,
A shank of lamb, a boiled ham,
Two bowls of grits, some black-eye peas,
Four chocolate shakes, eight angel cakes,
Nine custard pies with Muenster cheese
Ten pots of tea, and after he
Had eaten all that he was able,
He poured some broth on the tablecloth
And ate the kitchen table.

His parents said, "Oh Hungry Mungry, stop these silly jokes."
Mungry opened up his mouth, and "Gulp," he ate his folks.
And then he went and ate his house, all the bricks and wood,
And then he ate up all the people in the neighborhood.
Up came twenty angry policemen shouting, "Stop and cease."
Mungry opened up his mouth and "Gulp," he ate the police.
Soldiers came with tanks and guns,
Said Mungry, "They can't harm me."
He just smiled and licked his lips and ate the U.S. Army.

The President sent all his bombers—Mungry still was calm,
Put his head back, gulped the planes, and gobbled up the bomb.
He ate his town and ate the city—ate and ate and ate—
And then he said, "I think I'll eat the whole United States."

And so he ate Chicago first and munched the Water Tower,
And then he chewed on Pittsburgh but he found it rather sour,
He ate New York and Tennessee, and all of Boston town,
Then drank the Mississippi River just to wash it down.
And when he'd eaten every state, each puppy, boy and girl
He wiped his mouth upon his sleeve and went to eat the world.

He ate the Egypt pyramids and every church in Rome,
And all the grass in Africa and all the ice in Nome.
He ate each hill in Green Brazil and then to make things worse
He decided for dessert he'd eat the universe.

He started with the moon and stars and soon as he was done
He gulped the clouds, he sipped the wind and gobbled up the sun.
Then sitting there in the cold dark air,
He started to nibble his feet,
Then his legs, then his hips
Then his neck, then his lips
Till he sat there just gnashin' his teeth
'Cause nothin' was nothin' was
Nothin' was nothin' was
Nothin' was left to eat.

   Shel Silverstein

Activity A

Shel Silverstein exaggerated being hungry when he created "Hungry Mungry." See if you can exaggerate one of the following ideas. Write a short poem or paragraph.

A. Long song
B. Loud crowd
C. Tall Paul

Activity B

Complete each statement by giving an exaggerated response.

1. I'm so hungry _____ .
2. Frank talked so long _____ .
3. The grumpy man was so mean _____ .
4. The ship was so tall _____ .
5. The auditorium was so crowded _____ .
6. I'll love you until _____ .
7. There must have been a _____ people waiting for the bus.
8. The grandfather clock's gong was so loud _____ .
9. The plains are so flat _____ .
10. An eighty-year-old woman drove so slowly _____ .

Writer's Corner

▶ Write a poem or paragraph that exaggerates a talent you or a friend may have. Use one of the following or one of your own.

A. soccer	**E.** fishing
B. dancing	**F.** spelling
C. drawing	**G.** weight lifting
D. horseback riding	**H.** cooking

▶ Write a poem or paragraph that exaggerates an experience you or someone else has undergone. Choose one of the following experiences or think of one of your own.

A. first day in a new school
B. receiving your report card
C. keeping a surprise party a secret
D. your first job baby-sitting
E. being alone
F. tryouts for a sport
G. a watchdog that failed
H. attending a rock concert

Alliteration

Alliteration is the repetition of initial consonant sounds. It is a sound device that helps to create melody or mood.

Read "Foul Shot," looking and listening for words or phrases that begin with the same sound.

Foul Shot

With two 60's stuck on the scoreboard
And two seconds hanging on the clock,
The solemn boy in the center of eyes,
Squeezed by silence,
Seeks out the line with his feet,
Soothes his hands along his uniform,
Gently drums the ball against the floor,
Then measures the waiting net,
Raises the ball on his right hand,
Balances it with his left,
Calms it with fingertips,
Breathes,
Crouches,
Waits,
And then through a stretching of stillness,
Nudges it upward.

The ball
Slides up and out,
Lands,
Leans,
Wobbles,
Wavers,

Hesitates,
Exasperates,
Plays it coy
Until every face begs with unsounding screams—

And then

    And then

        And then,

Right before ROAR-UP,
Dives down and through.

      Edwin A. Hoey

1. How many different examples of alliteration can you find in the poem?

2. Can you hear repeated sounds in the middle and at the end of words? Give examples.

3. Because the author uses a predominance of certain sounds, he establishes a particular mood or tension. What is the mood of "Foul Shot"? What tension seems to be created?

Activity A

Write five poetic sentences using alliteration.

Example: The waves, wandering whitecaps of the sea, washed against the shore.

Writer's Corner

▶ Create some tongue twisters. Try them out on another student.

Example: Cookies crumbled crazily on kitchen cabinets and corner cupboards.

Onomatopoeia

Onomatopoeia is a sound device. Onomatopoetic words imitate the sound of a person, an animal, or a thing.

Hark, hark!
    Bow-wow
The watch-dogs bark!
    Bow-wow
Hark, hark! I hear
The strain of strutting chanticleer
Cry, "Cock-a-diddle-dow!"

William Shakespeare,
The Tempest,
Act i, sc. 2, l. 382

1. What words in the above poem are onomatopoetic?
2. Why do you think Shakespeare compares dogs with a rooster?

While some figures of speech may help you to see better, onomatopoeia helps you to hear better. Instead of writing,

The baseball flew by.

you can actually hear the sound when you write,

The baseball *whizzed* by.

Activity A

On a piece of paper, write the words that are listed below. Opposite each word, write an example of a person, an animal, or an object that could make that sound.

1. swish   **3.** varoom   **5.** ra-pa-pa-pum   **7.** gulp
2. splat   **4.** crackle   **6.** clackity-clack   **8.** sizzle

Activity B

Write the objects listed below and give the sound each one might make.

1. lightning
2. snoring
3. wind
4. snake
5. telephone
6. laughing
7. book hitting the ground
8. thunder

Activity C

Read the following poem to yourself and then orally as a class. Pronounce the onomatopoetic words carefully so that you can enjoy the sounds.

Cheers

The frogs and the serpents each had a football team,
and I heard their cheer leaders in my dream:

"Bilgewater, bilgewater," called the frog,
"Bilgewater, bilgewater,
Sis, boom, bog!
Roll 'em off the log,
Slog 'em in the sog,
Swamp'em, swamp'em,
Muck mire quash!"

"Sisyphus, Sisyphus," hissed the snake,
"Sibilant, syllabub,
Syllable-loo-ba-lay.
Scylla and Charybdis,
Sumac, asphodel,
How do you spell Success?
With an S-S-S!"

Eve Merriam

Writer's Corner

▶ Read the poem "Jabberwocky" on page 193. Practice reading it silently a few times before reading it aloud. Choose three onomatopoetic words that the author,

Lewis Carroll, used. Write your definition of each of the three words. Draw your own Jabberwock doing or saying the three onomatopoetic words.

Jabberwocky

'Twas brillig, and the slithy toves
    Did gyre and gimble in the wabe:
All mimsy were the borogoves,
    And the mome raths outgrabe.

"Beware the Jabberwock, my son!
    The jaws that bite, the claws that catch!
Beware the Jubjub bird, and shun
    The frumious Bandersnatch!"

He took his vorpal sword in hand:
    Long time the manxome foe he sought—
So rested he by the Tumtum tree,
    And stood awhile in thought.

And, as in uffish thought he stood,
    The Jabberwock, with eyes of flame,
Came whiffling through the tulgey wood,
    And burbled as it came!

One, two! One, two! And through and through
    The vorpal blade went snicker-snack!
He left it dead, and with its head
    He went galumphing back.

"And hast thou slain the Jabberwock?
    Come to my arms, my beamish boy!
O frabjous day! Callooh! Callay!"
    He chortled in his joy.

'Twas brillig, and the slithy toves
    Did gyre and gimble in the wabe:
All mimsy were the borogoves,
    And the mome raths outgrabe.

Lewis Carroll

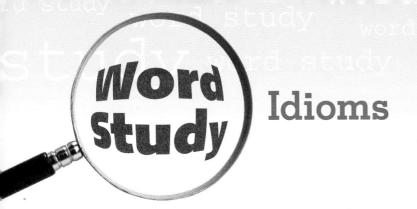

Word Study

Idioms

An idiom is an expression that has a meaning different from that indicated by its words.

Sometimes phrases cannot be understood word by word. They often have an entirely different meaning. For example,

> When giving your speech, put your *best foot forward.*

Does this mean

A. Make sure your best foot is in front of you?
B. Do the best you can?

If you interpret the words *best foot forward* by what each word means, then you have to choose *A*. But these words together are an idiom, a way of writing or speaking, that means "to do the best you can."

When searching for the meaning of an idiom in a dictionary, look under the most important word in the phrase. In the example above, you would look under *foot.* Your dictionary may also give you other idioms that use the same word, such as *put your foot down* or *put your foot in your mouth.*

Activity A

Write each idiom on a sheet of paper, underline the most important word, and then look for the meaning in a dictionary that includes idioms. Write the meaning next to each idiom.

1. right up my alley
2. my cup of tea
3. pulling my leg
4. go bananas

5. cream of the crop
6. eat your words
7. see eye to eye
8. jump in the lake

Activity B

Choose any four idioms from the list in Activity A. Write an original sentence for each one showing that you understand the meaning of the idiomatic expression. Add more idioms to the list and share them with your classmates.

WRITER'S WORKSHOP

A Poem About You

A famous television interviewer once asked, "What kind of tree are you?" The question may sound silly, but it really made her interviewee think. What kind of tree—or food or animal—are you? Write a poem to compare yourself to out-of-the-ordinary things. Publish your poem to make a class guessing game.

 Prewriting

Are you like a mighty oak because you feel powerful and strong? Or are you like a sapling because you feel that you still have a lot of growing to do? Questions like these will help you start thinking about things to which you can compare yourself.

- What kind of food am I like? Why?

- What kind of car am I like? Why?

- What kind of animal am I like? Why?

- What kind of sport or game am I like? Why?

- What time of day am I like? Why?

- What season of the year am I like? Why?

Write your answers to the questions. Then make up your own questions and answer them, too. Remember that you don't always feel the same way. You may want to answer some questions more than once for different moods or different times of day.

Avoiding Clichés

Remember that a simile is a figure of speech that compares two unlike things and usually includes the word *like* or *as.* You'll be using similes as you write your poem. But many similes, such as "as quiet as a mouse" or "like a ton of bricks," have become clichés. Clichés are expressions that have become overused and worn-out. So, try to avoid clichés. Stretch your mind to make up new, original similes.

Drafting

Reread your questions and answers, and circle the comparisons that tell the most about you. These are the similes you will use in your poem.

Then think about the format of your poem. The sample poem below may give you some ideas. Notice that this poem doesn't rhyme. It is a series of sentences written in a free verse poetry format.

Reread the circled ideas from your notes and number them in the order you will use them. Write your similes as sentences, adding words or phrases to clarify and expand your ideas.

The last few lines in your poem do not have to be comparisons. You may want to summarize the ideas you expressed or add a statement that tells a little more about you.

Finish by writing a title for your poem. A key phrase from the poem often makes a good title.

WRITER'S WORKSHOP

I'm Just Me!

Sometimes I'm like ice cream,
   all sugary and sweet.
Sometimes I'm like a prickly pine tree,
   ready to jab you
     with my sharp needles.
I'm like a sleek, red sports car,
   racing around in a cloud of dust.
I'm like a friendly puppy
   when I'm around my friends,
But I'm like a
   FIERCE, ROARING
     lion
      when I see an injustice.

When I'm unsure, I'm like a kite,
   blowing this way and that way
   in the wind.
I'm like a bright, sunshiny spring
   day,
   just waiting to turn into summer.
I'm like lots of different things,
   but I'm nothing like anybody else.
I'm just me.

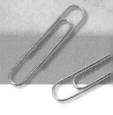

EDITOR'S WORKSHOP

Revising, Proofreading, and Publishing

Revising

Time to Take Another Look

Before you write your final copy, reread your draft to find ways to improve your poem.

Ask yourself these questions to help you revise.

❏ Do most of my sentences include a simile?

❏ Does each simile tell my reader something important about me?

❏ Do I need to rewrite any similes that are clichés?

❏ Do I need to substitute more vivid words for boring, overused words?

❏ Do I need to change the format of any of the poem's lines to make them easier to read aloud?

❏ Does my title reflect an important idea from the poem?

Reread the poem aloud to hear how it sounds. Ask yourself whether or not your poem describes you.

Make your revisions, using a colored pencil to emphasize your changes.

Listen to Your Poem

Ask a partner to read your poem aloud. Take notes as you listen. Does your partner pause in the places where you expected to hear a pause? If not, consider breaking some lines at a different part of the sentence.

Proofreading

Time to Look at Capitalization, Punctuation, and Spelling

Small errors can be distracting to your reader and destroy the flow of your poem. After you finish revising your draft, proofread it carefully to check capitalization, punctuation, spelling, and grammar.

Use the checklist below to edit and proofread your poem.

❑ Did I use commas correctly in complex sentences?

❑ Did I capitalize proper nouns correctly?

❑ Did I use the correct marks of punctuation?

❑ Did I spell each word correctly?

Start Backwards

To focus your attention as you proofread, try this technique. Begin with the last word of your poem and proofread backwards, one word at a time.

 ## Publishing

Time to Share

Publish your poem by displaying it so your classmates can enjoy guessing which poem is about you.

To publish, follow these steps:

1. Copy your revised draft in your neatest handwriting or type it on a computer.

2. Proofread your final copy one more time.

3. Glue your poem on a sheet of construction paper and write your name upside down on the back at the bottom of the page.

Make a class Guess Who bulletin board.

1. Stack the completed poems, poem side up.

2. Have one person pin the poems on the bulletin board, tacking only the top edge.

3. Read each poem and try to figure out who wrote it.

4. Carefully lift the bottom of the page to read the name to see if you were correct.

CHAPTER 8

Letter Writing

Writing Social Letters

A social letter is an informal letter written to friends and relatives.

A social letter is a very personal piece of writing. In it, you reveal yourself: your likes and dislikes, your feelings and attitudes. It is a reflection of your uniqueness.

Although the telephone and computer E-mail have replaced much of today's letter writing, there are still occasions when a thank-you, sympathy, or congratulatory note must be written. And for friends and relatives who live at a distance, there is nothing better than a long, chatty letter arriving in the mail.

About the Photograph

How do you keep in touch with friends and family? How do you express your gratitude or congratulations? A social letter can do all this for you.

The Parts of a Social Letter

There are five parts to a social letter.

Heading

The heading includes the address of the writer and the date. It is usually written on three lines in block form and begins about one inch from the top, slightly to the right of the center of the page. If you are writing to a person who knows you very well, you may omit the address but not the date.

6312 South Oakley Street
Chicago, Illinois 60626
September 20, 19___

Salutation

The salutation is the greeting at the beginning of the letter. It is written at the left-hand margin of the paper, below the heading, and is followed by a comma. The first word and the person's name are capitalized.

Dear Grandpa,   My dear Joan,

Body or Message

Your message is delivered in the body of the letter. This may take the form of a friendly conversation, an invitation, a request for information, an expression of gratitude, or a combination of all of these. Whenever you introduce a new subject, you must begin a new paragraph. The first word of every paragraph is indented.

Complimentary Close

The complimentary close is your word of farewell. It is written on a line by itself following the body of the letter and aligns with the heading at the top. Only the first word is capitalized. It is always followed by a comma. The words you use depend upon how well you know the receiver of your letter.

Your old pal,   Your friend,   Love,

Signature

The signature is begun under the first word of the complimentary close and should line up with it. When writing to a familiar person, you probably will sign only your first name. When writing to someone unfamiliar, you sign your full name.

Mike   Michael Brenner

Look for all five parts of a social letter in the model on page 204.

Since your letters represent you, it is important to be careful of their appearance as well as their contents. If a letter is handwritten, the writing should be clear and legible. If a letter is typed, it should be as perfect as possible, with no errors.

Model: A Social Letter

Lawnwood, Illinois 60626

September 20, 19___

Dear Dave,   SALUTATION

    You certainly are missed back here on Oakley Street. When I start out for school, I always want to stop by your house to see if you're ready. It's a strange feeling!   BODY

    How do you like your new school? It must seem funny to be in a place half the size of Lawnwood. I'll bet you know everyone from grades 1 to 8 by now. I think I might just like that family spirit.

    Remember the overgrown field behind the school? Mr. Wilkinson has decided to turn it into a baseball field. On Saturdays, some of us go over to help the men clear away the brush, but the bulldozer is really doing all the work. It should be ready by next spring.

    Let me hear from you soon, Dave. I'm anxious to know about life in your new town.

Your pal,   COMPLIMENTARY CLOSE

Mike   SIGNATURE

204

Finishing Touches for Letters

Folding the Letter

Some paper only has to be folded in half in order to fit into the envelope. The creased edge should be placed at the bottom of the envelope.

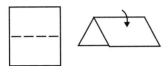

Sometimes you might want to write your letter on larger paper. Then, to fit it in a regular size envelope ($6\frac{1}{2}$" $\times$ $3\frac{3}{4}$"), you must first fold the paper in half, then fold the right side over a third of the way. Finally, fold the left side over. The letter should be inserted in the envelope with the last fold at the bottom.

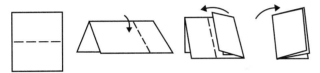

If you use a legal size envelope ($9\frac{1}{2}$" $\times$ 4"), large paper needs only to be folded in thirds to fit neatly into the envelope. The way to do this is to fold the bottom third of the paper a little past the halfway mark, then fold the top third over within an eighth of an inch of the bottom fold. Insert the letter in the envelope with the first fold at the bottom.

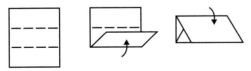

Addressing the Envelope

The envelope should contain the full name and address of the person to whom the letter is being sent. The first line contains the person's name and is begun just above the middle of the envelope and slightly to the left of center. The second line contains the street address, and the third line contains the city, two-letter postal abbreviation for the state, and zip code. It is customary to write your own address in the upper left-hand corner. This is called the return address.

Postal Abbreviations

AL	Alabama	**KY**	Kentucky	**OH**	Ohio
AK	Alaska	**LA**	Louisiana	**OK**	Oklahoma
AZ	Arizona	**ME**	Maine	**OR**	Oregon
AR	Arkansas	**MD**	Maryland	**PA**	Pennsylvania
CA	California	**MA**	Massachusetts	**RI**	Rhode Island
CO	Colorado	**MI**	Michigan	**SC**	South Carolina
CT	Connecticut	**MN**	Minnesota	**SD**	South Dakota
DE	Delaware	**MS**	Mississippi	**TN**	Tennessee
DC	District of	**MO**	Missouri	**TX**	Texas
	Columbia	**MT**	Montana	**UT**	Utah
FL	Florida	**NE**	Nebraska	**VT**	Vermont
GA	Georgia	**NV**	Nevada	**VA**	Virginia
HI	Hawaii	**NH**	New Hampshire	**WA**	Washington
ID	Idaho	**NJ**	New Jersey	**WV**	West Virginia
IL	Illinois	**NM**	New Mexico	**WI**	Wisconsin
IN	Indiana	**NY**	New York	**WY**	Wyoming
IA	Iowa	**NC**	North Carolina	**GU**	Guam
KS	Kansas	**ND**	North Dakota	**PR**	Puerto Rico
				VI	Virgin Islands

Tina Alvarado
8641 Winchester
Chicago, IL 60626

Melissa Hsu
2015 Decatur Drive
Atlanta, GA 30307

Activity A

Write each of the addresses and dates in the proper form for the heading of a letter.

1. Portsmouth, New Hampshire 03801; 171 Saratoga Way; September 12, 19____

2. June 27, 19____ ; 6333 Herbert Street; Detroit, Michigan 48210

3. 2219 Avenue H; May 3, 19____ ; Houston, Texas 77023

Activity B

Write a salutation for a letter addressed to each of the following persons.

1. your father   3. your teacher
2. a classmate   4. your cousin

Activity C

Write the following sentences in the form of a letter. Supply the missing parts, use capital letters as they are needed, and paragraph the letter properly.

i was so happy to see a letter from you on my desk when i got home from school. it was a rather dull day, so i was glad for a friendly note. thanks for sending your school picture. i especially liked the background of the library shelves. is that to make everyone believe you've read all those books? we are getting ready for a play, too, and i have a speaking part. i have to practice at a microphone, and you know how nervous i get when i read in front of others. here's hoping i don't lose my voice. if you have any ideas for a science project, let me know. my mom won't let me work with chemicals, so that's out. science is your favorite subject, so you must have some suggestions. keep in touch. it's nice to hear about what you're doing on the other coast.

Writer's Corner

▶ Choose one of the following ideas and write a letter. Make sure that the heading, salutation, complimentary close, and signature are properly written. Then draw an envelope on a piece of paper and address it correctly.

A. Write a letter to a pen pal telling him or her about interesting things to see and do in your hometown.
B. Write to a cousin or some other relative and tell about a recent trip you took.
C. Write a letter to someone you especially admire. Tell why you think so highly of the person.

Special Types of Social Letters

A Letter of Invitation

Keep invitations short, but be sure to include the time, the place, and the nature of the party or gathering.

1714 Ritner Street

Ogden, Utah 84400

April 28, 19___

Dear Victor,

    Are you in the mood for a few days in the mountains? Mom said that I may invite four friends to our cottage at Arrowhead for the weekend of May fifth, and I want you to be one of them.

    There will be much to do. We can hike the trails, swim in the lake, and go to the movie theater in town.

    Dad is driving up on Friday evening, and there will be plenty of room in the car for all of us. Let me know if you can join us, and I'll tell you what time we'll pick you up.

          Your friend,

          Eric

A Letter of Acceptance

A letter accepting an invitation should be brief and
enthusiastic.

5601 Moulton Street

Ogden, Utah 84400

April 30, 19___

Dear Eric,

I wouldn't miss this trip for anything. I love
hiking and swimming! It sounds like we'll have a
great time.

I'll be waiting with my bag packed at the front
door. Just let me know the time.

Your friend,
Victor

A Thank-You Letter

A thank-you letter will name the gift you have received and let the person know that the present is quite special.

July 27, 19____

Dear Grandmom,

You always buy me such unique things for my birthday. The skating passes are great, and the gift certificates to The Hamburger Shack will probably be used this weekend.

My friends think I have the best grandmom, and I agree. Thanks for everything.

Love,

Kim

Activity A

Try the following ideas for letters. Be sure that each letter contains the five essential parts: heading, salutation, body, complimentary close, and signature.

1. Invitation
   You are planning a New Year's Day party. Create your own original invitation. Be sure to include time, date, and place. Decorate the invitation appropriately.

2. Acceptance
   Your aunt (or friend) asks you to volunteer to be a clown at the children's hospital party. Accept the challenge.

3. Thank You
   Thank someone for providing a wonderful weekend of entertainment.

Writer's Corner

▶ **Choose two of the following ideas and write polished, courteous social letters.**

A. The holiday play at your school is on December 18. You have a special part and would like your grandparents (or other relatives) to come to see you. Write them an invitation they can't refuse.

B. At a country fair, you took a chance on a pony. A letter just arrived indicating that you won and are now the proud owner. You live in the city. Handle the situation courteously.

C. Your basketball team has made the playoffs for the district championship. Invite a former student (or someone else) to the series.

D. You have just won a food processor (something you don't want or need). Accept the prize graciously.

E. A student in your class has just received an award for an athletic event, a music recital, or a science contest. Write a note of congratulations.

F. A relative, who lives at a distance and hasn't seen you for a while, sends a gift that is too young for you. Write a gracious thank you for the gift.

G. Think of the events and activities of the last few weeks. Write to a friend and give him or her the latest news.

H. A gift for you from a special relative has arrived damaged. How would you respond to the sender?

I. Send a thank-you letter to your local newspaper editor who has awarded you a $500 savings bond for being "Outstanding Newspaper Carrier of the Year."

J. You have just had a new member added to your family. Describe your baby brother or sister to a friend or relative who lives at a distance.

Writing Business Letters

A business letter is a formal letter written to a company in order to obtain or give information, or to request specific merchandise.

Business letters should always be brief, courteous, and clear. The form of a business letter is very similar to that of a social letter. It does, however, contain one part that is not found in a social letter. This part is called the inside address.

The Parts of a Business Letter

Heading

This is the same and in the same location as the heading of a social letter.

> 607 Lincoln Drive
> Dubuque, Iowa 52001
> January 20, 19____

Inside Address

The inside address is not found in a social letter. It contains the complete name and address of the business or name and address of the person and business to whom the letter is written. It is placed at the left-hand margin above the salutation.

> E.M. Lohmann Company
> 314 Sibley Street
> St. Paul, Minnesota 55100

> Ms. Mary Callahan
> E.M. Lohmann Company
> 314 Sibley Street
> St. Paul, Minnesota 55100

Salutation

The salutation, or greeting, is very formal. It is best to use the person's name if it is known. The salutation is always followed by a colon.

Dear Sir or Madam: Dear Mrs. Rodriguez:
Dear Ms. Patel: Dear Dr. Levy:

Body or Message

The body of the letter contains the message. The message must be courteous, clear, accurate, and brief. Since a letter represents you before a business firm, you should try to be courteous in your manner, and to be clear and accurate in your statements. The letter must be brief so that the reader can pick out the necessary information as quickly as possible.

Please send, as soon as possible, the ivory and gold trophy listed in your catalog as S-214. Enclosed is a check for fifteen dollars ($15.00), as specified in your current price list.

Complimentary Close

The complimentary close is also more formal in a business letter. It consists of a short phrase indicating respect for the person addressed in the letter and is followed by a comma.

Sincerely,   Respectfully yours,
Respectfully,   Very truly yours,

Signature

The signature of a business letter contains the full name of the writer. The signature is always written, never typed. However, directly under your signature, you should type or neatly print your name.

Sarah J. Meier
Sarah J. Meier

(Ms.) Nicole Jones
(Ms.) Nicole Jones

Hakim I. Khallaq
Hakim I. Khallaq

Here is how a business letter should look.

607 Lincoln Drive
Dubuque, Iowa 52001   HEADING
January 20, 19____

Ms. Mary Callahan
E.M. Lohmann Company
314 Sibley Street   INSIDE ADDRESS
St. Paul, Minnesota 55100

Dear Ms. Callahan: SALUTATION

    Please send, as soon as possible, the
ivory and gold trophy listed in your catalog
as S-214. Enclosed is a check for fifteen   BODY
dollars ($15.00), as specified in your current
price list.

Sincerely yours,   COMPLIMENTARY CLOSE
Sarah J. Meier   SIGNATURE
Sarah J. Meier

Activity A

Rewrite the following inside addresses in correct order.

1. 189 Prospect Avenue; Soup to Nuts, Inc.; Buffalo, New York 14214

2. Homer, Louisiana 71040; 2922 Carlton Drive; Picture Perfect; Mr. James Snyder

3. Creative Gifts; Los Altos, California 94022; Ms. I. M. Merry; 18 North Second Avenue

Activity B

Draw three $9\frac{1}{2}$" × 4" rectangles on a piece of a paper to use as envelopes. Address the three envelopes, using the addresses in Activity A. Use the two-letter postal abbreviation for each state.

Activity C

Put the following sentences in business letter form. The punctuation and capitalization must be added. Use your own name and address and the present date.

ms. teresa vasquez librarian of children's department goshen public library goshen, indiana 46526 dear ms. vasquez: please consider me an applicant for the position of assistant library aide advertised in today's sentinel. i am fourteen years old and attend powell school. i have held a library card for five years. for references, i have permission to name the principal of our school, mrs. susan jardine, and my teacher, mr. mark niven. very truly yours,

Writer's Corner

▶ Write a business letter to your principal proposing an idea for the school to raise money for a charity.

Special Types of Business Letters

A Letter Placing an Order

When we need to place an order, often we call the 800 or 888 number. You can also fill out the form in the catalog and mail or fax it to the company. To write a letter to place an order, be sure to include the following information:

- names of items to be purchased

- catalog numbers if provided

- where the items were advertised

- the prices of the items

- how payment for the merchandise will be handled: cash, check, money order, C.O.D. (cash on delivery), charge card

Study the example letter on page 218.

1269 Asbury Street

Stone Harbor, New Jersey 08247

February 3, 19___

Junior High Book Club

110 Chestnut Street

Rockville, Maryland 20850

Dear Sir or Madam:

    Please send to the above address the following novels listed in your catalog:

1	The Sea-Wolf		
	by Jack London	(9046)	$3.95
1	Little Women		
	by L. Alcott	(9085)	2.50
			$6.45
		shipping	2.00
			$8.45

A check for $8.45 is enclosed.

Respectfully yours,

Karen L. James

Karen L. James

A Letter of Request

In this type of business letter, you are usually requesting information, catalogs, pamphlets, or samples. Be clear, brief, and polite.

Whitemarsh School
Dayton, Ohio 45400
November 6, 19___

Daily Local Times
1060 Morgan Avenue
Dayton, Ohio 45400

Dear Sir or Madam:

In our language arts class, we have been studying news and editorial writing. A friend and I thought it would be helpful if our class could see a real newspaper at work. Would it be possible for us to have a tour of the newspaper offices within the next two weeks? If so, please tell us what day and time would be convenient for you.

Very truly yours,
Scott Blum
Scott Blum

A Letter of Complaint or Adjustment

Give a clear and courteous explanation of your position on the matter. Be sure to mention the error by stating the name of the product and the date and place of purchase. Also, explain the action you are planning to take and the action you would like the business to take.

Bryn Mawr School
137 Locust Avenue
Spokane, Washington 99200
September 24, 19___

Enley Sport Shop
932 North Tacoma Street
Tacoma, Washington 98400

Dear Sir or Madam:

On September 9, we ordered one dozen blue-and-white football jerseys. The fuchsia-and-white ones that arrived today are not satisfactory substitutes since our school colors are blue and white.

I am returning these jerseys. Kindly send the colors ordered as soon as possible.

Very truly yours,
William Armstrong
William Armstrong

Activity **A**

Number a piece of paper from 1 to 10. Next to each number write the letter _a, b,_ or _c_ to tell whether the item refers to

       a. a business letter   **b.** a social letter   **c.** both

1. letter of invitation
2. heading
3. Dear Ms. McCole:
4. inside address
5. Your faithful friend,
6. letter of request
7. Love, Sandy
8. Respectfully,
9. letter of acceptance
10. salutation

Activity **B**

Write the following business letters. Use your home address as the heading and your own name for the signature.

1. Placing an Order
   You would like a subscription to _Popular Computer._ The cost is $8.98 for six issues. The magazine is published at 8219 Lindberg Boulevard; Seattle, Washington 98124.

2. Letter of Request
   You have written a marvelous short story, and your teacher suggests that you try to have it published. Write to a student publication called _Creative Corner;_ 6019 Penn Avenue; Santa Monica, California 90404.

3. Letter of Complaint or Adjustment
   You ordered a baseball mitt from Sporting Goods Unlimited; 19 Peterson Drive; Boise, Idaho 83742. Instead, you received a pair of mittens. Explain the problem.

Writer's Corner

▶ Here are ideas for business letters. Choose one and write a letter to the company. Then write an appropriate reply from the company to you. Create addresses and names as needed.

A. You have thought up a new computer game and would like a local company to see your idea. Write to them requesting an interview.

B. You ordered a poster of your favorite actor. Instead, you received a picture of a not-so-popular actor. Write to Picture Pinups; 1666 Star Road; Hollywood, CA 90210.

C. Your local paper states that by ordering two cassette tapes or CDs within the next week, you will get a third one free. Decide which ones you want and take advantage of the offer. Check page 217 for a list of what is included in an order. Write to Tons of Tapes; 3099 Market Street; Philadelphia, PA 19101.

D. You hosted a party at your home last week. The pretzels you bought were stale, even though the expiration date on the package was several weeks away. Write a letter of complaint to the company.

E. Write a letter to Montgomery Ward and Company; 618 W. Chicago Avenue; Chicago, IL 60652, to order the following items:

    1 tennis racket, No. 6H 1229, $24.00
    1 tennis cap, No. 6H 1259, Size 7, $6.95
    3 tennis balls, No. 6H 1231, $5.95

Add shipping charges and tell the method of payment. Use your own address and signature.

F. Your order of 100 personalized pencils arrived. Your name is misspelled. Write a letter of complaint to the company.

LESSON 5

Completing Forms

Completing a form is an orderly way of requesting information or materials.

Many companies, schools, clubs, and organizations ask that you fill out a form when requesting or ordering information or material. When businesses receive numerous requests, a form makes it easier for them to compile and process the information. Before you complete a form, you should do the following:

1. Read the entire form to find out what is being asked.
2. List on a piece of paper the information you must look up or ask about.
3. Collect the information needed to answer what you don't know.
4. Check to see how you will complete the form. Write? Print? Type?
5. Complete the form carefully and neatly.
6. Reread the form to see that all the information you have given is accurate and in the correct place.

Activity A

Study the form on page 224. Then answer the questions.

1. Is your information on the form to be written, printed, or typed?
2. What is the difference between Price Each and Total Price?
3. Why are there four columns under Item No.?
4. Why does the company request a page number?
5. What is meant by a subtotal?
6. How did Karen know to add $3.50 for shipping charges?
7. Why did she not include sales tax?
8. What does the statement "No cash or C.O.D." mean?

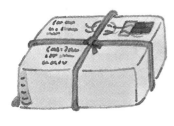

THE PERFECT GIFT
1039 Bryant Lane
Seattle, WA 98103

Please print or type all information.

Page No.	Name of Item	Item No.				QTY	Price Each	Total Price
18	White Porcelain Candlestick	9	0	1	6	1	4.98	4.98
22	Cookie Jar	7	7	7	6	2	8.98	17.96
29	Hand Puppet	3	9	5	0	1	12.98	12.98

Shipping/Handling				
Total of All Items	**Add**	**Subtotal**		$35.92
Up to $20.00 . . . .$1.50		**Shipping/Handling Charge**		3.50
$20.01 to $30.00 . . . .$2.50		**NY sales tax (residents only)**		——
$30.01 to $40.00 . . . .$3.50				
$40.01 to $50.00 . . . .$4.50		**Total**		$39.42
Over $50.00 . . . .$5.50				

(No cash or C.O.D.)

Ship to

Karen	L.	Dalesandro
first name	**middle initial**	**last name**
1659 Wellington Avenue		203
street address		**apt.**
Ann Arbor	Michigan	48107
city	**state**	**zip code**

Activity

Make a copy of the savings deposit form. Then complete it by using the information in the paragraph.

Keith Turner has savings account #00016767123. He wants to deposit $60.50 from his paper route earnings and a check for $25.00 he received on his birthday. He feels he should keep out $15.00 for expenditures for the coming week. Keith lives at 89 Marydell Lane in Mobile, Alabama 36604.

UNIVERSAL BANK	SAVINGS DEPOSIT		
	Dollars	Cents	
DATE _____			Cash
			Checks
NAME _____ (PRINT)			
ADDRESS _____			
_____			
_____ SIGNATURE			Total
			Less cash received
	$		Total deposit
ACCOUNT NUMBER			

Writer's Corner

▶ Copy the form for this check onto a piece of paper. Make out a check to cover the cost of the items purchased in Activity A. The signature in the right-hand corner should be the name that is printed at the top of the check.

Karen L. Dalesandro
1659 Wellington Avenue
Ann Arbor, MI 48107

139

_____ 19 _____ 2-7/310

PAY TO THE
ORDER OF _____ $ _____

_____ Dollars

UNIVERSAL BANK
Ann Arbor, MI **48108**

For _____

000111122   333 444 5 666

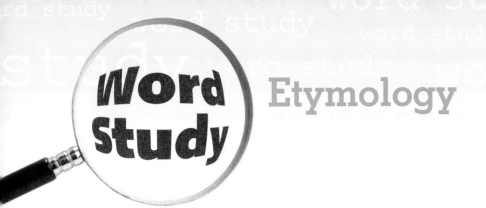

Etymology

Etymology is the study of the history of a word: where it came from, how it was originally spelled, and what it originally meant.

Many English words developed from other languages, such as Greek, Latin, French, and Old English. In most dictionaries, the history of a word, or etymology, is found in brackets either at the end or the beginning of the definition. Following are some symbols you should know in order to understand the information that is given in the etymology. Check the front of your dictionary for other abbreviations.

<	means "derived from or comes from"
<L	means "comes from the Latin language"
<Gk	means "comes from the Greek language"
<F	means "comes from the French language"
<OE	means "comes from the Old English language"
<ME	means "comes from the Middle English language"

Sometimes words come from two or more languages; for example, *anchor*. In some dictionaries, the etymology for *anchor* will look like this:

[<OE *ancor* <L *anchora* <Gk *ankyra*]

Our word *anchor* originally came to us from the Old English word. The Old English word came from Latin, and the Latin from the Greek word. Some dictionaries will only indicate that the word came from the Greek, since that is the earliest known form.

Activity **A**

Write each word on a piece of paper. Using a dictionary that provides etymologies, write the correct symbols to give the etymology of the word. If the word came from more than one language, use the symbols to indicate the various languages.

1. ranch
2. rotate
3. wharf
4. pepper
5. juvenile
6. monster
7. pentagon
8. cool
9. politics
10. censor
11. bonbon
12. manage

Activity **B**

Copy the words in column A onto a sheet of paper. Use a dictionary to find each word's etymology. Then next to each word, write the letter from column B that indicates the correct etymology of the word. Some letters will be used more than once.

COLUMN A	COLUMN B
1. nightingale	**a.** Spanish
2. stomach	**b.** Old English
3. siesta	**c.** Algonquian
4. school (of fish)	**d.** Latin
5. chauffeur	**e.** Italian
6. liberty	**f.** Dutch
7. piano	**g.** French
8. moccasin	**h.** Greek

A Whale of an Excuse

Something very strange happened to you yesterday. Because of this you missed a day of school. Now you're in real trouble, because you need an excuse to get back into school today. Write an absence excuse letter to explain what happened. Publish your letter so your classmates can vote on whether or not your absence will be excused.

 Prewriting

The body of your absence excuse will be like a tall tale. It may be something that could never really happen. Or it may be an exaggeration of something ordinary. Make a list of story ideas.

Ask yourself questions like these to help you think of an outlandish tale.

- What heroic deeds could you do that would be more urgent than getting to school?

- What obstacles might spring up in your path to keep you from getting to school?

- Who might you have met on the way to school?

Reread your list of tall tale topics and circle the one that sounds like it would be the most original and the most fun to write.

Then make a story map to develop your tall tale's plot.

Parts of a Story Map

Use an organizer like this one to help plan your story.

BEGINNING
Set the scene. You'll probably want to tell how your day began like an ordinary day or why you were especially looking forward to getting to school.

MIDDLE
Here's where your life gets complicated. How is this day different from your usual day? How do things keep you from getting to school? What happens as the day goes on?

ENDING
It's time to get yourself safely home. Tell how you do it.

Drafting

Tell your story as if you were writing a letter to your principal. You'd better use a formal style and a business letter format to make sure you'll be believed.

Begin by writing your heading clearly in the upper right corner. Include your address and the date below.

Below the heading and at the left margin of your stationery, write your principal's name and title and the school address.

Write your salutation. Since your letter is a business letter, your salutation will end with a colon.

Then start right in with the body of your letter. Begin by asking to be excused for yesterday's absence. Then explain what happened by telling your tall tale. Read the body of a letter below that one student wrote explaining her experience.

Conclude with a complimentary close and your handwritten signature, with your printed or typed name below it.

> Please excuse my absence from school yesterday. I was walking past the apple orchard when a spaceship landed right in front of me. Suddenly I was surrounded by little green people, who scooped me up and whisked me off to a distant planet. I told them I needed to go to school, so they sent me to one of theirs. Guess what! The space students were studying fractions, just like we are. Since I had studied so hard for my algebra test, I was able to teach them everything they needed to know. In gratitude, they brought me home at the end of the day. Of course I was sorry to miss school, but I'm sure you'll agree that my time was well spent.

EDITOR'S WORKSHOP

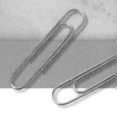

Revising, Proofreading, and Publishing

Revising

Time to Take Another Look

Reread your draft to find ways to make your letter's message funnier and more interesting.

Use these questions to help you revise your draft.

- ❏ Does my letter look like a real business letter?

- ❏ Does it include all the parts a business letter needs?

- ❏ Does the body of my letter tell a complete story?

- ❏ Do I need to add details to make the plot events clear?

- ❏ Do I need to take out any unnecessary details?

- ❏ Do I need to change the order of some details to tell the story in chronological order?

- ❏ Do I need to replace boring words with more vivid ones?

- ❏ Have I exaggerated the events?

- ❏ Does my story sound convincing?

Make your revisions with a colored pencil. Then read your revised draft to a partner and discuss your revisions.

Use Chronological Order

The body of your letter is just like a personal narrative. Relate your events in chronological, or time, order. Use words like *first, next, after,* and *finally* to help your reader follow the plot.

Proofreading

Time to Look at Capitalization, Punctuation, and Spelling

Before you make your final copy, check your capitalization, punctuation, spelling, and grammar.

Use the checklist below to edit and proofread your letter.

❏ Did I use a colon after the salutation?

❏ Did I use capital letters and commas correctly in the heading, inside address, and complimentary close?

❏ Did I use correct marks of punctuation in the body of my letter?

❏ Did I spell all the words correctly?

Take a Break
Take a short break before you begin proofreading. Think about something else for a few minutes. Taking time out will help you view your work with a fresh eye.

 ## Publishing

Time to Share

Publish your letter by reading it to your classmates and allowing them to determine whether or not you will be excused.

To publish, follow these steps:

1. Copy your revised draft in your neatest handwriting or type it on a computer.

2. Write your signature in your own handwriting.

3. Type or print your name below your signature.

4. Proofread your final copy one last time.

Share your letter.

1. Read your letter aloud to your classmates.

2. Even if you think your letter is funny, read it seriously as if you were reading it to your principal.

3. Have your classmates signal with a "thumbs up" or "thumbs down" to show whether or not they think your absence should be excused.

4. Offer to share your outlandish excuses with your principal.

CHAPTER 9

Speaking and Listening Skills

Speaking in Groups

Speaking skills enable us to give effective oral expression to ideas, while listening skills lead to proper perception and interpretation of spoken material.

In this chapter you will learn how to speak effectively when

- participating in a group discussion.
- giving a talk.
- reading poetry aloud.

You will also learn how to concentrate when someone else is speaking so that you can fully grasp the message being sent.

Much of your happiness in life will depend on your ability to work with others. No matter what your occupation may be, you will be a member of some group, club, association, or union. Decisions will be made that will affect your welfare. Will you be silent while questions are being discussed, or will you present your own ideas in such a way as to command respect?

It is important to practice interacting in a group—to learn to pool your bit of knowledge with that of others for the common good, to sift differences of opinion, to change your own opinion gracefully when you see that the arguments on the other side are stronger, and to defend your own view if you are certain that you are right. School offers many opportunities for practicing this kind of interaction.

About the Photograph

This teacher and his students are having an informal group discussion. Practicing your speaking and listening skills will help you in many situations both in and out of school.

Informal Class Discussions

Informal class discussions are those held when the class is not organized with elected officers. The teacher, or someone appointed by the teacher, presides as chairperson or leader. A day in advance of the time set for the discussion, the teacher may make an announcement like this: "Tomorrow during our English period we shall hold an informal discussion on the qualities of good sportsmanship. I should like the members of the class to come prepared to take part in the discussion by offering helpful suggestions. Elizabeth Stein, will you please act as leader of the discussion?"

Model: An Informal Discussion

(The English period is in progress. Elizabeth Stein is the discussion leader, or chairperson.)

ELIZABETH: We are here to discuss the qualities of good sportsmanship. Which do you think is the most important trait a person who practices good sportsmanship should possess?

MALIK: I think dedication heads the list. Good sportsmanship involves putting forth your best efforts at all times and under all circumstances, however trying they may be. You should never let down the other members of a team—nor yourself, for that matter.

SUSANA: Don't you want to put being a good loser high on this list? I like to see defeat acknowledged with a smile.

ELIZABETH: Of course, Susana. Everyone likes to see the loser sincerely congratulate the winner.

STEVEN: I think being a gracious winner is equally important. When a person is arrogant about having won, he or she is insulting the loser. And if the loser really wasn't very good, then it didn't mean much to win, did it? So what is there to be arrogant about?

MICHELLE: I agree, and I think we should add that *how* a person wins is part of good sportsmanship, too. In other words, winning through fair play is the only way to win. It would be better to lose every time than to try anything underhanded.

JAMES: That's a good point, Michelle. All the truly great athletes detest cheating. And if someone cheats at sports, it is likely to carry over into other parts of life. My grandfather had a favorite quote he used to repeat when he heard of someone cheating in a game: "He that will cheat at play will cheat you any way."

ELIZABETH: Will someone else express an opinion?

GEORGE: Being courteous is certainly part of good sportsmanlike conduct. There is no place in a game for a person who can't treat the other players with the respect he or she would like to receive personally.

ELIZABETH: That's a good thing to remember, George. It seems to me that we could sum up this discussion by putting all these qualities under one heading: courage. If a person has the courage to do the right thing, he or she will find that all these traits follow. Everything we mentioned calls for courage in some degree. Let's hope that from this talk we will all determine to possess these qualities when we are involved in competitive sports.

It is the duty of the discussion leader

- to see that the discussion is brief and orderly.
- to keep the discussion to the topic.
- to summarize the points discussed.

Notice that it is the leader's duty to keep the discussion moving in an orderly fashion and to sum up the suggestions at the end. Think about the discussion you just read. Was it lively? Did a number of persons participate and express their ideas? Did the leader state any conclusion arrived at by the group?

Activity A

Choose a leader and hold a group discussion. Select from the following list the topic you would like to discuss in class.

A. How does TV influence us?

B. What dangers are involved in the use of drugs?

C. Do you think that UFOs are really visitors from other planets?

D. Do Americans depend too much on their cars?

E. Would you like to have lived in another time?

F. What kind of person would you like to see be president of the United States?

G. If you won the lottery, what would you do with the money?

H. Why should we care about what we eat?

Writer's Corner

▶ Try holding an informal book discussion with several other students. Decide on a book you would all like to read, or one you have already read. Choose one person to be the chairperson and discuss the characters, plot, setting, and your general reactions to the book. It might be helpful to write your ideas and feelings out on paper before the discussion.

Speaking to Groups

It is only a step from group discussions to reports and formal talks to groups. Talks before an audience are more interesting if the speaker plans in advance what he or she is going to say. Having a good opening sentence prepared is important because it captures an audience's attention. The details that follow this good beginning sentence must likewise be carefully chosen. The best way to organize a talk so that it keeps to the topic and covers all the essential points is to make an outline.

Marcy Garcia decided to give a class talk on student councils, but this subject was too general. She therefore limited her talk to one topic: why we should form an eighth-grade student council. The following outline aided her in making the talk.

**Why We Should Form
an Eighth-Grade Student Council**

I. Structure
    A. Officers elected from the entire grade
    B. Representatives elected from each classroom
    C. Faculty advisor appointed by the principal
    D. Meetings held each month
    E. Agenda discussed each meeting

II. Advantages
    A. Mediator between faculty and students
    B. Aid to teachers in certain activities
    C. Student participation in school policy
    D. Development of individual responsibility and initiative

III. Results
    A. Increase in faculty-student rapport
    B. Reduction of discipline problems
    C. Preparation for service in higher levels of education
    D. Greater student contribution to school community

Model: A Class Talk

Why We Should Form
an Eighth-Grade Student Council

A profitable activity that is becoming quite popular with students is the formation of a student council. The main officers—president, vice president, secretary, and treasurer—are usually elected from the entire grade. They and the representatives from each classroom meet monthly with their faculty advisor. Their agenda includes the planning of school activities for the coming month and the discussion of suggestions submitted by the student body.

A student-oriented group such as this one offers many advantages to both faculty and students. Because the council serves as a mediator between these two groups, the teachers learn more about students' needs and are more likely to discuss their concerns about school situations. Faculty members also appreciate the assistance given to them by student representatives who organize sports and social activities. Students welcome the chance to take an active role in carrying out school activities. Perhaps the greatest advantage of a student council is that it offers students an opportunity to handle responsibilities similar to those they will have later in life. By acting on their own initiative, students gain self-confidence and a sense of achievement.

Furthermore, a student council often promotes a greater rapport between the faculty and students, which helps reduce disciplinary problems. In addition, the students become better prepared to participate in student government as they continue their education. Thus, the entire school community benefits from such a program.

Did the speaker explain why we should have a student council? Did she follow her outline? Was the beginning sentence interesting? Was it evident that the speaker had given some thought to her subject?

The Elements of a Good Speech

A good speaker has both mental and physical control. There are four elements to consider in preparing a talk, and each will play a role in how well your message is received by the audience:

- Ideas: What is said is of the most importance. Ideas are acquired from four sources: observation of life; conversation with experienced speakers; reading; and personal reflections on what is seen, heard, and read.

- Style: How ideas are presented also requires attention. The speech should be grammatically correct, with the words carefully chosen and the sentence structure varied.

- Voice: Let it be low in pitch and flexible. Speak distinctly, so that everyone understands what is said.

- Posture: Stand with body straight, head not too high, eyes focused on the audience, and hands relaxed.

Activity A

Prepare a short talk on any one of the following topics. You may use the beginning sentence, the details to be developed, and the ending sentence suggested for each topic, or you may alter them to suit your own speech.

A. Space Exploration

Beginning sentence:	In the early 1950s, few people could have dreamed that space exploration would achieve so much so quickly.
Details:	*Sputnik,* weather and communication satellites, exploration of Mars and Venus, manned spaceflights, moon landings, space stations, space shuttles
Ending sentence:	Today, the fact that vehicles travel to and from various points in space is an accepted part of life, and many of the former secrets of space are well known to us all.

B. How Baseball Is Played

Beginning sentence:	Because baseball is such a popular sport, we should have more than a superficial knowledge of the game.
Details:	playing field, position of players, object of the game, method of scoring
Ending sentence:	Whether you are a player or spectator of this great game, accurate knowledge should help you to enjoy it more.

C. Jane Addams

Beginning sentence: Jane Addams, winner of the Nobel Peace Prize, social reformer, and humanitarian, dedicated her life to helping the underprivileged in Chicago.

Details: founded Hull House, advocated labor reforms, including the eight-hour workday for women, supported suffrage for women, wrote several books on her experiences

Ending sentence: This courageous individual is an inspiration and model for all people.

Activity B

Prepare an original talk to be given in your classroom. These are the important steps to be followed.

1. Choose a subject.

2. Limit the subject to one topic that can be covered in a short speech.

3. Make an outline.

4. Prepare an interesting beginning sentence.

5. Follow the outline in developing the topic.

6. Think of a strong ending sentence. (The content of the speech and its desired effect will help you compose this final thought.)

Writer's Corner

▶ Think of something you've always been curious about and that might be of interest to your fellow students. Then research it in the library. Narrow the topic and write a short report to be presented as a brief class talk according to the steps given in Activity B.

Reading Poetry Aloud

Rhythm

Often we become aware of a particular mood or attitude when we read a poem. This mood may be one of joy or sorrow, excitement or humor. We can determine the mood of a poem by the words and thoughts contained in it, and also by its rhythm. The rhythm often matches or harmonizes with the mood. Light, quick-moving rhythm usually conveys a whimsical thought and creates a joyous mood. Slower rhythm generally suggests a more thoughtful theme, or it may communicate a feeling of sadness. Note how the rhythm in the following poem changes: it is slow when the poet talks about the city, and light and joyful when he reminisces about his island home.

When Dawn Comes to the City

The tired cars go grumbling by,
The moaning, groaning cars,
And the old milk carts go rumbling by
Under the same dull stars.
Out of the tenements, cold as stone,
Dark figures start for work;
I watch them sadly shuffle on,
'Tis dawn, dawn in New York.

But I would be on the island of the sea,
In the heart of the island of the sea,
Where the cocks are crowing, crowing, crowing,
And the hens are cackling in the rose-apple tree,
Where the old draft horse is neighing, neighing, neighing
Out on the brown, dew-silvered lawn,
And the tethered cow is lowing, lowing, lowing,
And dear old Ned is braying, braying, braying,
And the shaggy Nannie goat is calling, calling, calling
From her little trampled corner of the long wide lea

That stretches to the waters of the hill stream falling
Sheer upon the flat rocks joyously!
There, oh there! on the island of the sea,
There I would be at dawn.

The tired cars go grumbling by,
The crazy, lazy cars,
And the same milk carts go rumbling by
Under the dying stars.
A lonely newsboy hurries by,
Humming a recent ditty;
Red streaks strike through the gray of the sky,
The dawn comes to the city.

But I would be on the island of the sea,
In the heart of the island of the sea,
Where the cocks are crowing, crowing, crowing,
And the hens are cackling in the rose-apple tree,
Where the old draft horse is neighing, neighing, neighing
Out on the brown dew-silvered lawn,
And the tethered cow is lowing, lowing, lowing,
And dear old Ned is braying, braying, braying,
And the shaggy Nannie goat is calling, calling, calling
From her little trampled corner of the long wide lea
That stretches to the waters of the hill stream falling
Sheer upon the flat rocks joyously!
There, oh there! on the island of the sea,
There I would be at dawn.

Claude McKay

The following piece of writing looks like a paragraph, but it is actually a poem! Read it aloud and discover the rhythm.

Football

The Game was ended and the noise at last had died away, and now they gathered up the boys where they in pieces lay. And one was hammered in the ground by many a jolt and jar; some fragments never have been found, they flew away so far. They found a stack of tawny hair, some fourteen cubits high; it was the half-back, lying there, where he had crawled to die. They placed the pieces on a door, and from the crimson field, that hero then they gently bore, like a soldier on his shield. The surgeon toiled the livelong night above the gory wreck; he got the ribs adjusted right, the wishbone and the neck. He soldered on the ears and toes, and got the spine in place, and fixed a gutta-percha nose upon the mangled face. And then he washed his hands and said: "I'm glad that task is done!" The half-back raised his fractured head, and cried: "I call this fun!"

Walt Mason

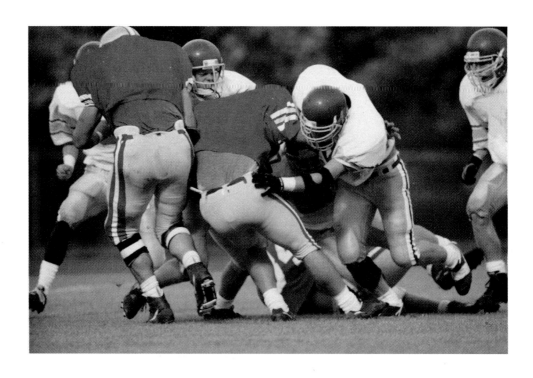

The Structure of a Poem

Just as prose is divided into paragraphs, so poetry is usually divided into stanzas. The number of lines in a stanza may vary. The poem "Some People" by Rachel Field has two stanzas, which are composed of four lines each.

Some People

Isn't it strange some people make
    You feel so tired inside,
Your thoughts begin to shrivel up
    Like leaves all brown and dried!

But when you're with some other ones,
    It's stranger still to find
Your thoughts as thick as fireflies
    All shiny in your mind!

Rachel Field

Note that the second and fourth lines of each stanza in the poem "Some People" rhyme. That means that the poem has a rhyme scheme of a-b-c-b. Note also that there are four beats, or stressed syllables (´), in the first line, three in the second, four in the third, three in the fourth, and so on. These beats give the poem a definite rhythm. Determine the number of beats in each of these two lines.

I wrote a letter to my friend today.
A shadow is floating through the moonlight.

Activity A

Read aloud the following poem. Discuss these points in relation to the poem.

1. Tell what experience the poet is sharing.
2. Describe the mood she conveys. Does it stay the same or change?
3. Give the number of lines in a stanza and the number of beats in a line.
4. Explain the rhyme scheme, if any.

Swift Things Are Beautiful

Swift things are beautiful:
Swallows and deer,
And lightning that falls
Bright-veined and clear,
Rivers and meteors,
Wind in the wheat,
The strong-withered horse,
The runner's sure feet.

And slow things are beautiful:
The closing of day,
The pause of the wave
That curves downward to spray,
The ember that crumbles,
The opening flower,
And the ox that moves on
In the quiet of power.

Elizabeth Coatsworth

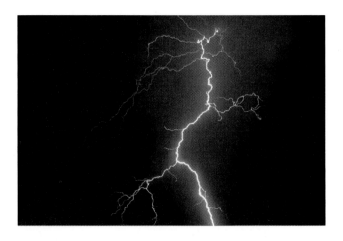

Activity B

Here is a poet's expression of how a perfect day by the sea made him feel. Practice reading it aloud until you think you have captured the feeling, and then recite it for the class. (*Spume* is the sea's spray or foam. It is pronounced spyūm.)

How instant joy, how clang
And whang the sun, how
Whoop the sea, and oh,
Sun, sing, as whiter than
Rage of snow, let sea the spume
Fling.

Let sea the spume, white, fling,
White on blue wild
With wind, let sun
Sing, while the world
Scuds, clouds boom and belly,
Creak like sails, whiter than,
Brighter than,
Spume in sun-song, oho!
The wind is bright.

Robert Penn Warren
(from "Mediterranean Beach, Day After Storm")

Writer's Corner

▶ What is your idea of the "perfect day"? What would you do? What friends would you see, if any? Write a paragraph or poem describing your day.

Learning to Listen

It is very important to develop your listening skills. Listening means more than just hearing. Hearing simply involves the ability of the ear to pick up and transmit sound waves to the brain. Listening, though, is a conscious activity. It involves your ability to concentrate on what you hear and get meaning from it.

Your teacher is going to read a selection to you. Focus your attention on what is being said and shut out all distracting noises or thoughts. Be prepared to answer these questions.

1. What is happening?
2. Where is it taking place?
3. Who is the most important person in the story?

Listen carefully!

Now that you have heard the story, answer these questions.

1. What is the story about?
   a. an operation
   b. an attack
   c. a routine drill

2. Where does the action take place?
   a. on a destroyer
   b. on a submarine
   c. in a hospital

3. Who is the most important person in the story?
   a. George Weller
   b. Dean Rector
   c. Wheeler B. Lipes

Like all other skills, the ability to listen requires practice. The following activities will improve your listening ability. Before you begin, it is important to remember two things:

- You must have a purpose for listening.

- You must shut out all distracting thoughts and sounds and concentrate on what is being said.

Activity A

In this activity you are going to name the sound or word that you hear. Your teacher will ask you either to write your answer on paper or give it orally.

Listen carefully for the sound and write/say what it is.

Make a list of ten sounds or words and be prepared to take a turn leading the activity for the class.

Activity B

In this activity you are going to demonstrate whatever you are told to do. You will be told three things. Ignore all but the one that is specified.

Example: Snap your fingers; clap your hands; pull your right ear—second.

Answer: In this instance you would clap your hands.

Listen carefully and demonstrate what you are told to do.

Make a list of ten actions and be prepared to lead the class in this activity.

Activity C

In this activity you will pick out the incorrect word in each sentence and give the correct word.

Example: The day was so cold I went for a swim.
Answer: incorrect—cold, correct—hot

Listen carefully and decide. Write/say the incorrect and correct words.

Make a list of ten sentences that contain a wrong word. Be prepared to take a turn leading the activity for the class.

Activity D

In this activity you will decide what word should come next.

Example: one-three-five-_____
Answer: seven

Listen carefully and decide. Write/say the correct word.

Make a list of ten sequences that are missing the last item. Be prepared to lead the activity for the class.

Activity E

In this activity you will decide what the classification of each selection is.

Example: Chris-Jim-Vanessa
Answer: names (or people)

Listen carefully and decide the classification. Write/say it.

Make a list of ten sets of items that have the same classification. Be prepared to lead the class in doing the activity.

Activity F

In this activity you will write/say one sentence that will summarize the selection read to you.

Example: This paragraph tells about a boy's close call with a shark.

Listen carefully. Think. Write/say the summarizing sentence.

Find two paragraphs in your social studies, science, or reading texts to read aloud. Be prepared to lead the activity in class.

Activity G

In this activity you will complete the analogies by determining the relationship that exists between the first two words.

Example: Door is to wood as window is to _____.
Answer: glass

Listen carefully. Think. Write/say the analogy.

Make a list of ten analogies. Be prepared to lead the activity in class.

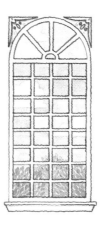

Writer's Corner

▶ Write a paragraph describing the qualities of a good listener. How could you use these qualities to help you succeed in life?

Discovering Meaning Through Context

By looking at words, phrases, or sentences that surround an unfamiliar word, you can often determine the meaning of that word.

You don't always have to consult a dictionary to discover the meaning of a new word. Many times the words that come before or after the unfamiliar word give you a clue to what it means. This is called finding the meaning from context.

Activity A

Sometimes the context gives a synonym for the unfamiliar word. Find the meaning of each italicized word by discovering the synonym or synonyms in the sentence.

1. Rose rarely makes a *conjecture* because her guesses are usually wrong.
2. The judge *exonerated* the alleged criminal and sent home a free man.
3. Dena's enthusiasm and excitement for acting made me wish that I had her *zeal*.
4. Since Jeff is a *novice* at skiing, he registered for the beginner's course.
5. Worn thin by hunger and disease, the *emaciated* children of our world need help.

Activity B

Sometimes the context gives an antonym for the unfamiliar word. Find the meaning of each italicized word by discovering the antonym in the sentence.

1. The teacher thought the young girl was *diffident,* but she displayed all the confidence in the world when she stood on the stage.
2. After the robbery, the whole house was *askew,* but with everyone's help it was soon straightened.
3. My sister never used her real name when she wrote a poem but used the *pseudonym* I.C. Ewe.
4. Melanie was an *avid* reader compared to Brian, who rarely picked up a book.
5. Skyler came to school looking *immaculate,* but by recess he had accumulated a pound of dirt.

Activity C

Find the meaning of each italicized word by searching the context. Choose the correct definition from the choices below the sentence.

1. I *concurred* with her decision. I would never disagree.
   a. disliked   **b.** agreed   **c.** appreciated

2. Eric really disliked staying in his room *isolated* from others.
   a. a part of   **b.** unaware   **c.** separated

3. Trying to resist with all her might, Natalia *succumbed* to a third slice of pizza.
   a. gave in   **b.** bought   **c.** saved

4. Hector's army was *invincible.* No enemy had overcome his forces.
   a. unconquerable   **b.** strong   **c.** well supplied

5. Even the most *callous* person had to feel compassion for the victims of the tragedy.
   a. sensitive   **b.** hardened   **c.** casual

WRITER'S WORKSHOP

Writing a Monologue

Have you ever visited a historic village? If so, you may have enjoyed interacting with interpreters, or people who act the parts of characters from an earlier era. You can interpret history, too. Choose a historical figure you find interesting. Use what you know to write a monologue that expresses that person's ideas and feelings. Perform your monologue for the class.

 Prewriting

Make a list of people from history whom you find interesting. Ask yourself questions like these to help you recall familiar historical characters.

- Which people from history did something very brave?
- Which historical characters overcame great obstacles?

- Which men or women from an earlier era were great leaders?
- Which people from an earlier era helped others?
- Which characters from history invented things that improved people's lives?
- Which men or women from history brought joy to others?
- What ordinary people's lives help us understand different historical periods?

Prepare to write your monologue, or one-person play. Choose a person from your list to be your character. To begin your prewriting notes, complete the first two columns of a chart like the one below. Skim books or an encyclopedia to fill in the gaps in your knowledge, and then complete your chart.

What I Know	What I Want to Find Out	What I Learned
Laura Ingalls Wilder wrote about her life as a pioneer child.	When did she live? Why did she write her books?	

Drafting

Set the scene for your monologue by imagining that you are sitting on a porch listening to your historical character reminisce about the past. Picture your character and imagine what he or she might sound like.

Review your notes and decide what you want to tell in your monologue. Remember that your speech will be short. You won't be able to tell everything about your character's life.

You'll need to choose one interesting incident or briefly summarize your character's accomplishments.

Remember that your monologue is a performance that represents a person speaking. Write informally, the way you talk. Use contractions and short sentences.

Be sure to introduce your character by name early in your monologue. Include any background information your listeners will need to understand your character's place in history.

Hello. I'm Laura Ingalls Wilder. I was born in 1867. When I was a little girl, I didn't think there was anything special about my life. All the other children I knew did the same things I did. My life with Ma and Pa and my sisters was just a series of ordinary events—chores, school, and play—in ordinary places. Sometimes it was fun, and sometimes it was boring. I grew up and moved away. I married and had a daughter. My husband and I built our own farm. And meanwhile everything was changing. Children rode in cars every day and couldn't imagine the slow pace of traveling in a covered wagon. Children growing up in cities didn't know the joys of growing up with nature on a solitary farm. Long after my childhood was far behind me, Ma died. I missed Ma, and I was homesick. But I was homesick for people and places that didn't exist any more. When I was 65, I began to write about my memories. Soon I had written a whole book. And what do you know! Lots of children wrote letters and asked me to write more books. I knew I wasn't a writer. "I went to little red schoolhouses all over the West and I was never graduated from anything," I told them. I was surprised, but I did what they asked. I wrote more books about my childhood. And this is what I found out: My life has been pretty interesting, after all!

EDITOR'S WORKSHOP

Revising, Proofreading, and Publishing

 Revising

Time to Take Another Look

Reread your draft carefully and revise it before making your final copy.

Ask yourself these questions to help you revise.

❑ Does my listener learn who my character is early in the monologue?

❑ Do I need to use contractions to make my monologue sound like natural speech?

❑ Do I need to substitute more vivid words for boring, overused words to make my monologue more interesting?

❑ Do I need to take out any unnecessary details that might be confusing?

❑ Do I need to add information to make clear my character's place in history?

Reread your monologue to find ways to make it clearer and more interesting.

Make your revisions stand out by using a colored pencil.

Use a Tape Recorder
Read your monologue into a tape recorder. Then listen carefully to the tape and make notes about ways to improve your monologue.

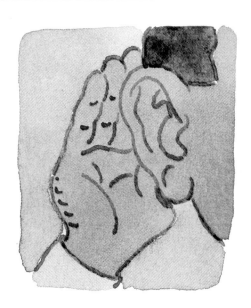

Proofreading

Time to Look at Capitalization, Punctuation, and Spelling

After you finish revising your draft, proofread it carefully to find capitalization, punctuation, spelling, and grammar errors that might distract you as you read aloud.

Use the checklist below to edit and proofread your monologue.

❑ Did I indent the first word of my paragraph?

❑ Did I capitalize proper nouns correctly?

❑ Did I use the correct mark of punctuation at the end of each sentence?

❑ Did I spell each word correctly?

Compare Final Copy and Draft

Ask a partner to follow along in your final copy as you read aloud from your revised draft. Tell your partner to stop you if he or she finds any differences between your final copy and the revisions you planned.

 Publishing

Time to Share

Publish your monologue by performing it for the class.

To publish, follow these steps:

1. Copy your revised draft in your neatest handwriting or type it on a computer.

2. Proofread your final copy one more time.

3. Check to make sure you have not left anything out.

Perform your monologue.

1. Rehearse your monologue in front of a mirror.

2. If you wish, wear a simple costume or hold props.

3. Read with expression, using gestures where they are appropriate.

4. Make eye contact with your listeners as you read your monologue aloud.

Finding Your Way Around the Library

The General Layout

A library consists of various sections, each one containing specific information that can help you with your school projects and research reports.

When you enter a library, one of the first places you encounter is the circulation desk. This is where you check out your books and where you might ask for information and help in locating needed reference materials. A large portion of the library contains circulating books. These are books that may be borrowed for a specified period of time.

The library also contains reference books, which give general, often-needed information to researchers. Because of their frequent use, these books usually are not loaned. Dictionaries, encyclopedias, and almanacs are examples of reference books.

Another section of the library contains videocassettes, films, audiocassettes, CDs, records, slides, art prints, microfiche, on-line periodical information, CD-ROMs, and miscellaneous audiovisual equipment. This section is known as the media center.

Still another section contains periodicals. The periodical section has the most recent copies of newspapers and magazines that would be of general interest to the population the library serves. Therefore, a school library subscribes to periodicals that would interest a school-age population.

About the Photograph

The library is more than just a quiet place to study. Think of it as a rich storehouse of information on almost any topic. When was the last time you visited your library?

Most libraries have a vertical file. This is a special cabinet that contains pictures, pamphlets, charts, and newspaper clippings about timely topics arranged by subject for quick and easy reference. Ask your librarian if your library has a vertical file.

Circulating Books

The books that you can check out of a library are called circulating books. Circulating books are classified into two groups: fiction and nonfiction.

Fiction Books

A fiction book relates an invented story. The people and events have been imagined by the author. Even when real people and events are used, the story is largely imaginary. Most libraries group fiction books together in one area and arrange them in alphabetical order according to the author's last name. When there are a number of books by the same author, the books are often alphabetized by the first word in the title. Words such as *The, An,* or *A* are not used for alphabetizing. If an author's last name begins with *Mc,* it is alphabetized as if it were spelled *Mac.* If an author's last name begins with *St.,* it would be considered *Saint.* In listing fiction books, write the author's last name followed by a comma and then the author's first name. The title of the book comes after the name of the author.

Activity A

Visit your school or local library. Draw a floor plan and label the following sections.

1. circulation desk
2. media center
3. reference books
4. vertical file
5. periodical section
6. fiction books
7. nonfiction books

Activity B

Arrange the following fiction books in alphabetical order as you would find them on a library shelf.

AUTHOR	TITLE
Herman Melville	*Moby Dick*
S.E. Hinton	*The Outsiders*
Marjorie K. Rawlings	*The Yearling*
Charlotte Brontë	*Jane Eyre*
S.E. Hinton	*That Was Then, This Is Now*
Robert Cormier	*I Am the Cheese*
Louisa May Alcott	*Little Women*
John Steinbeck	*The Grapes of Wrath*
Carson McCullers	*Clock Without Hands*
Samuel L. Clemens	*Adventures of Huckleberry Finn*

Nonfiction Books

Nonfiction books contain facts and true information. Because of the variety of subjects in the nonfiction area, some system of organization is necessary. Many libraries use the Dewey decimal system. This system was invented by an American librarian named Melvil Dewey, who divided all nonfiction books into ten major subject areas. He gave each major area a range of numbers so that all books on the same subject would be grouped together. Each book in an area is given a specific number called a call number. The ten major subject areas and their corresponding numbers are listed on page 262.

000–099	General Reference	Reference materials, encyclopedias, periodicals, almanacs
100–199	Philosophy	Beliefs, logic, morals, personality, psychology
200–299	Religion	Bible, mythology, theology
300–399	Social Sciences	Economics, education, government, law, customs, folklore
400–499	Languages	Foreign languages, dictionaries
500–599	Sciences	Biology, chemistry, mathematics, physics
600–699	Useful Arts and Technology	Aviation, business, cooking, engineering, farming, medicine, nursing, sewing, TV
700–799	Fine Arts	Acting, art, architecture, dancing, music, photography, sports
800–899	Literature	Novels, poetry, plays
900–999	Geography and History	Biography, travel

Activity C

Think about the subjects of the following books. Within which number range would you place each title?

1. *Learn Biology the Easy Way*
2. *World Book Encyclopedia*
3. *The Geography of Europe*
4. *Classic French Dictionary*
5. *Counseling Psychology*
6. *A Picture Salute to the Grand Canyon*
7. *Great Issues of American History*
8. *Middle English Literature*
9. *Great Dishes of the World*
10. *Current Issues in Theology*

Activity

The major subject areas are further subdivided into groups of ten. In the social sciences (the 300s), for example, the following subdivisions occur.

300	General Books on Social Sciences
310	Statistics
320	Political Science
330	Economics
340	Law
350	Government/Public Administration
360	Social Problems and Services
370	Education
380	Commerce/Communication/Transportation
390	Customs/Etiquette/Folklore

Study the following titles. Use the chart above to decide which number each title should be assigned.

1. *The Family and Its Legal Rights*
2. *Manners Made Easy*
3. *Theory of International Trade*
4. *Skills of the Economist*
5. *Introduction to Probability and Statistics*
6. *Essays in Political Theory*
7. *Law Enforcement*
8. *The Three Branches of Government*
9. *Saving American Rivers*
10. *Introduction to the Social Sciences*
11. *Treasury of American Folktales*
12. *Cultural Educational Issues*

Activity

Visit your library. During your visit, locate each section of the Dewey decimal system's major subject areas, starting with the 000–099 books. As you tour the various sections, do the following activities.

1. Biology books have the number 574. Name a title and author from this area of your library.
2. Books about domestic animals have the number 636. Locate this area and name a title and author with this call number.
3. Photography books are classified in the 770 section. Name one title and author from this section.
4. Athletic and outdoor sports have a call number starting with 796. Locate the books beginning with this number. Write down one title and author from this section.
5. Books about the United States have a call number beginning with 973. List one title and author having this call number.

The Card Catalog

Suppose you were assigned a project on vitamins. What books could you use for your report? Suppose you want to know what stories Ray Bradbury or Jules Verne have written. Where can you locate books by these authors? Suppose your friend has recommended the story *Stone Pony* or *The Hobbit* to you. How can you find these books in your library?

The easiest way to locate information is through the library's catalog. The catalog might be a computer terminal, or it might be a cabinet with small drawers containing 3" x 5" cards. In either case, the catalog entries will be arranged in alphabetical order and will fall into three groups: author, title, and subject. Fiction books have a title and author card. Nonfiction books have title, author, and one or more subject cards. For books with two or more authors, there is an individual author card for each of the authors. If you know the author's name and you need the title of the book, look under the author's last name to find the author card. The author's name appears first on this card.

Here is an example of an author card.

745.5
V394 **Van Zandt, Eleanor R**

       Crafts for fun and profit, by Eleanor Van Zandt.
       Garden City, N.Y., Doubleday, 1974 [c1973]

           144 p.   illus.   27 cm. $6.95
           Bibliography: p. 143–144.

If you know the title of the book, then locate the title card.
Words such as *A, An,* and *The* are not used in alphabetizing
the cards. The name of the book appears first on a title card.
Here is an example of a title card.

          Crafts for fun and profit

745.5
V394 **Van Zandt, Eleanor R**

       Crafts for fun and profit, by Eleanor Van Zandt.
       Garden City, N.Y., Doubleday, 1974 [c1973]

           144 p.   illus.   27 cm. $6.95
           Bibliography: p. 143–144.

If you need information on a particular subject, look for the subject card. The general subject area is the first information on this card. Here is an example of a subject card.

Handicrafts

745.5
V394 **Van Zandt, Eleanor R**

Crafts for fun and profit, by Eleanor Van Zandt. Garden City, N.Y., Doubleday, 1974 [c1973]

144 p.   illus.   27 cm. $6.95
Bibliography: p. 143–144.

Each card contains the call number so that you can locate the book on your library shelves. All three cards contain the publisher and date of publication, the number of pages in the book, and sometimes cross-references to related subjects.

Activity F

Answer the following questions about the sample library cards on pages 265 and 266.

1. What is the main subject area on the subject card?
2. What publishing company printed the book?
3. When was the latest printing of the book?
4. How many pages does the book have?
5. Where would one find the bibliography?
6. Does the book contain illustrations?
7. What is the call number?

Activity G

Visit your library and find the following information in the card catalog.

1. Locate the author card for Cynthia Voigt. List two books written by this author.
2. Locate the title card for *The Case of the Baker Street Irregular.* Who is the author? What is the call number for this book?
3. Locate the subject cards for sports. Name two titles and authors found in this subject area.

Activity H

Tell whether you would use a title, an author, a subject card, or a combination of cards to locate the information below. Give the general call number range (100–199, 600–699, etc.) for each item, using the chart on page 262, or write *fiction*.

1. plays by William Shakespeare
2. books about the people of Japan
3. *Stories from Around the World*
4. a book on the beginning of space exploration
5. Stephen Dunning's poetry
6. *The Reluctant Dragon*
7. *The World of the Greek Gods* by T. J. Rowan
8. a collection of Irish folktales
9. a book on ballet by Marcia E. Ellis
10. information on climbers who have made it to the top of Mount Everest

Writer's Corner

▶ A new student has recently moved to your school. Write a paragraph detailing how this student could locate a book in your library.

Using the Dictionary

Alphabetical Order

A dictionary is one of the most frequently used reference books in the library. This book helps you with the spelling, pronunciation, and various meanings of words. However, in order to use a dictionary in the most beneficial way, certain basic skills need to be mastered. You already have mastered alphabetical order. But how quickly can you alphabetize words that begin with the same three, four, or five letters? Activity A gives you practice in doing this kind of alphabetizing. Time yourself and see how proficient you are.

Guide Words

Guide words are the two words printed in heavy type at the top of each dictionary page. They name the first and last words on that particular page so you can locate a word faster. Because guide words may have the same spelling until the third, fourth, or fifth letters, you will have to be careful to check that far into a word to determine if it would appear before, on, or after that page.

204 full • furnace   furnish • fuzzy 205

Activity A

Divide your paper into four columns. As quickly as possible, alphabetize each column.

1.
shovel
sheath
shuttle
shilling
shaman
shrimp

2.
conjugation
conform
consumer
coniferous
conquest
contrast

3.
repel
repercussion
repetition
repent
repeat
repeople

4.
underfoot
understand
underweight
undertow
underline
underbrush

Activity B

Above each column are possible guide words for a dictionary page. If a word in the column would appear on that page, write *on* next to the word; if the word would appear before the page, write *before*; if the word would appear after the page, write *after*.

COTTAGE—COUNTERBLOW

1. counselor
2. counterfeit
3. countdown
4. cotillion
5. cottage cheese
6. countenance

MAGNITUDE—MAIZE

7. majority
8. maid of honor
9. magnificent
10. maim
11. maharaja
12. magnetic

Activity C

1. **Using your dictionary, copy the two guide words from the page where you would find each word.**

   a. blossom   **e.** polarity
   b. tenuous   **f.** clandestine
   c. frivolous   **g.** incognito
   d. stoic   **h.** ornithology

2. **Give your dictionary and answers to your partner. Have him or her check your work for accuracy.**

Reading Dictionary Entries

When you read a dictionary entry, you are able to learn a great deal about a word. The following information appears in most dictionary entries:

1   A   B   C   D   E

show er (shaù ´ər) *n.* [Old English scūr, Middle English shoure] **F 1** a brief fall of rain, sleet, or hail: **G** *The shower lasted five minutes.* **2** abundant flow resembling a rain shower: *A shower of letters followed the performance.* **3** a party at which gifts are presented to a guest of honor: *She enjoyed her bridal shower.* **4** a bath in which water is splashed on the body: *Take a shower daily.* **H Syn.** rain, abundance, bath **I** <-y, adj.>

       A. Syllabication
       B. Pronunciation
       C. Accent
       D. Part of speech
       E. Etymology
       F. Word definition
       G. Sample phrase or sentence
       H. Synonyms
       I. Other forms of word

2

show er (shaù ´ər) *v.* **1** to pour down copiously and rapidly; to bestow liberally: *She showered her dog with attention.* **2** to make wet with water or other liquid: *He showered after gym class.* **H Syn.** pour, lavish, deluge **I** <-ed, -ing>

Some dictionaries print all parts of speech under one dictionary entry. The following entry demonstrates this idea:

> **trans plant** (*v.* tran splant´; *n.* tran´splant), *v.t.*
> **1** plant again in a different place: *We grow the flowers indoors and then transplant them to the garden.* **2** remove from one place to another: *A group of farmers was transplanted to the island by the government.* **3** transfer (skin, an organ, etc.) from one person, animal, or part of the body to another: *transplant a kidney.* —*v.i.* bear moving to a different place. —*n.* **1** the transfer of skin, an organ, etc., from one person, animal, or part of the body to another: *a heart transplant.* **2** something that has been transplanted. —**trans plant´a ble,** *adj.* —**trans´plan ta´tion,** *n.* —**trans plant´er,** *n.*

Etymology is the history of the development of a word. The etymological information given in the dictionary might appear at the beginning of an entry, right after the part of speech, or at the end of an entry. The order in which the entry information is presented varies slightly with each dictionary. Also, not every dictionary entry will include every item listed on page 270.

Activity D

From the three sample dictionary entries given on pages 270 and 271, answer the following questions on a sheet of paper.

1. How many definitions does *shower* have as a noun?
2. As a verb, *transplant* is accented on which syllable?
3. From which language does *shower* originate?
4. How can *shower* be used as an adjective?
5. Copy the sentence that uses *transplant* as "remove from one place to another."
6. Write the adjective form of *transplant.*
7. List three synonyms for *shower* as a verb.

Choosing the Right Meaning

Many words in the English language have more than one meaning. Words also may have more than one part of speech. Once you locate a word in the dictionary, your next job is to find the part of speech and meaning that best corresponds to the sense of your sentence.

Suppose you read this sentence:

> To *rehabilitate* a person after an accident can be a long, tedious process.

In the following dictionary entry, *rehabilitate* has three meanings. Which of the three meanings best fits how *rehabilitate* is used?

> **re ha bil i tate** (rē´hə bil´ə tāt), *v.t.,* **-tat ed, -tat ing.**
> **1** restore to a good condition; make over in a new form: *The old neighborhood is to be rehabilitated.* **2** restore to former standing, rank, rights, privileges, reputation, etc.: *The former criminal was rehabilitated and became a respected citizen.* **3** restore to a condition of good health, or to a level of useful activity, by means of medical treatment and therapy. [< Medieval Latin *rehabilitatum* made fit again < Latin *re-* + *habilis* fit]
> —**re´ha bil´i ta´tion,** *n.*

Suppose you read this sentence in your history textbook:

> Nicholas II *reigned* over Russia for twenty-three years.

In the following dictionary entry, *reign* has two parts of speech and two or three meanings for each part of speech. Which part of speech and which definition best fit the way *reign* is used in the sentence?

> **reign** (rān), *n.* **1** period of power of a ruler: *Queen Victoria's reign lasted sixty-four years.* **2** act of ruling; royal power; rule: *The reign of a wise ruler benefits a country.* **3** existence everywhere; prevalence. —*v.i.*
> **1** be a ruler; rule: *A monarch reigns over a kingdom.*
> **2** exist everywhere; prevail: *On a still night silence reigns.*
> [< Old French *reigne* < Latin *regnum* < *regem* king]

Activity E

The following words have two parts of speech and several different meanings. For the italicized words in sentences 1–8 on page 274, give the part of speech and the number of the most accurate meaning.

ac claim (ə klām´), *v.t.* **1** welcome with shouts or other signs of approval; praise highly; applaud: *The crowd acclaimed the winning team.* **2** proclaim or announce with approval: *The newspapers acclaimed the results of the election.* —*n.* a shout or show of approval; approval; applause. [< Latin *acclamare* < *ad-* to + *clamare* cry out] —**ac claim´er,** *n.*

al ien (ā´lyən, ā´lē ən), *n.* **1** person who is not a citizen of the country in which he or she lives; a resident foreigner whose allegiance is owed to a foreign state. **2** person belonging to a different ethnic or social group; stranger; foreigner. —*adj.* **1** of or by another country; foreign: *an alien language, alien domination.* **2** having the legal status of an alien: *an alien resident.* **3** entirely different from one's own; strange: *alien customs.* **4** not in agreement; opposed, adverse, or repugnant: *Cruelty is alien to his nature.* [< Latin *alienus* < *alius* other]

com pli ment (*n.* kom´plə mənt; *v.* kom´plə ment), *n.* **1** something good said about one; something said in praise of one's work, etc. **2** a courteous act: *The town paid the old artist the compliment of a large attendance at his exhibit.* **3** **compliments,** *pl.* greetings: *In the box of flowers was a card saying "With the compliments of a friend."* —*v.t.* **1** pay a compliment to; congratulate; praise: *The principal complimented me on my good grades.* **2** give something to (a person) in order to show one's regard. [< French < Italian *complimento* < Spanish *cumplimiento* < *cumplir* fulfill < Latin *complere* fill up, complete] See **complement** for usage note.

de lib er ate (*adj.* di lib´ər it; *v.* di lib´ə rāt´), *adj., v.,*
-at ed, -at ing. —*adj.* **1** carefully thought out
beforehand; made or done on purpose; intended:
deliberate lie. See synonym study below. **2** slow and
careful in deciding what to do; thoughtful; cautious.
3 not hurried; slow: *walk with deliberate steps.* See
slow for synonym study. —*v.i., v.t.* **1** think over carefully;
consider. **2** discuss reasons for and against something;
debate. [< Latin *deliberatum* carefully weighed < *de-* +
librare weigh] —**de lib´er ate ly,** *adv.* —**de lib´er ate**
ness, *n.* —**de lib´e ra´tor,** *n.*
Syn. *adj.* **1 Deliberate, intentional** mean done after
thinking something over. **Deliberate** suggests full
thought before acting: *The lawyer made a deliberate*
attempt to confuse the jury. **Intentional** means done
on purpose, with a definite end in mind: *His mean*
remark was intentional; he wanted to make you angry.

1. Thoughtful and *deliberate* consideration preceded the
   important voting.
2. Theresa discovered interesting *alien* customs while visiting
   that country.
3. The newscaster *acclaimed* the unexpected victory.
4. We received a *compliment* for our honesty.
5. The *aliens* studied industriously to obtain their citizenship.
6. The athlete was *complimented* on her excellent victory.
7. Congress will *deliberate* the repeal of the law.
8. The crowd demonstrated their *acclaim* with applause.

Writer's Corner

▶ Here is a list of eight words for you to locate in your
dictionary. After reading the definition, write an original
sentence using the word as the part of speech indicated,
give the guide words at the top of the page, name any
other part of speech given for the word, and, finally, put
all words in alphabetical order.

1. loathe (v)	**5.** scuttle (v)
2. characteristic (adj)	**6.** clangorous (adj)
3. resilience (n)	**7.** periwig (n)
4. bounteous (adj)	**8.** galleon (n)

Using Other Reference Tools

Reference books are designed to give information on a wide variety of subjects. Probably the most frequently used and most familiar reference books in the library are dictionaries, encyclopedias, almanacs, and the *Readers' Guide to Periodical Literature.* You've already learned about the information contained in dictionaries, so it's time to see what these other resources offer.

Encyclopedias

An encyclopedia is a set of books giving information on many branches of knowledge. *Encyclopedia* is a Greek word that means a "well-rounded education." Articles in an encyclopedia are arranged in alphabetical order. Guide letters on the spine of each encyclopedia volume indicate that articles beginning with those letters will be found in that particular volume. So an article on Quebec, for instance, would be found in the Q–R volume.

Sometimes you might not be able to locate an article on a particular subject you desire. In that case, you need to think of similar topics and titles that might incorporate your idea. For example, if you want to obtain information about the summer solstice or the autumnal equinox, you might have to look under the broader topic Seasons. Most encyclopedias have index volumes that can help you determine which broad subject to look under for your information.

There are guide words at the tops of encyclopedia pages that are used in a similar manner as the guide words in a dictionary. Encyclopedias, however, have only one guide word per page. Any article that can be alphabetized between the guide words on two facing pages will be found on either of those pages. An example of guide words appears on page 276.

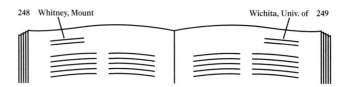

An article titled "Whittier, John Greenleaf" would be located on one of these two pages.

To keep an encyclopedia current, a yearbook is added at the end of a calendar year. The yearbook includes important events, discoveries, changes, and developments of the past year. Yearbooks are usually shelved after all the other volumes of the encyclopedia.

Activity A

Choose eight of the following topics. For each topic chosen, write the title of the encyclopedia article in which the topic is discussed, the name of the encyclopedia, and the volume and page numbers where the topic is found. Then state two major ideas contained in the topic.

A. Groundhog or Woodchuck
B. Uses of water
C. Running
D. Tourist attractions of Rome
E. Space travel
F. Shelter around the world
G. Manufacturing of glass
H. Parts of a microscope
I. Red Cross

J. Seven wonders of the ancient world
K. Florence Nightingale
L. Germany
M. Montana
N. History of the Olympic Games
O. Metabolism

Almanacs

An almanac is a reference book that contains current facts, data, and statistics of miscellaneous information. Some topics included in the almanac are:

government officials	information on states
current events	and foreign countries
astronomical data	weather predictions
entertainment	sports
important people	recent population figures
historical records	holidays

You must use the almanac's index or table of contents to locate the desired information, since the data is not alphabetically arranged. Two important almanacs are:

The World Almanac and Book of Facts
Information Please Almanac

Activity B

Using a recent almanac, answer the following questions.

1. What were two of the top ten news stories in the year covered by the almanac?
2. Which state had the highest number of deaths due to automobile accidents in the last year reported? How many people died?
3. What was the population of the United States in 1990? In 1980?
4. Name the six areas in which the Nobel Prize is given.
5. What is the origin of the name of the state of Colorado?
6. Where is the highest point in the world? How high? Where is the lowest point in the world? How low?
7. Where were the Summer Olympic Games held in 1932?
8. Who was the National Basketball Association's Rookie of the Year in 1990?

Atlases

An atlas is a reference book of maps. It gives information on population, rivers, mountains, climate, geography, and airline distances. Every atlas has an index to help you locate the appropriate continent, country, or state.

Activity C

Consult an atlas to answer the following questions.

1. In what state would you find most of Yellowstone National Park?
2. What mountain range is in New Hampshire?
3. Which ten states have borders along the Mississippi River?
4. Name the north/south interstate highway that goes through Alabama.
5. What Canadian province borders both Montana and North Dakota?
6. Name the long, narrow country on the western coast of South America and give its capital.
7. What five countries border Switzerland?
8. In what country is the Tiber River and through what capital city does it flow?
9. What countries border Lake Victoria in Africa?
10. Sumatra is one of the large islands contained in the Republic of _____ .

Biographical References

A biographical reference is a book or set of books that gives a short biography of famous people—past and present. The most commonly known biographical reference books include:

American Men and
Women of Science
Contemporary Authors
Current Biography

International Who's Who
Webster's New Biographical
Dictionary
Who's Who in America

Activity D

Look up these five people in a biographical reference book. On a separate sheet of paper, give a brief description of why they are famous.

1. History: Mahatma Gandhi
2. Science: Linus Pauling
3. Government: Geraldine Ferraro
4. Sports: Roger Staubach
5. Art: Georgia O'Keeffe

Readers' Guide to Periodical Literature

One final reference source that can help you with your research reports is the *Readers' Guide to Periodical Literature*. This is a subject and author guide to magazine articles that have been published in a variety of popular magazines about many contemporary events. It comes out twice a month, so it is a good source for obtaining current information.

Since much of the information in this guide is reported in abbreviated form, it is important to check the abbreviation key in the front of the book in order to understand each entry. Turn to page 280 and study the sample page from the *Readers' Guide*.

Activity E

Use information from the example page of the *Readers' Guide to Periodical Literature* on page 280 to answer the questions.

1. Give a cross-reference for "Temperature."
2. When did *Tennis* publish an article titled "Fit Player: Wristy Business"?
3. Who wrote this article?
4. On what page or pages is it located?
5. In what volume of *U.S. News and World Report* will you find an article titled "Were Dinosaurs Cold-Blooded?"
6. Are there any illustrations with this article?
7. What abbreviation indicates this?
8. Name an article written by M. Webb on Telluride, Colorado.
9. In what magazine was this article published?
10. If you needed information for a research paper on television viewers, to what other topic would you refer?

TELEVISION TRANSMISSION
See also
High definition television
Scrambling systems (Telecommunication)
Wide screen television
Video, video editing, character generators, and more. D. Lancaster. il *Electronics Now* v68 p63-8 Ap '97
TELEVISION VIEWERS *See* Television audiences
TELEVISION WRITING *See* Television authorship
TELEVISIONS *See* Television receivers
TELEWORKING *See* Telecommuting
TELLER
Mr. Teller builds his dream house . . . il pors *Gentlemen's Quarterly* v67 p246-9 My '97
TELLER MACHINES, AUTOMATED *See* Automated teller machines
TELLIER, PAUL
about
Back on the rails. P. Kaihla. il por *Maclean's* v110 p36-8 Ja 13 '97
TELLURIDE (COLO.)
Architecture
Telluride elevation: inventive stone-and-wood buildings form a family compound in Colorado [designed by M. Appleton for E. Glazer] M. Webb. il *Architectural Digest* v54 p216-22+ Je '97
TELOMERASE
Enzyme rare in adults may signal cancers. N. Seppa. *Science News* v151 p333 My 31 '97
The immortality enzyme [cloning of gene that controls telomerase may lead to development of drugs that inhibit diseases linked to aging; research by Thomas Cech and Robert Weinberg] J. M. Nash. il *Time* v150 p65 S 1 '97
Protein of cancer enzyme identified [p123 protein similar to reverse transcriptase; research by Joachim Lingner] J. Travis. *Science News* v151 p389 Je 21 '97
TELOMERES
Ndj1p, a meiotic telomere protein required for normal chromosome synapsis and segregation in yeast. M. N. Conrad and others. bibl f il *Science* v276 p1252-5 My 23 '97
Sticky endings; separating telomeres. R. S. Hawley. bibl f *Science* v276 p1215 My 23 '97
TELSTAR SATELLITES
Russian Proton challenges Ariane [launch of Telstar 5] C. Covault. il *Aviation Week & Space Technology* v146 p29 Je 2 '97
TEMAGAMI WILDERNESS (ONT.)
Studying protests in Temagami; native people and environmentalists both fight logging, but their goals are at odds [study by S. Teitelbaum] E. Shilts. il *Canadian Geographic* v117 p102+ My/Je '97
TEMPE (ARIZ.), STATE UNIVERSITY *See* Arizona State University
TEMPER
See also
Anger
TEMPER TANTRUMS *See* Tantrums
TEMPERAMENT
Squares live longer [study by George E. Vaillant] B. Bower. *Science News* v151 p352 Je 7 '97
TEMPERATURE
See also
Atmospheric temperature
Climate
Heat
Hot weather
Ocean temperature
TEMPERATURE, ANIMAL AND HUMAN
See also
Cattle, Effect of temperature on
Hypothermia
Insects, Effect of temperature on
Honeybee thermoregulation. B Heinrich and others. bibl f *Science* v276 p1015-17 My 16 '97
Noses show dinosaurs were cold-blooded [CAT scans of nasal bones; research by John Ruben] il *USA Today (Periodical)* v125 p12 Je '97
Were dinosaurs cold-blooded? B. Koerner. il *U.S. News & World Report* v123 p40-2+ Ag 18-25 '97
TEMPLE UNIVERSITY
Basketball
"You need to keep crying": grief-stricken coach John Chaney leads Temple through a succession of tragedies. G. Smith por *Sports Illustrated* v87 p142 Ag 25 '97
TEMPLES
California
See also
Hsi Lai Buddist Temple

Cambodia
See also
Angkor (Ancient city)
TEMPLES, BUDDHIST
See also
Hsi Lai Buddhist Temple
TEMPLES, SIKH
Canada
See also
Guru Nanak Sikh Temple (Surrey, B.C.)
TEMPLETON GROWTH FUND, LTD.
These first-class funds go round the world for profits. L. R. Cullen. il *Money* v26 p50-2 My '97
TEMPORARY EMPLOYMENT
See also
Adecco (Firm)
MacTemps, Inc.
The audition: a new trend in hiring. S. C. Libes. il *USA Today (Periodical)* v126 p54-5 Jl '97
A creative way to avoid layoffs [employee-exchange program at Rhino Foods] T. Castle. il por *Nation's Business* v85 p6 Ag '97
Organizing temps [Carolina Alliance for Fair Employment] R. Nixon. il *The Progressive* v61 p16 Jl '97
TEMPTRESS MOON [film] *See* Motion picture reviews—Single works
TEN COMMANDMENTS
Kieslowski on the mountaintop [The Decalogue; cover story] J. Cunneen. il por *Commonweal* v124 p11-14 Ag 15 '97
Ten commandments ruled off-limits [case of Charleston County Council, S.C.] *The Christian Century* v114 p720 Ag 13-20 '97
TENAX SOFTWARE ENGINEERING (FIRM)
Super speed-reading. N. Hutheesing. il por *Forbes* v160 p123 Ag 11 '97
TENG, HSIAO-P'ING *See* Deng Xiaoping, 1904-1997
TENGGER (INDONESIAN PEOPLE)
Photographs and photography
Dust, dirt, danger—and fantastic photo opportunities in East Java [Kasada religious festival] H. Hollitzer and A. Hollitzer. il pors *Popular Photography* v61 p34-6+ Mr '97
TENNECO INC.
The private sector [address, April 16, 1997] D. G. Mead. *Vital Speeches of the Day* v63 p565-8, Jl 1 '97
TENNER, EDWARD
How the chair conquered the world. il *The Wilson Quarterly* v21 p64-70 Spr '97
about
Biting back [interview] K. L. Adelman. por *Washingtonian* v32 p35-9 My '97
TENNESSEE
See also
Air pollution—Tennessee
Caves—Tennessee
Cumberland River (Ky. and Tenn.)
Dale Hollow Lake (Tenn. and Ky.)
Fishing—Tennessee
French Broad River (N.C. and Tenn.)
Great Smoky Mountains National Park (N.C. and Tenn.)
Hardin County (Tenn.)
Historic houses, sites, etc.—Tennessee
Pigeon River (N.C. and Tenn.)
Trials—Tennessee
Water pollution—Tennessee
Wildlife management—Tennessee
Politics and government
See also
Tennessee, Legislature
TENNESSEE, LEGISLATURE
The sick legislature syndrome and how to avoid it [cover story] C. Mahtesian. il map *Governing* v10 p16-20 F '97
TENNESSEE OILERS (FOOTBALL TEAM)
Home alone [small crowd sees Tennessee Oilers defeat Oakland Raiders] J. Pearlman. il *Sports Illustrated* v87 p34-6 S 8 '97
TENNIS
See also
Table tennis
Wheelchair tennis
Accidents and injuries
Fit player: wristy business [wrist injuries among tennis players] S. F. Fiske. il *Tennis* v32 p76-8 Mr '97
How to handle an injury. J. E. Loehr. il *Tennis* v32 p64 Mr '97
Anecdotes, facetiae, satire, etc.
Sometimes, the cliche's the thing [tennis cliches] C. Nicholson. il *Tennis* v33 p24 My '97

Activity **F**

Use the *Readers' Guide* to locate a recent article on ten of the following topics. Write down the author of the article (if given), the title, the name of the magazine, the volume number, the pages, and the date.

A. Motion picture industry
B. Aerobics
C. Radio broadcasting
D. Basketball, professional
E. Fashion
F. Photography
G. Marriage
H. Video games
I. Women—employment
J. High schools

K. Farmers
L. Nutrition
M. Rock music
N. Short stories
O. Medical care
P. Transportation
Q. Music festivals
R. Day care
S. Journalism
T. United Nations

Writer's Corner

▶ Number your paper from 1 to 10. Name the reference books to which you would refer if you wanted to obtain the following information. Next, choose one idea to develop into an expository paragraph. See Chapter 5 for helpful tips on writing a good expository paragraph.

1. the six major divisions/countries of Australia
2. information on bread as the "staff of life"
3. the most current information on the president's economic policy
4. background information on John Glenn
5. the names of the governors of each state and the political parties to which they belong
6. a diagram of the human skeleton
7. the cities and geographical features of Nicaragua
8. information on future solar and lunar eclipses
9. information on Dr. Thomas Dooley
10. the airplane and how it flies

WRITER'S WORKSHOP

Finding the Answer

Is there something you've always wondered about? A question you've always wanted answered? This is your chance. Think about a question that has perplexed you for a long time. Research the answer and write a report. Include your report in a class Book of Knowledge.

 Prewriting

Make a list of questions that have always puzzled you. Use the questions below to help you think about your ideas. Substitute your own word for the words in parentheses.

- What causes (a particular weather phenomenon) to happen?

- How do (machines you use every day) work?

- Where did (a special tradition) begin?

- What's the story behind (an idiom like "let the cat out of the bag")?

- Why is (a person from history) still remembered?

- How do you (do something you've always wanted to learn)?

- What was the (any historical term you've heard but don't understand)?

Begin your prewriting activities by writing your question at the top of a sheet of paper. Circle key words you will use as you look up the answer.

Then look up your key words in a variety of sources and take notes on individual note cards. Remember to write the source of each note at the bottom of the card.

Use the checklist to help you recall good places to find information.

Research Source Checklist
❑ Card Catalog
❑ Dictionary
❑ Encyclopedia
❑ Almanac
❑ Atlas
❑ Biographical References, such as *Webster's New Biographical Dictionary*
❑ *Readers' Guide to Periodical Literature*
❑ Vertical File

Drafting

After you've completed your research, organize your note cards in the order you plan to use each bit of information in your report. Rearrange the cards until you feel that they are in logical order and that one idea flows smoothly into the next.

Begin your draft by writing your question at the top of the page. Write a brief answer as your beginning sentence.

Explain your beginning sentence more fully in the body of your report. Expand your notes into sentences to complete the body.

End your report with a sentence that sums up your ideas or restates your beginning sentence.

Creating a Bibliography

A bibliography is a formal list of the sources you used in your report. Bibliographies are helpful to readers who want to learn more about your topic. All the entries in a bibliography follow a special format.

Prepare for your bibliography as you do your research by filling out a note card for each source you use. When you complete your report, arrange your note cards in alphabetical order by author's last name and copy the information in a list titled *Bibliography*. If the article's author is not listed, omit it and use the first word of the article's title to alphabetize.

Magazine Article

Schmart, Jackie. "How Airplanes Fly." *Science for Everyone*, September 30, 1998, pp. 35–39.

Encyclopedia Article

Wright, George. "Principles of Aviation." *Whole World Encyclopedia*, Vol. 1, 1996 ed., pp. 210–213.

Book

Hopkins, Herman. *Inventing the Airplane*. New York: Books Unlimited, Inc., 1997.

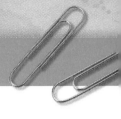

EDITOR'S WORKSHOP

Revising, Proofreading, and Publishing

 Revising

Time to Take Another Look

Reread your draft. As you read, ask yourself if the answer to your question is complete and clearly explained.

Use these questions to help you revise.

❏ Does my beginning sentence summarize the answer to my question?

❏ Do the ideas in my report flow logically from one to another?

❏ Does my explanation include all the necessary facts?

❏ Does my explanation need to be written more clearly so my readers will understand it easily?

❏ Does my report sound as if I wrote it in my own words, not the words of my sources?

❏ Do I need to add diagrams, drawings, or maps to clarify my explanation?

❏ Do I need to verify any facts?

Make your revisions using a colored pencil so they will be easy to see as you write your final copy.

Quick Quiz
Read your report aloud to a partner who does not know the answer to your question. Ask your partner to listen carefully. Then quiz your partner about key points in your explanation. If there is anything your partner doesn't understand, you may need to revise your report by adding information or by rewriting to clarify some of your ideas.

 **Proofreading**

Time to Look at Capitalization, Punctuation, and Spelling

When you are satisfied with the content of your report, proofread it to correct capitalization, punctuation, spelling, and grammar errors.

Use the checklist below to edit and proofread your report.

❑ Did I indent the first word of each paragraph?

❑ Did I use capital letters for proper nouns?

❑ Did I follow the correct format for each source in my bibliography?

❑ Did I spell all the names of people and places correctly?

One Line at a Time

To focus your attention as you proofread, place a blank sheet of paper under the top line of your report. Proofread the line you see, concentrating on capitalization, punctuation, spelling, and grammar, and then move your paper down to the next line and proofread it. Continue reading one line at a time until you've completed your proofreading.

 Publishing

Time to Share

Share your report by publishing it in the class Book of Knowledge.

To publish, follow these steps:

1. Copy your revised draft in your neatest handwriting or type it on a computer.

2. After you finish, proofread your final copy one more time.

3. Check to make sure you did not leave anything out as you copied your revised draft.

4. If you used diagrams, drawings, or maps, be sure to include them.

Make the class book.

1. Collect everyone's report.

2. Group the reports according to subject area.

3. Make a table of contents.

4. Bind the pages together.

5. Place the book in the class library so everyone can enjoy reading the answers to your intriguing questions.

PART 2
Grammar, Usage, and Mechanics

NOUNS

PRONOUNS

ADJECTIVES

VERBS

VERBALS:
PARTICIPLES,
GERUNDS, INFINITIVES

ADVERBS

PREPOSITIONS,
CONJUNCTIONS,
INTERJECTIONS

PHRASES,
CLAUSES,
SENTENCES

PUNCTUATION/
CAPITALIZATION

MODEL
DIAGRAMS

287

LESSON 1

Kinds of Nouns

A noun is a name word.

Proper Nouns and Common Nouns

There are two main classes of nouns, proper nouns and common nouns.

A proper noun names a particular person, place, or thing.

A common noun names any one of a class of persons, places, or things.

The *Pharaohs* were the *rulers* of ancient *Egypt.*
   (proper)   (common)   (proper)

Which *actor* starred in the *movie* <u>Titanic</u>?
   (common)   (common) (proper)

Collective Nouns

A collective noun denotes a group of persons, animals, or things considered as one.

An attentive *audience* heard the *symphony* play last evening.

The *assembly* was made up of sailors from the U.S. *fleet.*

Exercise 1

First make a list of all the proper nouns in the following sentences. Then make a list of the common nouns.

1. Robert Frost was an American poet.
2. Florence Nightingale was a nurse in the Crimean War.
3. Some games require great skill.
4. Athletes practice long hours when training for the Olympics.
5. Gold is a highly valued metal mined from the earth.
6. In England many people carry umbrellas.
7. Nina received a gold chain as a gift.
8. Samantha and her brother live in New York City.
9. The president of the United States lives in the White House.
10. Many citizens live in cities.

Exercise 2

Make a list of all the collective nouns in the sentences.

1. All members of the Senate are elected officials.
2. The Spanish Armada sailed in 1588.
3. A herd of pigs swarmed through the streets of the capital city.
4. Our class is going on a field trip Friday.
5. Beverly saw the bunch of sweet red grapes on the table.
6. Juan saw a flock of wild geese.
7. The Latin club meets on Friday.
8. The track team practices every morning at seven o'clock.
9. Sometimes the team divides into squads for special drills.
10. At the aquarium, we will see small schools of rare fish.

Concrete Nouns

Most nouns are concrete nouns. A concrete noun names a person, a place, or a thing that can be seen or touched.

The following are examples of concrete nouns: *lily, flame, tower, snow, crystal.*

Abstract Nouns

An abstract noun expresses a quality, a condition, or an action apart from any object or thing.

Justice should be tempered with *mercy.*
Toby's *leadership* was invaluable.

Words Used as Nouns and Verbs

A noun is a name word. A verb generally expresses action or being.

The play has three *acts.* (noun)
Henry *acts* like a gentleman. (verb)

Exercise 3

Make a list of all the concrete nouns in the sentences.

1. The hawk soars above the field.
2. The roaring train woke everyone in the house.
3. They drilled a well behind the barn.
4. The cat purred softly.
5. Subways can be crowded.
6. His brother plays the saxophone.
7. Our librarian is an excellent storyteller.
8. The stapler is on the desk.
9. The music entertained the children.
10. Enough sleep helps people stay healthy.

Exercise 4

List all the abstract nouns in the sentences.

1. Ramona showed courage in defending her brother.
2. Tenderness spilled from every line of Michael's letter.
3. Trust is important in friendship.
4. Carol's health failed.
5. The man retained his cheerfulness even after he lost his job.
6. That young woman has a flawless reputation.
7. People kept in slavery respond in different ways.
8. Some people see beauty everywhere.
9. Violence does not solve problems.
10. Jonathan won our confidence.

Exercise 5

Tell whether each word in italics is a verb or a noun.

1. *Drink* the milkshake slowly.
2. Milk is a nourishing *drink*.
3. *Stand* quietly in the corner.
4. Kate left her music on the *stand*.
5. Dr. Wilson will *sign* your note.
6. That *sign* must be removed.
7. Thunder *alarms* some animals.
8. We were awakened by the sound of the *alarms*.
9. Mary Jo took a *walk* through the garden.
10. *Walk* when the light turns green.

Practice Power

▶ Write ten original sentences using the five kinds of nouns in this lesson: proper, common, collective, concrete, and abstract. Find and label an example of each kind in your sentences.

▶ For each of the following five words, write two sentences, one using the word as a noun, the other, as a verb: *laugh, crown, rest, watch, catalog.*

LESSON 2

Person, Number, and Gender

Person

Person is that quality of a noun through which the speaker, the one spoken to, or the one spoken about is indicated.

The first person denotes the speaker.
> We, the *citizens,* petitioned the mayor.

The second person denotes the one spoken to.
> *Peter,* please bring me the tools.

The third person denotes the one spoken about.
> The *Apennine Mountains* run the entire length of Italy.

Exercise 1

Give the person of each noun printed in italics.

1. You are late, my *friend.*
2. I, the *president,* do not really care what you choose.
3. My *brother* saw a raccoon running away with our sandwiches.
4. "Stop, *sir,*" the crossing guard called.
5. We, the *students,* wondered why humans wanted to explore space.
6. *Stephano,* did you see a store nearby with a new sign?
7. Someone, perhaps *Stephano,* had removed the sign.
8. *Neighbors,* it is your duty to vote.
9. We, the *pedestrians,* demand proper crosswalks.
10. *Bicyclists,* too, need more protection.

Number

Number is the quality of a noun that denotes whether it refers to one person or thing (singular number) or more than one (plural number).

One of the three *branches* of the government is the executive *branch*. (*branches*, plural; *branch*, singular)

Methods of Forming the Plural

There are seventeen well-known rules for forming the plurals of various types of nouns. If you wish to use the plural of some noun that does not seem to be included in the rules, consult the dictionary. A choice of plural forms is given for some words; for example, the plural of *scarf* may be *scarfs* or *scarves*.

1. Most nouns form the plural by adding *s* to the singular.

   SINGULAR: miracle   PLURAL: miracles

2. For the sake of a pleasing sound (euphony), nouns ending in *s, x, z, ch,* and *sh* form the plural by adding *es* to the singular.

   SINGULAR: tax   PLURAL: taxes

3. Nouns ending in *y* preceded by a consonant form the plural by changing the *y* to *i* and adding *es.*

   SINGULAR: victory   PLURAL: victories

   Nouns ending in *y* preceded by a vowel form the plural by adding *s* to the singular.

   SINGULAR: valley   PLURAL: valleys

4. The following nouns form the plural by changing the *f* or *fe* to *ves: calf, elf, half, knife, leaf, life, loaf, self, shelf, thief, wife, wolf.*

   SINGULAR: leaf   PLURAL: leaves

5. Nouns ending in *o:*

   a. All nouns ending in *o* preceded by a vowel form the plural by adding *s* to the singular.

   > **SINGULAR:** ZOO   **PLURAL:** ZOOS

   b. Nouns ending in *o* preceded by a consonant generally form the plural by adding *es* to the singular.

   > **SINGULAR:** potato   **PLURAL:** potatoes

   c. Some nouns ending in *o* preceded by a consonant form the plural by adding *s* or *es* to the singular.

   > **SINGULAR:** buffalo   **PLURAL:** buffalos or buffaloes

6. A few nouns form the plural by a change within the singular.

   > **SINGULAR:** man   **PLURAL:** men

7. A few nouns form the plural by the addition of the Old English ending *en.*

   > **SINGULAR:** OX   **PLURAL:** oxen

8. A few nouns retain the same form in the plural as in the singular.

SINGULAR	PLURAL	SINGULAR	PLURAL
series	series	corps	corps
species	species	salmon	salmon
sheep	sheep	cod	cod
deer	deer	trout	trout
swine	swine	Portuguese	Portuguese

9. When a name is preceded by a title, either the name or the title may be pluralized.

SINGULAR	PLURAL
Miss Lee	the Misses Lee, the Miss Lees, or the Ms. Lees
Mr. Snyder	the Messrs. Snyder or the Mr. Snyders
Dr. Heard	the Doctors Heard or the Dr. Heards

   NOTE: The title *Mrs.* is an exception to this rule, as it cannot be pluralized.

   > **SINGULAR:** Mrs. Fisher   **PLURAL:** the Mrs. Fishers

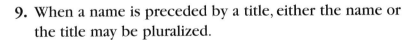

10. Some nouns taken from foreign languages retain their foreign plurals.

SINGULAR	PLURAL	SINGULAR	PLURAL
radius	radii	crisis	crises
alumna	alumnae	oasis	oases
alumnus	alumni	larva	larvae
basis	bases	thesis	theses
analysis	analyses	stratum	strata
synopsis	synopses	vertebra	vertebrae
datum	data	bacterium	bacteria

11. Some nouns taken from foreign languages have both a foreign and an English plural. The English form is preferred.

SINGULAR	ENGLISH PLURAL	FOREIGN PLURAL
formula	formulas	formulae
memorandum	memorandums	memoranda
curriculum	curriculums	curricula
appendix	appendixes	appendices
index	indexes	indices
tableau	tableaus	tableaux

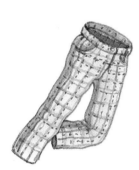

12. Some nouns are used only in the plural.

trousers	pliers	clothes
goods	scissors	tweezers

13. Some nouns are plural in form, but singular in meaning and use.

civics	physics	aeronautics
mathematics	measles	news

14. Compound nouns usually form the plural by adding *s* to the most important word or words.

SINGULAR	PLURAL
governor general	governors general
brother-in-law	brothers-in-law
drive-in	drive-ins

15. Compound nouns ending in *ful* form the plural by adding *s* to the last syllable.

SINGULAR: handful   PLURAL: handfuls

NOTE: Another way to form the plural is to use two words, as in *two hands full, three glasses full.*

16. Letters form the plural by adding *s* or *'s*. Lowercase letters and capital letters that would be confusing if *s* alone were added form the plural by adding *'s*.

SINGULAR	PLURAL
TV	TVs
i	*i*'s
A	*A*'s

17. The plural of numbers is formed by adding *s* with no apostrophe.

SINGULAR	PLURAL
1980	1980s
87	87s

Exercise 2

Write the plural of each noun.

1. lady	**8.** John	**15.** 8	**22.** infant
2. suffix	**9.** chimney	**16.** sketch	**23.** politics
3. trespass	**10.** kimono	**17.** salmon	**24.** Mrs. Teng
4. sash	**11.** mumps	**18.** dishful	**25.** child
5. dispatch	**12.** shelf	**19.** floor	**26.** radio
6. heresy	**13.** alumnus	**20.** pulley	**27.** Chinese
7. jockey	**14.** appendix	**21.** tiff	**28.** parenthesis

Gender

Gender is that quality of a noun by which sex is distinguished. There are three genders: masculine, feminine, and neuter.

The masculine gender denotes the male sex.
man, boy, uncle, brother

The feminine gender denotes the female sex.
woman, girl, grandmother, niece

The neuter gender denotes objects that have no sex.
house, football, telephone, tree

Some nouns may be taken as either masculine or feminine.
teacher, senator, writer, supervisor

NOTE: Several nouns that traditionally denoted the masculine gender in certain occupations are no longer used. One form is now used for both genders.

TRADITIONAL	CURRENT
fireman	firefighter
repairman	repairer
mailman	mail carrier
policeman	police officer

The gender of a pronoun should agree with that of its antecedent. When the antecedent of a singular possessive pronoun may be either masculine or feminine, the form *his or her* is now considered acceptable.

Exercise 3

Give the gender of each noun.

1. invalid
2. relative
3. juror
4. costume
5. ewe
6. alumnus
7. scout
8. ladder
9. prophet
10. ship
11. lamp
12. Marie
13. lad
14. book
15. goddess
16. kitchen
17. friend
18. bridesmaid
19. library
20. cousin

Practice Power

▶ **Write ten sentences. Each one should contain the kind of noun or nouns specified.**

1. a third person, plural, neuter noun
2. two third person, singular, masculine nouns
3. a second person, plural, feminine noun
4. a first person, plural, masculine noun
5. a third person, singular, feminine noun
6. a third person, plural, feminine noun
7. a second person, singular, masculine noun
8. a second person, singular, feminine noun
9. two third person, plural, masculine or feminine nouns
10. a first person, singular, masculine or feminine noun

LESSON 3

Nominative Case

**Case is that quality of a noun that shows its relation to some other word or words in the sentence.
There are three cases: nominative, possessive, and objective.**

Before a noun can be classified according to case, its use, or syntax, must be determined. The uses of the nominative case that have been studied in previous years are as follows:

Subject. A noun used as the subject of a finite verb is in the nominative case.

Cairo is the capital of Egypt.
Through the Panama Canal sail *ships* of many nations.
An important *crop* of France is the grape.

Subjective Complement. A noun used as a subjective complement is in the nominative case.

A noun that follows a copulative, or linking verb, is in the nominative case if it refers to the same person or thing as its subject.

Winston Churchill became *prime minister* of England during World War II.
The child was named *John.*
Sherlock Holmes is a famous *detective* in English fiction.

Apposition. **A noun in apposition is in the same case as the noun it explains.**

A noun that explains a subject or a subjective complement is in the nominative case.

> Rome, the *capital* of Italy, is called the "Eternal City."

> Margaret Chase, the *mayor,* was reelected to a third term.

> Wanda's favorite food is pizza, a tomato-cheese *pie.*

Address. **A noun used in direct address is in the nominative case.**

> *Tony,* will you go with me to the game?
> *Senators,* let us vote on the resolution.
> Obey the traffic signals, *drivers.*

Exclamation. **A noun used independently to express a strong emotion is in the nominative case.**

> *Action!* The play needs action.
> *Theresa!* She has won the award.
> The poor *man!* We feel so sorry for him.

Nominative Absolute. **A noun before a participle in an independent phrase is in the nominative case absolute.**

A participle, a word that does the twofold work of a verb and an adjective, is sometimes used with a noun or a pronoun in an independent adverbial phrase. The phrase may express the time, the condition, the cause, or the circumstances of the main verb's action. The noun or the pronoun used in this absolute construction is in the nominative case.

> The *salute* having been given, the soldier marched on.
> The *work* having been completed, we went to the zoo.
> *Winter* coming on, the geese flew south.

Exercise 1

Select the nouns in the nominative case and give the use, or syntax, of each.

1. Water power is sometimes called white coal.
2. Lincoln having been assassinated, Johnson succeeded him.
3. Brussels is the capital of Belgium.
4. Steve, the new librarian, works evenings and Saturdays.
5. The river! It is flooding the town.
6. Jerome remained captain of the team.
7. My aunt, Barbara, works as a nurse.
8. The play being delayed slightly, the director addressed the audience.
9. Ricardo won ten dollars in the raffle. Lucky boy!
10. Ms. Tobias, may we race to the corner?

Exercise 2

Complete each sentence with a noun in the nominative case, and tell how the noun is used in the sentence.

1. _____ has been a good friend of mine for many years.
2. Into the fort stumbled the exhausted _____ .
3. _____ encouraged the team.
4. Our lifeguard, _____ , is very concerned about water safety.
5. Brian is a talented _____ .
6. It was _____ who set off the fire alarm by mistake.
7. Keep your hands inside the windows, _____ .
8. My cousin, _____ , visited China.
9. Her computer _____ would not work properly.
10. _____ used a power saw to remove the dead branches.

Practice Power

▶ Compose a total of six sentences illustrating each type of noun in the nominative case.

Possessive Case

> **A noun that expresses possession, ownership, or connection is in the possessive case.**

The sign of the possessive case is the apostrophe and *s*.

    Beethoven's "Eroica" is a popular symphony.

Methods of Forming the Possessive Case of Nouns

- To form the singular possessive, add *'s* to the singular form of the noun.

    Joseph, Joseph's   captain, captain's

The apostrophe and *s* is *not* used with nouns relating to inanimate things.

    steeple of the church (not church's steeple)

The apostrophe and *s* is used with the names of certain inanimate objects that have become idiomatic from common usage.

    sun's rays   earth's surface

- To form the plural possessive of nouns ending in *s*, add the apostrophe only.

    boys, boys'   babies, babies'

If the plural form of the noun does not end in *s*, add *'s*.

    children, children's   oxen, oxen's

- Proper names ending in *s* usually form the possessive case by adding *'s*.

    Mr. Burns, Mr. Burns's   Dickens, Dickens's

● In compound nouns the *'s* is added to the end of the word.

NOUN	SINGULAR POSSESSIVE	PLURAL POSSESSIVE
father-in-law	father-in-law's	fathers-in-law's

Separate and Joint Possession or Ownership

If two or more nouns are used together to indicate separate ownership—that is, to show that each person possesses something independently of the other—the *'s* is used after each noun.

> *Irving's and Scott's* literary works are well worth reading.
>
> *Webster's and Hayne's* speeches have been studied by many orators.

If two or more nouns are used together to indicate joint ownership—that is, to show that one thing is possessed by the group jointly—the *'s* is used after the last noun only.

> *The secretary and the treasurer's* office is on the third floor.
>
> *Garcia and King's* store has been remodeled.

Exercise 1

Write the singular possessive form and the plural possessive form of each noun.

1. brother-in-law	**9.** student	**17.** professor	**25.** mouse
2. woman	**10.** man	**18.** gentleman	**26.** horse
3. mayor-elect	**11.** lady	**19.** sister	**27.** lion
4. father	**12.** child	**20.** Thomas	**28.** deer
5. attorney general	**13.** Jane	**21.** king	**29.** goose
6. stepsister	**14.** boy	**22.** princess	**30.** bird
7. Mr. Swenson	**15.** scout	**23.** pupil	**31.** animal
8. maid of honor	**16.** girl	**24.** sheep	**32.** ox

Exercise 2

Write the possessive form of the word in parentheses that will correctly complete each sentence. In some sentences, you will use the singular number and in other sentences, the plural.

1. Beth put some food in the (dog) dish.
2. The (child) classmates study with her.
3. You may enjoy reading (Shakespeare) *Romeo and Juliet.*
4. The (deer) horns are shed and renewed annually.
5. The (boy) team finished third.
6. In February we celebrate (Washington) birthday.
7. Jean works in her (sister) store.
8. The general tried to discover the (enemy) strategy.

Exercise 3

Number a sheet of paper from 1 to 8 and write the correct possessive forms of the nouns.

1. Janice and Maria compositions describe the animal life in caves.
2. Campbell and Luciano market sells imported cheese.
3. Patty and Richard father's blood pressure is too high.
4. We received the doctor and the nurse reports.
5. Keats and Tennyson poems are among my favorites.
6. Da Vinci and Picasso paintings hang in important museums.
7. Laura and Katie mother seems very young.
8. Did you see Pedro and Dianne new town houses?

Practice Power

▶ Compose six sentences using nouns from Exercise 1 on page 303. Be sure to use both singular and plural possessives. Then write four sentences using separate and joint ownership correctly.

LESSON 5

Objective Case

The uses of the objective case are as follows:

Direct Object. **A noun used as the direct object of a verb is in the objective case.**

Tadeusz Kosciuszko sought a *commission* in the
   Continental Army.
Dylan Thomas wrote beautiful *poems*.
The villagers planned a *celebration*.

Indirect Object. **A noun used as the indirect object of a verb is in the objective case.**

Terri sent *Benjamin* the directions.
Buy your *brother* some candy.
They gave the *bride* beautiful flowers.

NOTE: The preposition *to* or *for* can usually be inserted before the indirect object without changing the meaning of the sentence.

Object of a Preposition. **A noun used as the object of a preposition is in the objective case.**

Water evaporates in *sunlight*.
The lawyer performed his duties with great *courage*.
The farmers objected to a protective *tariff*.

Apposition. A noun in apposition is in the same case as the noun it explains. A noun that explains a direct object, an indirect object, or an object of a preposition is in the objective case.

Kent Jackson won the first prize, an *automobile*.

We gave Rose, our *captain*, the trophy.

John gave the message to the coach, his *uncle*.

Adverbial Objective. A noun used as an adverbial objective is in the objective case.

An adverbial objective is a noun used as an adverb. Adverbial objectives may tell *when, where, how long,* or *how far.*

The athlete exercises every *day.*
Linda can jump five *feet.*
This *morning* the ground was covered with frost.

Objective Complement. A noun used as an objective complement is in the objective case.

Some common verbs that may take objective complements are *appoint, call, choose, elect, make,* and *name.*

The team chose Saul *captain.*
The owner appointed Julia *treasurer.*
The parents named the baby *Paul.*

NOTE: In the last sentence, the noun *Paul* completes the meaning of the verb *named* and refers to the direct object, *baby.*

Cognate Object. **A noun used as a cognate object is in the objective case.**

A cognate object is a noun that repeats the meaning of and closely resembles the verb of which it is the object.

> He dreamed a *dream* of future greatness.
> The boxer fought a good *fight.*
> Anne sang a *song* of joy.

Exercise 1

Each italicized noun is in the objective case. Give the use, or syntax, of each.

1. Many people take the *train* to *work.*

2. Bette sang a very unusual *song.*

3. The team selected *Albert* team *captain.*

4. Going into the New York *subway* is an artistic experience.

5. The author told the *class* a *story.*

6. We must wait two *hours.*

7. Ross Brown, our group leader, gave *Scott* a new *program.*

8. The commissioner gave *Reggie Jackson* a batting *award.*

9. The actors danced the *dance* of the sea *creatures.*

10. Hyunah waited twenty *minutes* at the *station.*

11. Sarah consulted *Jennie,* her *doctor.*

12. Oscar named his *dog Dynamite.*

13. He gave *George,* my *brother,* his old *watch.*

14. The class called *Eddie "Whiz Kid."*

15. The president can veto *acts* of *Congress.*

Exercise 2

Choose a noun in the objective case to complete each sentence, and then tell how the noun is used in the sentence. Be sure to use each of the seven possible uses of the objective case.

1. Jerry gets up every morning three _____ before he has to leave for school.

2. Florence, the _____ , read the minutes of the last meeting.

3. José spoke the _____ of a seasoned politician.

4. Judy painted a small _____ .

5. The students chose _____ captain.

6. Ben, my _____ , enjoyed the book.

7. Lisa gave _____ some flowers.

8. They elected Robert _____ .

9. The coach taught _____ a new _____ .

10. Orbiting satellites travel around _____ .

Putting It All Together

Play a game of twenty questions in which each question must be a grammar question. Think of a noun known to all your classmates. (You may want to limit the pool of nouns by restricting the game to nouns in the classroom.)

Allow your classmates to ask yes/no questions about the noun, such as *Is it singular?* or *Can it be used as a verb?* Encourage your classmates to guess the word before they have asked twenty questions.

Chapter Challenge

Read this selection carefully and answer the questions that follow.

¹In the Louvre in Paris hangs a painting by the celebrated American artist James McNeill Whistler. ²*An Arrangement in Gray and Black* is the imposing title of this portrait, but to the millions who know and love it, the likeness is known as "Whistler's Mother." ³The picture, when it first appeared, was given very little attention, and it brought the artist scant recognition. ⁴Many years later, however, it was the opinion of more than one committee of critics that this picture alone would have made Whistler a leader among painters. ⁵For connoisseurs of art, the beauty of this painting lies in the harmony achieved by perfect spacing and the many tones of gray produced by skillful blending. ⁶Its appeal to the heart of the ordinary person rests in the noble traits of motherhood that Whistler has captured and enshrined forever on canvas.

1. Name the proper nouns in the first sentence.

2. What is the subject in the first sentence? What is its case?

3. Find an appositive in the first sentence. What is its case?

4. What is the case of the noun *Whistler's* in the second sentence?

5. In what case is the noun *title* in the second sentence? Why?

6. Find the direct and the indirect objects in the third sentence.

7. Find a masculine noun and a neuter noun in the third sentence.

8. Find an adverbial objective in the fourth sentence.

9. Select a collective noun in the fourth sentence.

10. Name an objective complement in the fourth sentence.

11. Write the singular form of *connoisseurs* in the fifth sentence.

12. Which nouns in the fifth sentence are objects of prepositions?

13. Name the abstract and concrete nouns in the sixth sentence.

14. In what person is this selection written?

LESSON 1

Personal Pronouns: Review, Nominative Case

A pronoun is a word used in place of a noun.

> When Claude felt the sting of the jellyfish, he was swimming.

The word to which a pronoun refers is called its antecedent. In this sentence, the antecedent of the pronoun *he* is *Claude.*

Personal Pronouns: A Review

A personal pronoun is a pronoun that denotes by its form the speaker, the person spoken to, or the person or the thing spoken of.

> *You* and *I* believe the alibi.
> *It* belongs to *him* or *her.*

The pronouns of the first person (the speaker) are *I, mine, me, we, ours,* and *us.* The pronouns of the second person (the person spoken to) are *you* and *yours.* The pronouns of the third person (the person, the place, or the thing spoken of) are *he, she, it, his, hers, its, him, her, they, theirs,* and *them.*

Pronouns change form to denote case and number. The nominative case is used when the pronoun is the subject of a sentence or a subjective complement. The possessive case is used to denote possession. The objective case is used for a direct object, an indirect object, or the object of a preposition.

About the Photograph

Just about any time you talk or write about yourself, your friends, or your things, you'll use personal pronouns.

The personal pronouns are declined in the following way. In the third person singular, there are distinct forms for masculine, feminine, and neuter genders.

Declension of the Personal Pronouns

First Person

CASE	SINGULAR	PLURAL
NOMINATIVE	I	we
POSSESSIVE	my, mine	our, ours
OBJECTIVE	me	us

Second Person

CASE	SINGULAR	PLURAL
NOMINATIVE	you	you
POSSESSIVE	your, yours	your, yours
OBJECTIVE	you	you

Third Person

CASE	SINGULAR	PLURAL
NOMINATIVE	he, she, it	they
POSSESSIVE	his, her, hers, its	their, theirs
OBJECTIVE	him, her, it	them

Exercise 1

Name the personal pronouns and give the person, number, gender, and case of each.

1. She called him as he entered the room.
2. Bring it with you to the beach.
3. I told her that she was mistaken.
4. He reminded you that it would happen.
5. They come when they are called.

Practice Power

▶ Write a conversation that could be taking place between the two boys pictured on page 310. Work first, second, and third person personal pronouns into the conversation.

Correct Use of the Nominative Case

Subject of a Verb

A pronoun used as the subject of a verb is in the nominative case.

Grace and (I, me) swim together.

The correct form is: Grace and *I* swim together.

Subjective Complement

A pronoun that follows a linking verb is used as a subjective complement and is in the nominative case.

It is (he, him).

The correct form is: It is *he*. *He* follows the linking verb *is* and refers to the word *it*.

Exercise 1

Select the correct form of the personal pronoun and give the reason for your choice.

1. (He, Him) and (her, she) drove here together.
2. Ira and (me, I) will pack the lunch.
3. The group leader and (he, him) wrote the script for the variety show.
4. (Her, She) and Adrienne wrote last year's variety show.
5. (They, Them) and (us, we) live on the same street.

Exercise 2

Select the correct form of the personal pronoun and give the reason for your choice.

1. The winner of the prize was (she, her).
2. This is (him, he).
3. Did you know it was (me, I) who called?
4. The youngest couple could be (they, them).
5. The people called were (we, us).

Exercise 3

Of the two words in parentheses in each sentence, select the word that correctly completes the sentence. Then tell whether the word selected is used as a subject or as a subjective complement.

1. Margie and (I, me) saw the snake shed its skin.
2. Ernesto and (they, them) are sky divers.
3. It was (he, him) who found the binoculars.
4. It was (us, we) whom they met at the studio.
5. Doug, Joan, and (me, I) toured NASA in Houston.

Practice Power

▶ **Choose a personal pronoun to complete each sentence. Tell whether the pronoun is used as a subject or a subjective complement.**

1. _____ am eager to see the World Series in person.
2. Is that you? Yes, it is _____ .
3. Corita and _____ met at the library.
4. _____ intends to study Aztec civilization.
5. Joe and _____ will compete in the race.
6. It was _____ who wrote the poem.
7. Was it _____ who answered the door?
8. Will _____ be ready on time?
9. The best hula dancer is _____ .
10. Vince and _____ were playing hockey.

Personal Pronouns: Objective Case

LESSON 3

Direct Object

A pronoun used as the direct object of a verb is in the objective case.

I met David and (he, him) at the station.

The correct form is: I met David and *him* at the station.

Indirect Object

A pronoun used as the indirect object of a verb is in the objective case.

Give Coretta and (I, me) the stamps.

The correct form is: Give Coretta and *me* the stamps.

NOTE: The preposition *to* or *for* can usually be inserted before the indirect object without changing the meaning of the sentence.

Give *to* Coretta and me the stamps.

Exercise 1

Copy each sentence, using the correct form of the pronoun. Give the reason for your choice.

1. Carmela took Monica and (I, me) for a ride in her new car.
2. The guard helped (he, him) look for the lost keys.
3. The teacher rewarded Tom and (her, she) for their consistent effort.
4. Mr. Winslow directed Kathleen and (I, me) in the school play.
5. The judge warned Kristine and (her, she) about riding their bicycles on city streets.
6. They thanked the police officer and (him, he) for helping.
7. The firefighter congratulated (we, us) on our fire prevention activities.
8. Ten people helped Nicholas and (me, I) find the dog.
9. Charles instructed (they, them) in the art of wood carving.
10. Grandfather took Stella and (us, we) out for dinner.

Exercise 2

Copy each sentence, using the correct form of the pronoun. Mentally insert the preposition before the indirect object.

1. Bryan wrote Kevin and (me, I) a long letter.
2. He told (we, us) facts about life in Thailand.
3. Marita brought Carl and (her, she) some fresh pineapple.
4. A guide showed Rosemary and (them, they) the exhibit.
5. My brother lent Bill and (he, him) the car.
6. The bullfighter gave (me, I) his red cape.
7. Todd threw (her, she) the ball.
8. The vendor offered (he, him) and (I, me) some peanuts.
9. We owe Mrs. Fernandez and (him, he) ten dollars.
10. Ellen lends (we, us) her computer on Tuesdays.

316

Object of a Preposition

A pronoun used as the object of a preposition is in the objective case.

I have not heard from Jean or (she, her).

The correct form is: I have not heard from Jean or *her.*

Exercise **3**

Copy each sentence, using the correct form of the pronoun. Give the reason for your choice.

1. This puzzle is too difficult for (I, me).
2. We went sledding with him and (her, she).
3. Lloyd gave the keys to (him, he).
4. Maria voted for (they, them).
5. John showed his mother a painting by (her, she).
6. Eric, sit between (he, him) and (I, me).
7. Alfred walked beside (us, we) toward the fire.
8. We went to the computer store with (her, she).
9. The man did not want to talk with (we, us).
10. Lenny may stand between Mark and (she, her).

Exercise **4**

Write the correct form of the personal pronoun in the objective case.

1. The mouse was behind Helen and (2nd person, sing.).
2. Is this mail for (3rd person, sing., masc.) or (1st person, sing.)?
3. Regina is singing with (2nd person, sing.).
4. The artist painted a picture of (3rd person, sing., fem.).
5. Al brought (3rd person, sing., masc.) a puppy.
6. The salesperson helped (3rd person, plural).
7. Andrew told (1st person, sing.) an exciting story.
8. The crowd separated Greg from (1st person, plural).
9. Shelly invited Dave and (3rd person, sing., fem.).
10. Take (3rd person, plural) with you.

Exercise 5

Copy these sentences, filling in each blank with the proper form of a personal pronoun. Tell how the pronoun is used: direct object, indirect object, or object of a preposition.

1. We went with _____ to see the game.
2. The English prizes were won by Mary and _____ .
3. Wanda gave _____ her fishing pole.
4. His father promised _____ a trip to the lake.
5. They visited _____ over the weekend.
6. He saw _____ at the theater.
7. Jim offered _____ some popcorn.
8. The noise startled _____ .
9. Will you take _____ to the basketball game?
10. Did you call _____ before school?
11. The storm carried _____ out to sea.
12. They want to take us with _____ .
13. The magician divided the cards between _____ and _____ .
14. Tyrone showed _____ the secret formula.
15. Theresa gave Chris and _____ this intricate teapot.

Practice Power

▶ Write three sentences for each of the following personal pronouns. Use the pronoun first as a direct object of a verb, second as an indirect object of a verb, and third as the object of a preposition.

1. me   2. you   3. him   4. them

LESSON 4

The Case Used After *Than, As,* and *Before*

After the conjunctions *than, as,* and *before,* there is an omission of words. The pronoun following these conjunctions must be in the same case as the word with which it is compared.

Marcia reads better than (she, her).

The correct form is: Marcia reads better than *she* (reads).

We saw him before (she, her).

The correct form is: We saw him before (we saw) *her.*
or
We saw him before *she* (saw him).

Exercise 1

Select the correct form of the pronoun. Then give the words that are omitted but understood.

1. Evelyn walks more quickly than (she, her).
2. Fred sings better than (I, me).
3. Anne swims as fast as (he, him).
4. That band is as good as (we, us).
5. Bernie is older than (I, me).
6. I hope to be as proficient as (she, her).
7. Francine finished her homework before (I, me).
8. She prepares her work better than (I, me).
9. Dale is not so witty as (he, him).
10. Antonio climbs as well as (she, her).
11. He drove no faster than (we, us).
12. Sarita skied down a steeper trail than (he, him).
13. I wish I had arrived at the movies before (he, him).
14. Ed recognized the star sooner than (she, her).
15. Our sprinters are faster than (they, them).

EXERCISE 2 REVIEW

Choose the correct pronoun in each of the following sentences. Give the reason for your choice.

1. We thought that it was (she, her).
2. May (we, us) three leave early?
3. The cat followed (he, him) and (I, me).
4. Did the nurse ask Ted and (she, her) a question?
5. That tall boy is (he, him).
6. Ana gave (she, her) a CD as a present.
7. (He, Him) and (I, me) were invited to the costume party.
8. It was (I, me) who called.
9. The woman saw (they, them) from her kitchen window.
10. Is it (she, her) you want?

Exercise 3 REVIEW

Substitute a pronoun for the italicized words in each sentence. Tell the case of the pronoun and how it is used in the sentence.

1. The best musician in the class is *Francine.*
2. The tour continued without *the three children.*
3. *The group* sat in a circle around the campfire.
4. My mother told Carmen and *Jeff* a bedtime story.
5. The firefighters saw *the cat* hanging from the roof.
6. I knew it was *Gabrielle* as soon as I turned the corner.
7. *Jason and I* signed up for the field trip.
8. *The field trip* was a tour through the Air Force Academy.
9. Jason and I were grateful to *the tour guides* for their time.
10. I had seen *the academy* from the outside but never the inside.

Practice Power

▶ Write a note to someone in your family explaining what you and a friend are planning for the day. Underline the pronouns you use. Show the correct case of a pronoun that follows *than, as,* or *before* in one sentence of the note.

LESSON 5

Possessive and Compound Personal Pronouns

Possessive Pronouns

A possessive pronoun is a pronoun used to denote possession or ownership by the speaker, the person spoken to, or the person, place, or thing spoken of.

The possessive pronouns *mine, ours, yours, his, hers, its,* and *theirs* are sometimes called independent possessives because they may be used alone to take the place of nouns. *My, our, your, his, her, its,* and *their* modify nouns. The possessives that modify nouns are called possessive adjectives.

POSSESSIVE PRONOUNS	POSSESSIVE ADJECTIVES
Mine is blue.	*My* uniform is blue.
This is *yours.*	This is *your* pen.
Mr. Cook sold *his.*	Mr. Cook sold *his* car.
They have examined *theirs.*	They have examined *their* posters.

When a possessive pronoun or a possessive noun is used independently, its case is determined by its use in the sentence.

Leo's is here.	*His* is here.	(subject)
She saw *Helen's.*	She saw *yours.*	(direct object)
This is *Kelly's.*	This is *mine.*	(subjective complement)

Compound Personal Pronouns

Compound personal pronouns are pronouns made by adding *-self* or *-selves* to certain forms of the personal pronouns.

Forms of the Compound Personal Pronouns

	SINGULAR	PLURAL
FIRST PERSON	myself	ourselves
SECOND PERSON	yourself	yourselves
THIRD PERSON	himself, herself, itself	themselves

A compound personal pronoun may be used to give emphasis to a noun, or as an object referring to the subject.

An intensive pronoun is used to emphasize a preceding noun or pronoun.

The land *itself* was very fertile.

A reflexive pronoun is used as an object referring to and denoting the same person or thing as the subject.

We must prepare *ourselves* for the examination.

Agreement of Compound Personal Pronouns

A compound personal pronoun must agree with its antecedent in person, number, and gender.

Compound personal pronouns have two distinct uses, as intensive and as reflexive pronouns.

King Ethelbert *himself* received the explorers. (intensive)
We seldom see *ourselves* as others see us. (reflexive)

The antecedent of *himself* is *King Ethelbert. King Ethelbert* is third person, singular, masculine; so, too, is *himself.* The antecedent of *ourselves* is *we. We* is first person, plural, masculine or feminine; so, too, is *ourselves.*

Exercise 1

Complete each sentence with an appropriate possessive pronoun.

1. That blue sweater is not _____ .
2. Take _____ but leave _____ .
3. _____ is not as warm as _____ .
4. This book is _____ but that is _____ .
5. Mrs. Rodriguez sold _____ .
6. _____ ran away.
7. The umbrella with purple stripes is _____ .
8. Someone stole _____ .
9. _____ was left on their beach.
10. _____ were in a box on my desk.

Exercise 2

List the compound personal pronouns and tell whether they are intensive or reflexive.

1. I myself could not explain my behavior.
2. Rome took its name from Romulus himself.
3. Napoleon crowned himself emperor.
4. The people support themselves by working.
5. Pat yourself on the back, Jillian.
6. The children saw a reflection of themselves in the store's spotless windows.
7. The baby frightened himself.
8. A customer herself complained to the manager.
9. The bank guard himself was surprised by the president's kindness.
10. The police officers put themselves between the accident and the onlookers.

Exercise **3**

Select the correct compound personal pronoun for each of the following sentences. Then tell whether the selected pronoun is intensive or reflexive, and give its antecedent.

1. Roger blamed _____ for the misunderstanding.
2. Margie cut _____ on the pieces of the broken ketchup bottle.
3. Every woman must answer for _____ .
4. The firefighters _____ could not find the source of the smoke.
5. Allen _____ had been hiking in the forest that afternoon.
6. You _____ heard the verdict.
7. The fugitives hid _____ from the sheriff.
8. We _____ were responsible for the broken window.
9. Kim's turtle hid _____ behind a pile of stuffed animals.
10. The voters disagreed among _____ .
11. She _____ did the job.
12. The couple _____ had not seen the videotape of the wedding.
13. Louis XIV called _____ the Sun King.
14. Ben _____ changed the tire.
15. Ellen _____ composed the song for the school play.

Practice Power

▶ You took your brother's (sister's) books to school. He (she) took yours. In five or six sentences, explain how this happened. Use possessive and compound personal pronouns.

LESSON 6

Interrogative Pronouns

An interrogative pronoun is a pronoun used in asking a question.

The interrogative pronouns are *who, whose, whom, which,* and *what.* They are used in both direct and indirect questions.

DIRECT QUESTIONS:	By *whom* was it written?
	Who is Tom?
INDIRECT QUESTIONS:	She asked *whom* we wanted.
	He wondered *whose* book it was.

Use *who, whose,* and *whom* in speaking of persons. Use *which* in speaking of places and things or to denote one of a definite class. Use *what* in speaking of places and things and in seeking information.

Declension of *Who*

	SINGULAR	PLURAL
NOMINATIVE	who	who
POSSESSIVE	whose	whose
OBJECTIVE	whom	whom

Correct Use of Interrogative Pronouns *Who* and *Whom*

The interrogative pronoun *who* is used when the sentence requires a pronoun in the nominative case.

The interrogative pronoun *whom* is used when the sentence requires a pronoun in the objective case.

To help determine the correct use of *who* and *whom,* answer the question by filling in a name.

Subject—Nominative Case
Who picked the winning number?
Jack picked the winning number.

Object of a Preposition—Objective Case
With *whom* does Anita plan to work?
Anita plans to work with *Sally.*

Direct Object—Objective Case
Whom did you invite to your party?
I invited *the entire class* to my party.

Exercise 1

List the interrogative pronoun in each sentence and tell what it refers to by writing *person(s), thing(s),* or *information.* Then give the case of each interrogative pronoun.

1. What were the direct causes of the First World War?
2. To whom did you give your job application?
3. Whom did you meet at the White House?
4. From what is rayon made?
5. Which of those movies would you like to see?
6. Whom will you escort to the dance?
7. Rose asked who lived in that house.
8. Of whom did you ask the question?
9. Who wrote *The Mill on the Floss?*
10. What was the result of the recycling project?

Exercise 2

For each blank, provide an appropriate interrogative pronoun.

1. _____ led the fight for Haitian independence?
2. _____ was the result of the election?
3. By _____ were the votes tallied?
4. For _____ did you cast your ballot?
5. By _____ of the political parties was he nominated?

Exercise 3

Complete each sentence with the correct form of
who **or** *whom.*

1. _____ is the first person in line?
2. By _____ were you told?
3. _____ do you think is at the door, wearing pink tennis shoes?
4. With _____ did you come to the party?
5. _____ went with you to see the blue whale?
6. To _____ do we owe thanks for these season theater tickets?
7. _____ brought the pizza?
8. _____ was chosen to be captain of the soccer team?
9. To _____ did you explain your absence?
10. By _____ was this video game created?
11. _____ usually picks the flowers in the morning?
12. For _____ are these remarks intended?
13. _____ left the test tube where that child could get near it?
14. _____ will they choose to explain the problem?
15. _____ do you think will have the graduation party?
16. _____ are your friends?
17. _____ shall we invite this time?
18. To _____ have you already mailed cards?
19. By _____ was that documentary on nuclear power prepared?
20. _____ can it be?

Practice Power

▶ Compose six questions showing the correct use of interrogative pronouns. Answer your own questions.

Relative Pronouns

A relative pronoun is a pronoun that does the work of a conjunction. A relative pronoun joins the subordinate clause to the antecedent in the principal clause.

Examine these two sentences:

Dominic went to the house of his friend *who* was ill.

The bear *that* roamed the countryside was honey-colored.

In the first sentence, *who* joins the subordinate clause *who was ill* to the antecedent *friend* in the principal clause. In the second sentence, *that* joins the subordinate clause *that roamed the countryside* to the antecedent *bear* in the principal clause.

The relative pronouns *who, whose,* and *whom* refer to persons; *which* refers to animals and things; *that* refers to persons, places, or things; and *what* refers to things.

Correct Use of Relative Pronouns *Who* and *Whom*

The relative pronoun *who* is used when the pronoun is the subject of a verb.

The relative pronoun *whom* is used when the pronoun is the object of a verb or of a preposition.

Christina Rossetti is the person *who* wrote that poem. (subject of *wrote*)

Louisa is the one *whom* they selected for the play. (object of *selected*)

328

Since the relative pronoun relates to a word (antecedent) in the principal clause, you can discover whether you are using the correct pronoun with these two steps.

1. Write the sentence as two sentences, substituting the antecedent for the relative pronoun.

   Christina Rossetti is the person. Christina Rossetti wrote that poem.

   Louisa is the one. They selected Louisa for the play.

2. Determine whether the antecedent in the second sentence is in the nominative case or the objective case.

   Christina Rossetti is the person. *Christina Rossetti* wrote that poem. (nominative case)

   Louisa is the one. They selected *Louisa* for the play. (objective case)

Exercise 1

Name the relative pronouns and their antecedents.

1. The Goldbergs, who moved into the house next door, have three cats and two dogs.
2. There is no person here who can solve the math problem.
3. The letter that you wrote to the mayor is quite good.
4. Ms. Sysmanski was the lawyer who handled Ronald's case.
5. The rug that I wove has been entered in the art show.
6. He who debates the issue is a fool.
7. Thomas Jefferson, who wrote the Declaration of Independence, also owned slaves.
8. None who do battle want to die in the process.
9. They redesigned the museum that overlooks the river.
10. People who race in marathons must run many miles.
11. The storm, which kept us from getting to the store, left twelve inches of snow on the ground.
12. Dublin is located on the Liffey, which is a principal river of Ireland.
13. The river that divides the United States is the Mississippi.
14. The Andes, which run the length of South America, are rugged and beautiful.
15. Only those who are prepared finish the race.

Exercise 2

Choose the correct pronoun to complete each sentence.

1. The senator is a woman in (who, whom) I have great confidence.

2. I will send a messenger (who, whom) you can trust.

3. Paul is a nurse (who, whom) will give good care.

4. Michael Hopkins, from (who, whom) we bought the car, is an honest person.

5. We have a friend (who, whom) will entertain you.

6. We have a friend (who, whom) you will like.

7. Was it Joanne to (who, whom) you spoke?

8. Thom is the person for (who, whom) you have been waiting.

9. Do you know the person with (who, whom) he is sitting?

10. Are they the cousins (who, whom) are visiting you?

11. Someone (who, whom) she respects will have to tell her.

12. The boy (who, whom) owns that blue convertible is my neighbor.

13. Kelsey, (who, whom) has a very clear voice, will introduce the speaker.

14. Reiko was the only player (who, whom) scored a point.

15. We watched the workers (who, whom) were building the bridge.

Practice Power

▶ **Write your own six sentences using the following relative pronouns:**

1. who   3. whom   5. that

2. whose   4. which   6. what

330

LESSON 8 Agreement of Relative Pronouns

A relative pronoun agrees with its antecedent in person, number, and gender, but its case depends upon its use in the subordinate clause.

> Jane Hamlin, to *whom* we gave this award, was very happy.

In this sentence, the relative pronoun is in the third person, singular number, feminine gender to agree with its antecedent, *Jane Hamlin*. It is in the objective case because it is the object of the preposition *to*.

Compound Relative Pronouns

Compound relative pronouns are pronouns formed by adding *ever* or *soever* to *who*, *whom*, *which*, and *what*.

The compound relative pronouns usually contain their own antecedents.

> Give the letter to *whoever* answers the door. (subject of *answers)*
>
> He needs *whatever* is on the desk. (subject of *is)*

REMEMBER: The case of a relative pronoun depends on its use in the subordinate clause.

Exercise 1

For each of the following sentences, name the relative pronoun and its antecedent. Give the person, number, gender, and case of each relative pronoun.

1. The skiers who swooped down the snowy hill seemed to enjoy the cold.
2. The workers voted for the person whom they knew best.
3. The jockey who rode the winning horse was very happy.
4. Scott's shirt is made of cotton, which is a natural fabric.
5. The nerves that carry messages to the brain are called sensory nerves.

Exercise 2

Give the use, or syntax, of the compound relative pronouns in the following sentences. The subordinate clauses are italicized.

1. The prize goes to *whoever achieves the highest score.*
2. The campers took *whatever was necessary for the trip.*
3. You may keep *whatever you desire.*
4. We rewarded *whoever was most diligent.*
5. *Whoever wants this map* may have it.
6. Write about *whatever interests you.*
7. *Whoever is easily moved* cries often.
8. Mr. Pisani gives pie to *whoever wants some.*
9. Do *whatever you can for your friend.*
10. Jack spoke to *whomever he met.*

Practice Power

▶ Expand each sentence with a relative pronoun and a subordinate clause in the place indicated (^).

1. The campground ^ was open all year round.
2. My friend and I were lucky to have a large camper ^.
3. My friend ^ loved to see as many interesting places as possible.
4. Most of our vacation days ^ were sunny and warm.
5. On the morning we left, we vowed to take another trip^.

Pronominals

A pronominal is a pronoun that can also be used as an adjective.

In this lesson, all pronominals will be used as pronouns. The common pronominals are possessive, interrogative, demonstrative, indefinite, and distributive pronouns.

Demonstrative Pronouns

A demonstrative pronoun is a pronoun that points out a definite person, place, or thing.

The demonstrative pronouns are *this, that, these,* and *those.* *This* and *these* denote objects that are near. *That* and *those* denote distant objects.

Indefinite Pronouns

An indefinite pronoun is a pronoun that points out no particular person, place, or thing.

Many of the conquistadors suffered hardships.
Some returned to Europe, but *some* remained.

In all, there are about thirty indefinite pronouns. The most commonly used indefinite pronouns are

all	anything	few	no one	some
another	both	many	nothing	somebody
any	everybody	much	one	someone
anybody	everyone	nobody	same	something
anyone	everything	none	several	such

Distributive Pronouns

A distributive pronoun is a pronoun that refers to each person, place, or thing separately.

Each of the soldiers reported promptly.

The distributive pronouns are *each, either,* and *neither.*

Exercise 1

Choose an appropriate demonstrative pronoun to complete each of the following sentences. Then tell whether the pronoun you have selected refers to things near or to things distant.

1. _____ were grown in Israel.
2. _____ is from the South.
3. Do you prefer _____ ?
4. _____ is not balanced.
5. _____ is the best food you can eat.
6. I have never seen a river as polluted as _____ is.
7. _____ are located on the fall line.
8. Is _____ a model of *Apollo 11?*
9. _____ did not end the debate.
10. _____ is the only white tiger in captivity.

Exercise 2

Find the indefinite pronouns in the sentences and tell how they are used: subject, direct object, or object of preposition.

1. No one saw the comet.
2. Everybody on the team ran his or her best.
3. Anyone who works hard enough can achieve his or her goal.
4. Much of this is news to me.
5. Few of us wanted to do the extra work.
6. You may have both.
7. Someone saw the gorilla eat the hat.

8. Many of the South American rivers are infested with piranhas.
9. Have they questioned everyone about the accident?
10. Several should be able to complete the project.
11. Before the Industrial Revolution, much of the work was done in the home.
12. The tornado lifted everything in its path.
13. Some work at night.
14. All of the cows rested in the shade of the huge oaks.
15. Is Cheryl waiting for somebody?

Exercise 3

Identify the distributive pronouns in the sentences.

1. Each of the objects is crafted by hand.
2. Hank will be pleased with either.
3. Neither of the countries turned away the refugees.
4. Each was told to take care of his or her own things.
5. Do you prefer either of these clocks?
6. Each expected the other to make the decision.
7. Neither wanted to take the risk.
8. Either of the men could have spoken first.
9. Sheila may be living in either of the provinces.
10. Each of the burglars blamed the others.

Practice Power

▶ Describe a collection of things, such as the contents of your backpack, bookshelf, or dresser drawer. Use and underline the demonstrative, indefinite, and distributive pronouns in your paragraph.

Agreement with Distributive and Indefinite Pronouns

Personal pronouns and possessive adjectives must agree with their antecedents in person, number, and gender.

The distributive pronouns *each, either,* and *neither* and the indefinite pronouns *one, anyone, no one, anybody, nobody, everyone, everybody, someone,* and *somebody* are always singular. Pronouns and possessive adjectives referring to these pronouns as antecedents must be singular in number.

Such indefinite pronouns as *all, both, few, many, several,* and *some* are generally plural. Pronouns and possessive adjectives referring to these pronouns as antecedents must be plural.

Each did *her* best.
Both did *their* best.

Exercise 1

Identify the indefinite or distributive pronoun in each sentence. Then select the pronoun or adjective that agrees with the indefinite or distributive pronoun.

1. Everyone wore (his or her, their) best outfit to school that morning.

2. Neither of the little girls lost (her, their) bonnet in the wind.

3. Everyone in the class agreed to give some of (his or her, their) money to the Save the Whales fund.

4. Each of the students thought that (his or her, their) own social studies project should win first prize.

5. Neither of the runners thought that (she, they) had tripped the other in the race.

6. Everyone must wait (his or her, their) turn to work on the computer.

7. Many of the employees ate (his or her, their) lunch at Ernie's Diner.

8. Everybody who has red hair was asked if (he or she, they) would try the new shampoo.

9. All of the candidates did (his or her, their) best to win.

10. A few of the students complained that (his or her, their) names were misspelled in the yearbook.

11. Both of the boys forgot to bring (his, their) skates.

12. If everyone does (his or her, their) best, it doesn't matter if we lose the game.

Exercise 2

Complete each sentence with a pronoun or posessive adjective that agrees with its antecedent.

1. Anyone who has finished _____ dinner may help clear the table now.

2. Both of the scouts spent an hour loading _____ camping equipment into the old blue truck.

3. Each of the newspaper carriers was given a bonus at the end of the year based on _____ service to customers.

4. No one could take any of the tiny kittens into _____ home until we had taken them to the veterinarian.

5. If anyone wishes to start the program with a song, _____ may do so now.

6. Is anyone willing to donate _____ time to help serve food at the shelter tonight?

7. Each student received a grade that equaled _____ effort throughout the entire class project.

8. All at the high school agreed that _____ float was the best one in the parade.

Putting It All Together

Look through a favorite short story or article and write notes about the tone of the piece. What kind of person do you imagine the author or narrator to be?

Then make a list of the pronouns the story or article uses. Replace each pronoun with the noun it represents. How does the lack of pronouns change the tone of the article or story? How do your ideas about the author or narrator change?

Chapter Challenge

Read the paragraph carefully and then answer the questions that follow.

[1]Each of you, boys and girls, belongs to two important societies: the family and the state. [2]"What," you may ask, "is the obligation that is imposed by membership in these societies?" [3]The answer is this. [4]You must give a respectful obedience to those in authority, perform your duties conscientiously, and strive to live in harmony with other persons. [5]In other words, you must develop in yourself whatever will make you a valued member of each group. [6]Such is the attitude of every worthwhile person. [7]It should also be yours.

1. Name a personal pronoun found in the first sentence.

2. In what person is the pronoun *you* in the second sentence?

3. Name the demonstrative pronoun in the third sentence.

4. In the fourth sentence, select a personal pronoun that is used as the subject.

5. Find a compound personal pronoun in the fifth sentence.

6. Is the compound personal pronoun in the fifth sentence used intensively or reflexively?

7. Find an interrogative pronoun in the second sentence.

8. In what case is the interrogative pronoun?

9. Name a personal pronoun in the seventh sentence that is neuter in gender.

10. Find a relative pronoun in the second sentence. What is the antecedent of that relative pronoun?

11. What kind of pronoun is the first word in the paragraph?

12. What kind of pronoun does the sixth sentence contain?

13. Name the possessive pronoun in the seventh sentence.

ADJECTIVES

Descriptive Adjectives

An adjective is a word that describes or limits a noun or a pronoun.

Adjectives may be divided into two general classes, descriptive adjectives and limiting adjectives. Limiting adjectives will be studied in Lesson 2.

A descriptive adjective is an adjective that describes a noun or a pronoun.

> He pulled out the *crumpled red* handkerchief.

There are two types of descriptive adjectives, proper adjectives and common adjectives.

A proper adjective is an adjective that is formed from a proper noun.

A common adjective is an adjective that expresses the ordinary qualities of a noun or a pronoun.

> Mia has a *Persian* cat. (proper adjective)
> The author was an *intelligent* girl. (common adjective)

NOTE: Many participles may be used as descriptive adjectives.

> A happy, *laughing* group of boys returned from the amusement park.
> (*Laughing* comes from the verb *laugh*.)

About the Photograph

What adjectives would you use to describe your school activities?

Exercise 1

Find all of the descriptive adjectives. Tell whether they are common or proper.

1. Canada is famous for picturesque lakes and majestic mountains.
2. Athenian citizens participated in their ancient democracy.
3. Amateur photography is an absorbing hobby.
4. The old buildings of European cities amaze American visitors.
5. Good health requires fresh air and abundant sunshine.
6. Byzantine culture spread to Europe from the Middle East after the Crusades.
7. Colorful pennants decorated the walls of the school gym.
8. Rubber trees flourish in Amazon jungles.
9. Eudora Welty, a Southern writer, lived in rural Mississippi.
10. Foamy waves had washed all of the white pebbles.

Exercise 2

Complete each of the following sentences with adjectives. Remember to use both common and proper adjectives.

1. The _____ guard has _____ eyes.
2. In the _____ museum, we saw paintings of _____ artists.
3. Remember that _____ objects break easily.
4. Dan's _____ bicycle has _____ handlebars.
5. _____ citizens vote in _____ elections.
6. Many nations import _____ oil.
7. The _____ mountains tower above the _____ ravine.
8. People from _____ climates have trouble adjusting to weather.
9. Ms. Keller, the _____ coach, gave us some _____ cake.
10. Sometimes _____ diplomats work in _____ places.

Position of Descriptive Adjectives

The usual position of a descriptive adjective is before a noun, but sometimes it comes after the noun.

> Eric has *bright blue* eyes.
>
> The colors, *sharp* and *vivid,* helped make the picture come alive.

A descriptive adjective used as a subjective complement follows and completes a linking verb.

> The room is *large* and *comfortable.* (This is a *large* and *comfortable* room.)

A descriptive adjective that follows the direct object and at the same time completes the thought expressed by a transitive verb is called an objective complement.

> The announcement made him *angry.*

Exercise 3

Identify the descriptive adjectives. Tell if each adjective comes before or after the noun, or if it is a subjective or an objective complement.

1. Sam keeps his motorcycle clean.
2. The gray cat is blind.
3. Philadelphia pretzels are famous around the world.
4. The new car, small and sporty, drives like a dream.
5. Nicole appears indifferent.
6. Workers paved the road smooth.
7. She painted the house red.
8. The baby's high fever caused alarm.
9. Steven looks ill.
10. The pizza, hot and bubbly, arrived exactly at noon.

Words Used as Nouns and Adjectives

The use of a word in the sentence determines the part of speech. Very frequently the same word may be used both as a noun and as an adjective.

A noun is a name word; an adjective describes or limits a noun.

> The *iron* is very hot. (noun)
>
> An *iron* pot hung over the fireplace. (adjective)

Exercise 4

Identify each word in italics as a noun or an adjective.

1. The white *brick* became the cornerstone of the building.
2. The *brick* wall cracked this morning.
3. The *inside* door to their building opened with a triangular key.
4. Let me see the *inside.*
5. Leroy has a new hat with a *feather* in it.
6. Grandmother has *feather* pillows on her bed.
7. Draw a *square* figure at the top of the page.
8. The town *square* was full of people.
9. The *past* cannot be relived.
10. The telephone has rung seven times during the *past* hour.
11. Some *metal* hung down from the back of the car.
12. The table was supported by firm *metal* legs.

Practice Power

▶ Write a paragraph about the picture on the opposite page. Use different kinds of descriptive adjectives in various positions in the sentences.

Limiting Adjectives

A limiting adjective is an adjective that either points out an object or denotes number.

The limiting adjectives may be subdivided into the following three classes: (1) articles, (2) numeral adjectives, and (3) pronominal adjectives.

The articles *the*, *an*, and *a* show whether the noun is used definitely or indefinitely.

The parade was very colorful. (definite: a specific parade)

An artist must use his imagination. (indefinite: any artist)

A numeral adjective is an adjective that denotes exact number.

Matt paid *fifty* cents for his *second* game.

A pronominal adjective is an adjective that may also be used as a pronoun.

Pronominal adjectives are usually divided into the following five classes:

A demonstrative adjective is an adjective that points out a definite person, place, or thing *(this, that, these, those).*

A possessive adjective is an adjective that denotes ownership *(my, our, your, his, her, its, their).*

A distributive adjective is an adjective that refers to each person, place, or thing separately *(each, every, either, neither).*

An indefinite adjective is an adjective that points out no particular person, place, or thing *(any, all, another, both, few, many, much, several, some, such).*

An interrogative adjective is an adjective that is used in asking a question *(which, what).*

Exercise 1

Find the limiting adjectives in the following sentences. Identify each as an article, a numeral adjective, or a pronominal adjective.

1. Several airplanes flew over the stadium.
2. Do you know the names of the ten animals?
3. Many actors will appear in the play.
4. His baseball bat was lost.
5. Which debater gave the longest speech?
6. The United States has five important forest belts.
7. That bag is filled with her candy.
8. A man took Michiko's twenty dollars and gave it to two other people.
9. The sailors saved many lives.
10. Each member of the board cast one vote.
11. The truck hit my car.
12. The diameter of that rock is twelve centimeters.

Exercise 2

Select the pronominal adjectives and tell to which of the five classes found on page 347 each belongs.

1. Some clowns arrived early.
2. We had never seen such outfits before.
3. Each clown had brought an extra arm.
4. The clowns shook hands with a few people.
5. Several people were shocked when they found themselves holding rubber arms.
6. Those people were fooled.
7. There was much laughter as many clowns tumbled out of a tiny car.
8. Which person in my family laughed the hardest?
9. Even my grandparents enjoyed the antics of those clowns.
10. We had such fun we wanted to see every performance.

Practice Power

▶ Complete the sentences with appropriate pronominal adjectives.

1. _____ member of the panel gave a short talk on _____ part of the topic.
2. _____ work requires great strength.
3. Our vacation was terrible because of _____ rudeness.
4. _____ politicians talk too much.
5. _____ worker has _____ job to do.
6. Mike wants _____ day to be more fun than the one before.
7. _____ tree is an elm.
8. _____ state has two senators in Congress.
9. You may have _____ chance.
10. _____ statue was given to _____ country by France.

348

More About Limiting Adjectives

Correct Use of Demonstrative Adjectives *This* and *That, These* and *Those*

The demonstrative adjectives agree in number with the nouns they modify.

This and *that* are singular and modify singular nouns.

this book
that kind of shoe

These and *those* are plural and modify plural nouns.

these books
those kinds of shoes

This and *these* denote objects that are near. *That* and *those* denote more distant objects.

Exercise 1

Choose the correct form of the indicated type of demonstrative adjective.

1. _____ coffee tastes bitter. (near)
2. My mother has one of _____ pink toasters. (distant)
3. _____ computer has enough memory to run any program on the market. (distant)
4. _____ hybrid tulip came from Holland. (near)
5. Why does she refuse to watch _____ kind of TV show? (distant)
6. _____ shoes may not last until the end of the day. (distant)
7. What did _____ men say to you? (distant)
8. She has many agates of _____ color in her rock collection. (distant)

The Repetition of the Article

The repetition of the article changes the meaning of a sentence.

> I know *the* director and *the* producer.

Here the article is placed before both nouns to show that they refer to two separate persons.

> I know *the* director and producer.

In this sentence, the article is placed only before the first noun to show that both positions (director and producer) are held by one individual.

Exercise 2

Determine whether the article in parentheses is needed. Give a reason for your choice.

1. We had a plum and (a) peach for our lunch.
2. The Danube and (the) Rhine are major German rivers.
3. The co-captain and (the) center is wearing number 51.
4. A blue and (a) yellow pencil are in the case.
5. The French bakery and (the) café has moved to a new location.
6. The president and (the) manager have gone to Madrid.
7. The secretary and (the) treasurer has written the report about the meeting.
8. The captain and (the) pilot were asking the ground crew for help.
9. The ranchers and (the) farmers made a treaty.
10. A canoe and (a) rowboat were still on the lake when the storm hit.

Practice Power

▶ Imagine that you are in a store to buy popcorn. Write a comparison of two brands. You might compare price, package size, preparation time, and flavor. Use the demonstrative adjectives in your comparison.

Using Adjectives to Compare

Comparison is the change that adjectives undergo to express different degrees of quality, quantity, or value.

Most adjectives have three degrees of comparison: positive, comparative, and superlative.

> This is a *large* apple. (positive degree)
>
> This is a *larger* apple than yours. (comparative degree)
>
> This is the *largest* apple in the basket. (superlative degree)

The positive degree denotes the quality.

The comparative degree denotes the quality in a greater or a lesser degree.

The superlative degree denotes the quality in the greatest or the least degree.

Methods of Comparison

Most adjectives of one syllable and some adjectives of two syllables (generally those ending in *ow, y,* and *e*) form the comparative degree by adding *-er* to the positive, and the superlative degree by adding *-est* to the positive.

POSITIVE	COMPARATIVE	SUPERLATIVE
nobl*e*	nobl*er*	nobl*est*
merr*y*	merri*er*	merri*est*
narr*ow*	narrow*er*	narrow*est*

Adjectives of three or more syllables, and some of two syllables, form the comparative and the superlative degrees by using *more* and *most* or *less* and *least* with the positive form of the adjective.

POSITIVE	COMPARATIVE	SUPERLATIVE
industrious	more industrious	most industrious
thoughtful	less thoughtful	least thoughtful

Certain adjectives are compared irregularly, such as

POSITIVE	COMPARATIVE	SUPERLATIVE
little	less	least
bad	worse	worst
good	better	best
many, much	more	most
late	later, latter	latest, last
far	farther	farthest
—	*further	furthest
—	*inner	innermost, inmost
—	*outer	outermost, outmost
—	*upper	uppermost, upmost

*These adjectives have no positive degree.

Some adjectives cannot be compared, such as *perfect, dead, perpendicular, eternal, supreme,* and so forth.

Exercise 1

Identify the adjectives and give the degree of comparison.

1. Aaron wore his newest shirt.
2. Natalie had a small radio clipped to her belt.
3. Chicago gets more snow than Los Angeles does.
4. Isabel is taller than her sister.
5. Derek thought they were his worst enemies.

Practice Power

▶ Retell a fairy tale that has three characters, such as The Three Pigs or The Three Bears. Be sure to include adjectives in the three degrees of comparison in your tale.

Correct Use of Comparative and Superlative Degrees

The comparative degree of an adjective is used when two nouns or pronouns are compared. The superlative degree is used when more than two are compared.

Which river is *longer,* the Ohio or the Mississippi? (comparative)

The Mississippi is the *longest* river in North America. (superlative)

Exercise 1

Select the correct degree of the adjective to complete each sentence.

1. Which is (more useful, most useful), copper or silver?
2. The Pacific is the (larger, largest) ocean.
3. Hakeem knew a (quicker, quickest) way home than Paula.
4. Which of the two buildings is (more modern, most modern)?
5. Of the two, the hare was the (better, best) runner.
6. Was the hare or the tortoise the (faster, fastest)?
7. Which are the (more precious, most precious) gems, diamonds or rubies?
8. They rented the (newer, newest) model of VCR.
9. Who did the (better, best) work, Joe, Maureen, or Kenny?
10. Gina is (faster, fastest) than Greg.

Correct Use of *Fewer* and *Less*

Use *fewer* when number is indicated. Use *less* when degree is indicated. Usually, *fewer* is used with a plural noun and *less* is used with a singular noun.

> There are *fewer* players than spectators.
> We have had *less* snow this winter than last winter.

Exercise 2

Choose the correct word, *fewer* or *less*, to complete each sentence.

1. _____ people go camping in the winter than in the summer.
2. This farmer has _____ cherry trees and _____ corn than that one.
3. This test allows _____ time and has _____ questions than the one you took last week.
4. Carol had _____ books in the bookcase than on her bedroom floor.
5. _____ students chose to attend the class play this year than last.
6. Roberto found _____ worms in the garden today than yesterday.
7. _____ guests than expected came to the wedding.
8. Greater diligence results in _____ mistakes.
9. Jo had _____ time to practice than I did.
10. As many jobs become automated, _____ workers are needed.

Putting It All Together

Write four sentences containing simple observations. Add two or more adjectives to each sentence. Then delete all the words in the sentence except the nouns and adjectives. Rearrange the remaining words to create an adjectival poem.

If you like, give the poem a specific structure. You might place all your adjectives in the same position or give your poem the same number of words per line, the same number of syllables per line, or verses with the same number of lines per verse.

Chapter Challenge

Read this paragraph carefully and answer the questions.

¹Have you ever considered what would happen to us if our American bird life became extinct? ²To appreciate the dire consequences of such a misfortune, we must consider the many ways in which birds help us. ³The destruction of harmful insects is perhaps their most important work. ⁴This constant war on one natural enemy of humankind makes the farmers' task easier. ⁵The seed diet of some birds helps to keep the weed crop under control, while many of the larger birds prevent mice and rats from becoming intolerable pests. ⁶What good reasons we have for valuing these small creatures! ⁷They are among our greatest benefactors.

1. What kind of pronominal adjective is *our* in the first sentence?

2. Find a proper adjective in the first sentence.

3. How is the adjective *extinct* in the first sentence used?

4. What is the comparative form of the adjective *extinct?*

5. Name the definite and indefinite articles in the second sentence.

6. What kind of pronominal adjective is *their* in the third sentence?

7. Give the comparative degree of *harmful* found in the third sentence.

8. Give the positive and the comparative degrees of *important* found in the third sentence.

9. Name a numeral adjective in the fourth sentence.

10. What is the use of the word *easier* in the fourth sentence?

11. Find a singular and a plural demonstrative adjective in the fourth and sixth sentences.

12. Name an indefinite adjective in the fifth sentence.

13. Name the adjective that modifies the subject of the fifth sentence. Can this word be used as any other part of speech?

14. In the sixth and the seventh sentences, name the adjectives in the positive degree and the superlative degree.

Regular and Irregular Verbs

A verb is a word used to express action, being, or state of being.

Carol *speaks* Polish and German. (action)

Iron *is* a strong, useful metal. (being)

A large picture *hangs* on the wall. (state of being)

Without a verb there can be no sentence.

The principal parts of the verb are the present, the past, and the past participle, because all other forms of the verb are determined from these.

A regular verb forms its past and its past participle by adding *d* or *ed* to the present form.

An irregular verb does not form its past and its past participle by adding *d* or *ed* to the present form.

	PRESENT	PAST	PAST PARTICIPLE
REGULAR VERB:	walk	walked	walked
IRREGULAR VERB:	rise	rose	risen

Review the principal parts of the irregular verbs listed on pages 358–360.

Review the principal parts of the irregular verbs listed on pages 358–360.

About the Photograph

These volleyball players *are participating* in an important match. They *have* to *serve, jump, dive,* and *spike* during the game.

PRESENT	PAST	PAST PARTICIPLE
am (is, be)	was	been
awake	awoke, awaked	awaked
beat	beat	beat, beaten
begin	began	begun
bend	bent	bent
bet	bet	bet
bind	bound	bound
bite	bit	bitten
blow	blew	blown
break	broke	broken
bring	brought	brought
build	built	built
burn	burned, burnt	burned, burnt
burst	burst	burst
catch	caught	caught
choose	chose	chosen
come	came	come
creep	crept	crept
do	did	done
draw	drew	drawn
dream	dreamed, dreamt	dreamed, dreamt
drink	drank	drunk
drive	drove	driven
dwell	dwelt, dwelled	dwelt, dwelled
eat	ate	eaten
fall	fell	fallen
find	found	found
flee	fled	fled
fly	flew	flown
forget	forgot	forgotten
freeze	froze	frozen
give	gave	given
go	went	gone
grow	grew	grown
hang	hung	hung
have	had	had
hide	hid	hidden, hid
hold	held	held
hurt	hurt	hurt
keep	kept	kept
kneel	knelt, kneeled	knelt, kneeled

PRESENT	PAST	PAST PARTICIPLE
knit	knit, knitted	knit, knitted
know	knew	known
lay	laid	laid
lead	led	led
leave	left	left
lend	lent	lent
let	let	let
lie (recline)	lay	lain
light	lighted, lit	lighted, lit
lose	lost	lost
make	made	made
mean	meant	meant
meet	met	met
read	read	read
ride	rode	ridden
ring	rang	rung
rise	rose	risen
run	ran	run
say	said	said
see	saw	seen
seek	sought	sought
set	set	set
shake	shook	shaken
show	showed	shown, showed
sing	sang	sung
sink	sank	sunk
sit	sat	sat
sleep	slept	slept
slide	slid	slid
smell	smelled, smelt	smelled, smelt
sow	sowed	sown, sowed
speak	spoke	spoken
spend	spent	spent
spill	spilled, spilt	spilled, spilt
stand	stood	stood
steal	stole	stolen
stick	stuck	stuck
sting	stung	stung
stride	strode	stridden
swim	swam	swum
swing	swung	swung

PRESENT	PAST	PAST PARTICIPLE
teach	taught	taught
tear	tore	torn
throw	threw	thrown
wake	waked, woke	waked, woken
wear	wore	worn
weave	wove	woven
win	won	won
wind	wound	wound
wring	wrung	wrung
write	wrote	written

Exercise 1

Test your knowledge of irregular verb forms by copying these sentences and filling in the blanks with the past tense or the past participle of the verbs in parentheses.

1. He _____ the book from the shelf. (take)
2. The storm _____ early this morning. (begin)
3. Have you ever _____ the subway? (ride)
4. The cat _____ into the room. (steal)
5. Paul has never _____ a car. (drive)
6. I have _____ my coat. (lose)
7. The enemy _____ the ship. (sink)
8. Have you ever _____ the Roman Forum? (see)
9. He has _____ the land by now. (sell)
10. The Chengs have _____ to their cottage. (go)
11. The judge _____ every word he said. (mean)
12. The workers have _____ down the old building. (tear)
13. I have _____ the date of my appointment. (forget)
14. They have _____ the dessert for dinner. (freeze)
15. We have _____ friends for many years. (be)
16. Have you _____ your arm? (hurt)
17. Last night I _____ I could fly. (dream)
18. Rose says that she has never _____ through the night. (sleep)
19. Sean _____ the flares to warn the other drivers. (light)
20. Who has _____ in this pool? (swim).

Troublesome Verbs

The verb pairs *lie* and *lay, sit* and *set, rise* and *raise, let* and *leave, borrow* and *lend, learn* and *teach,* and *bring* and *take* are sometimes confused with each other. Give special attention to the meanings of these verbs when they are used in sentences.

Lie, lay, lain

This verb means "to rest or recline."

> I like to *lie* on the beach.

Lay, laid, laid

The meaning of this verb is "to put or place in position."

> The company will *lay* our wall-to-wall carpeting today.

Sit, sat, sat

This verb means "to have or keep a seat."

> Janie always *sits* in that big, overstuffed chair.

Set, set, set

The meaning of this verb is "to place or fix in position."

> *Set* the plant by a window that faces south.

Rise, rose, risen

This verb means "to ascend."

> Smoke *rose* lazily from the chimney.

Raise, raised, raised

This verb means "to lift."

Raise the window to let in some fresh air.

Let, let, let

This verb means "to permit or allow."

Please *let* me go to the movies tonight.

Leave, left, left

This verb means "to abandon or depart from."

I *left* my glasses at school.

Borrow, borrowed, borrowed

This verb means "to obtain something from another person with the intention of returning it." It is often followed by *from*.

Don hasn't paid back the money he *borrowed* from me.

Lend, lent, lent

This verb means "to let another person have or use something for a time."

I think Don *lent* the money to his sister.

Learn, learned, learned

This verb means "to receive instruction or to acquire knowledge."

Do you want to *learn* how to knit?

Teach, taught, taught

This verb means "to give instruction or to impart knowledge."

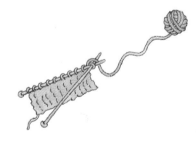

My mother *taught* me how to knit.

Bring, brought, brought

This verb means "to come with some person or thing from another place." The verb denotes motion toward the speaker.

Ana *brought* her dog to my house.

Take, took, taken

This verb means "to go with a person or something to another place." The verb denotes motion away from the speaker.

Tom, *take* your little brother with you.

Exercise 2

Choose the correct verb.

1. The clerk has (lain, laid) the package on the counter.
2. The golf ball (lay, laid) just a foot from the hole.
3. The customer had been (sitting, setting) patiently.
4. The burglar (brought, took) our TV.
5. My father (let, left) my sister drive the car.
6. She (rose, raised) her head and watched him go.
7. After a few minutes, she (rose, raised) slowly.
8. Katie asked a friend to (borrow, lend) her some money to take the bus home.
9. Please (let, leave) Mary go with you.
10. Did the dough (rise, raise) on the warm windowsill?
11. The Boy Scouts have (risen, raised) the flag over their cabin.
12. The baby has (lain, laid) there gurgling for hours.
13. We shall (let, leave) him know our answer soon.
14. (Let, Leave) Bill do the work in his own way.
15. The dog has (lain, laid) under the tree all day.
16. Mark (sit, set) the table for breakfast.
17. Elena (sat, set) at the table for breakfast.
18. Gary said he would (let, leave) the package at the door.

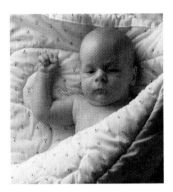

Exercise 3

Insert an appropriate troublesome verb from pages 361–363 to complete each sentence.

1. _____ this file to the mayor's office.

2. The books _____ on the library tables where we left them.

3. Neil's doctor would not _____ him swim.

4. Our class _____ many poems.

5. Dianna _____ me how to swim.

6. Banks _____ money to people.

7. The waiter _____ me a clean glass.

8. Jorge _____ me his bicycle for an hour.

9. If you come, be sure to _____ your hiking boots.

10. _____ me show you the penguins.

Practice Power

▶ Write a short paragraph about a special event you have attended. Use some of the irregular verbs from the list on pages 358–360. Underline the verbs and then label them as auxiliary or main verbs.

Transitive, Intransitive, and Linking Verbs

Transitive Verbs

A transitive verb expresses an action that passes from a doer to a receiver.

DOER	ACTION	RECEIVER
Joel	opened	the door.

Opened is a transitive verb because the action passes from the doer, *Joel,* to the receiver, the *door.*

To determine the receiver of the action, ask the question *whom* or *what* after the verb. Joel opened what? The answer to this question determines the receiver of the action.

The action may pass from the doer to the receiver in two different ways.

>   The team *enjoyed* the trip.
>
>   The trip *was enjoyed* by the team.

Team is the doer of the action in both sentences, and *trip* is the receiver. Since the action passes from the doer to the receiver in each case, the verb *enjoyed,* whether in the form of *enjoyed* or *was enjoyed,* is a transitive verb.

The doer is not always expressed when a transitive verb is used in the passive voice.

>   News *is broadcast* by many commentators.
>   (doer expressed)
>
>   News *is broadcast* every hour. (doer not expressed)

VERBS

Intransitive Verbs

An intransitive verb has no receiver of its action.

DOER	ACTION	RECEIVER
The general	hastened away.	—

The action of the verb *hastened* begins and ends with the doer, or the subject of the verb. The question *whom* or *what* after the verb will receive no answer because there is no receiver.

Intransitive verbs are always in the active voice since a verb is in the active voice when its subject is the doer of the action.

Some verbs may be transitive or intransitive according to their use in the sentence.

> Experience *develops* character. (transitive verb)
> Manufacturing *developed* rapidly in England. (intransitive verb)
> The sun *melted* the ice. (transitive verb)
> The ice *melted* slowly. (intransitive verb)

Cognate Verbs

A cognate verb is a verb whose object repeats the meaning implied by the verb itself.

> Walter *dreamed* a pleasant dream.

A cognate verb is usually an intransitive verb that becomes transitive by taking an object derived from the verb itself.

Exercise 1

Name the verbs and tell whether they are transitive, intransitive, or cognate. For each transitive verb, name the receiver of the action and tell whether it is the subject or the object of the verb.

1. Joseph Lister introduced antiseptics into surgery.
2. What movies are shown at that theater?
3. Sidney Hillman organized labor unions.
4. British rule of India started in the nineteenth century.
5. Betsy washes inside the cabinets.
6. Workers paved the road three times last summer.
7. Alicia purchased a summer cottage.
8. Every group member helped an older person in some way.
9. The leaves were raked into a huge pile.
10. The performance bored the hot, tired audience.
11. The elves danced a dance of boundless glee.
12. The rabbits scattered in all directions.
13. Multicolored shells were tossed up on the beach.
14. Nothing remains of the old temple.
15. Edna St. Vincent Millay wrote lyrical, romantic poems.

Linking Verbs

A linking verb couples, or links, the subject with a noun, a pronoun, or an adjective.

A word or group of words used to complete the meaning of a linking verb is called a subjective complement. The complement may be a noun, a pronoun, or an adjective.

SUBJECT	LINKING VERB	COMPLEMENT
His name	is	Paul. (noun)
I	am	she. (pronoun)
The room	seems	cold. (adjective)

The verb *be* in its various forms is the most common linking verb. Some other verbs that may be used as linking verbs are *appear, become, continue, feel, grow, look, remain, seem, smell, sound,* and *taste.*

Exercise 2

Name the linking verbs in each of the following sentences. Tell whether the verb links the subject with a noun, a pronoun, or an adjective.

1. Beatriz's new car is green.

2. We are competitive swimmers.

3. Paul grew restless during the lecture.

4. The optic nerve is the nerve of sight.

5. The captain seemed eager to set sail before the seas got too rough.

6. Red and yellow were the leaves on the trees in Michigan.

7. Samantha always remains cool, calm, and collected.

8. A tome is a large, scholarly book.

9. Carl's latest plan sounds exciting.

10. King Richard and King John were brothers.

11. Skin feels drier in the winter.

12. Kevin remained the person with the highest score.

13. Who is that?

14. The orange tasted bitter.

15. Liz's perfume smells wonderful.

Practice Power

▶ Using the linking verbs *appear, feel, look, seem, smell, sound,* and *taste,* write five sentences describing one of the following: pizza, popcorn, fried chicken, or spaghetti.

Active and Passive Voice

Voice is the quality of a verb that shows whether the subject is the doer or the receiver of the action.

In the active voice, the subject is the doer of the action. In the passive voice, the subject is the receiver of the action.

> Alexander Graham Bell *invented* the telephone.
> The telephone *was invented* by Alexander Graham Bell.

In the first sentence the subject, *Alexander Graham Bell,* is the doer of the action, *invented;* therefore, *invented* is in the active voice. The receiver of the action is the direct object, *telephone.* In the second sentence the subject, *telephone,* is the receiver of the action, *was invented;* therefore, *was invented* is in the passive voice.

Only transitive verbs are used in the passive voice. Intransitive verbs have no receivers of the action.

Formation of the Passive Voice

The passive voice is formed by using some tense of the verb *be* as an auxiliary with the past participle of the verb. Therefore, the verb *be* (and its tenses), used before a past participle, is generally the sign of the passive voice.

> *was + called* = passive voice

Two sentences may convey the same idea, the one expressed by a verb in the active voice and the other by a verb in the passive voice. When a verb in the active voice is changed to the passive voice, the subject of the active verb is usually made the object of a preposition, and the object of the active verb becomes the subject of the passive verb.

VERBS

The brain *keeps* the body under control. (active voice)
The body *is kept* under control by the brain. (passive voice)

In each of these sentences, the *brain* performs the action, and the *body* receives the action. In the first sentence *brain* is the subject of the verb *keeps;* in the second sentence it becomes the object of the preposition *by.*

Body, the receiver of the action, is the direct object of the active verb *keeps,* but in the second sentence it becomes the subject of the passive verb *is kept.*

Exercise 1

Change the verbs in the following sentences from active to passive voice.

1. Cliff walked his dog in the park.

2. The dog snapped the leather leash.

3. Cliff frantically called the dog.

4. The park guard would close the gate at sunset.

5. Cliff and his dog left the park just in time.

Change the verbs in the following sentences from passive to active voice.

6. The mouse is killed by the cat.

7. The cat is eaten by the snake.

8. The snake is attacked by the mongoose.

9. The mongoose is destroyed by the hunter.

10. The hunter is fined by the judge.

Exercise 2

Determine whether the verbs in the following sentences are in the active or passive voice. Then rewrite the sentences, changing active verbs to passive voice and passive verbs to active voice.

1. Terry wrote a very simple word-processing program.

2. The incandescent lamp was invented by Edison.

3. The teacher sent cards to all of her students.

4. Canadian wood pulp is sold to the United States.

5. The Panama Canal connects the Caribbean Sea and the Pacific Ocean.

6. Exercise strengthens the heart and lungs.

7. The president is guarded by Secret Service agents.

8. Jackie lost a moon-shaped earring.

9. Frank's car was stored at the body shop.

10. The Greeks established many colonies in Italy.

Practice Power

▶ **Model your own passive voice poem after the one below.**

The tree is
    planted by the gardener
    strengthened by the sun
    nourished by the rain
    bent by the wind
    uprooted by the storm

Simple and Compound Tenses

Tense is the quality of a verb that denotes the time of the action, the being, or the state of being.

Simple Tenses

Present tense signifies action, being, or state of being in present time.

Past tense signifies action, being, or state of being in past time.

Future tense signifies action, being, or state of being in future time.

PRESENT:	Lorrie *studies* diligently.
PAST:	Lorrie *studied* diligently.
FUTURE:	Lorrie *will study* diligently.

In the passive voice the tense is shown by the auxiliary verb.

PRESENT:	The lesson *is studied.*
PAST:	The lesson *was studied.*
FUTURE:	The lesson *will be studied.*

Exercise 1

Give the tense and voice of each verb.

1. Our class will study some poems by Gerard Manley Hopkins.

2. The drowning of five nuns in an 1875 shipwreck was memorialized by Hopkins in his poem "The Wreck of the Deutschland."

3. The nuns left Germany because of religious persecution.

4. Hopkins was inspired by their courage.

5. Many people study his poem.

6. They will be moved by his emotional appeal.

7. I read the poem several years ago.

8. I still find it poetically pleasing.

9. Hopkins is studied as part of the Victorian period.

10. His poetry will be read for years to come.

Use of *Shall* and *Will*

To express future time or expectation, use *shall* in the first person and *will* in the second and the third persons.

> I *shall* go tomorrow.
> You *will* go tomorrow.
> He *will* go tomorrow.

Shall and *Will* in Questions

To ask a question that requests an opinion or permission, use *shall* when the subject is the first person. In the second and the third persons, use the same word, either *shall* or *will,* that is expected in the reply.

QUESTION	EXPECTED REPLY
Shall we help him?	We *shall.*
Shall you see him?	Yes, I *shall.*
Will you help me?	Yes, I *will* help.
Will the concert begin soon?	It *will.*

Exercise 2

Fill in each blank with *shall* or *will*.

1. My friends _____ not be home this evening.
2. All the nations _____ be represented at the meeting.
3. My little sister _____ be three years old tomorrow.
4. The swimming meet _____ be moved to another pool.
5. I must hurry or I _____ be late for class.
6. We _____ study the causes of the war.
7. The peace talks _____ start again tomorrow.
8. The doctor _____ be here soon.
9. This Saturday I _____ go to the photography exhibit.
10. Susan's parents _____ pick her up at the park.

Exercise 3

Choose *shall* or *will* to complete each sentence. Give a response to the question that fits your verb choice.

1. When _____ the next bus leave?
2. _____ I meet you at the corner?
3. _____ he show us how to configure the system?
4. Where _____ I find the information?
5. _____ somebody please carry this chair?
6. _____ you give me a ride to the circus?
7. _____ we walk there together?
8. _____ anyone see us?
9. _____ Christmas be on a Sunday this year?
10. Who _____ create a better theory?

Compound Tenses

Present perfect tense signifies action, being, or state of being completed or perfected in present time.

Past perfect tense signifies action, being, or state of being completed or perfected before some definite past time.

Future perfect tense signifies action, being, or state of being that will be completed or perfected before some specified time in the future.

	ACTIVE VOICE
PRESENT PERFECT:	Lorrie *has* always *studied* diligently.
PAST PERFECT:	Lorrie *had studied* diligently before the examination.
FUTURE PERFECT:	Lorrie *will have studied* diligently before the examination.

	PASSIVE VOICE
PRESENT PERFECT:	The lesson *has been studied.*
PAST PERFECT:	The lesson *had been studied.*
FUTURE PERFECT:	The lesson *will have been studied.*

Exercise 4

Give the tense and voice of each verb.

1. Carlos has purchased a new camera.
2. The check will have been mailed before the payment is due.
3. I shall have completed this grammar exercise before class tomorrow.
4. The laundry had been left out in the rain.
5. That solution has been tried.
6. Have you read *Huckleberry Finn?*
7. Elaine had trained hard before the race.
8. The act will have been performed by the time you get there.
9. Wendy has told us her view of the subject.
10. The results had been announced.
11. Heavy fog has shrouded the little town.
12. The bicycle has been repaired.

Practice Power

▶ You must complete certain chores before you can go to your class party this evening. Write a note and tell in the first paragraph what you *had* already *completed* before you were told about the chores. In the second paragraph, tell what you *have completed* this morning, and in the third paragraph, tell what you *will have completed* by this evening.

Mood

Mood is the attribute or quality of a verb that denotes the manner in which the action, the being, or the state of being is expressed.

Indicative Mood

The indicative mood is used to state a fact, to deny a fact, or to ask a question.

STATES A FACT:	The population of Alaska *has increased* in recent years.
DENIES A FACT:	It *is* not always cold in Alaska.
ASKS A QUESTION:	When *was* the Alcan Highway *completed?*

All the six tenses are found in the indicative mood.

PRESENT:	She *writes* letters.
PAST:	She *wrote* the letters yesterday.
FUTURE:	She *will write* the letters today.
PRESENT PERFECT:	She *has written* many letters today.
PAST PERFECT:	She *had written* the letters before noon.
FUTURE PERFECT:	She *will have written* the letters before tomorrow.

Progressive Form of the Indicative Mood

The progressive form of the verb denotes an action as going on or in progress. In the active voice the various tenses of the verb *be* are used with the present participle of the main verb to form the progressive verb phrases.

PRESENT:	She *is writing* letters.
PAST:	She *was writing* letters yesterday.
FUTURE:	She *will be writing* letters today.
PRESENT PERFECT:	She *has been writing* many letters today.
PAST PERFECT:	She *had been writing* the letters before noon.
FUTURE PERFECT:	She *will have been writing* the letters before tomorrow.

The present and the past tenses of the progressive form are the two tenses most frequently used in the passive voice.

PRESENT:	The letter *is being written.*
PAST:	The letter *was being written.*

Exercise 1

Find the progressive verb phrases and give the tense and the voice of each.

1. Cory is teaching his dog a new trick.
2. She will be washing the dog tomorrow.
3. Hot chocolate was being served in the lodge.
4. Harriet was hiking when the snake bit her.
5. We had been talking for hours before the show.
6. Those people have been fishing all night.
7. Where is your new home being built?
8. As of tomorrow, we will have been training a week.
9. Helen has been feeding the tigers.
10. Four purple airplanes were flying over the field.

Practice Power

▶ Write a short paragraph describing a recent news event. Underline all the verbs in the indicative mood. Include at least one verb in the progressive form.

VERBS

Emphatic and Potential Forms of the Indicative Mood

Emphatic Form of the Indicative Mood

Use the emphatic form to give emphasis to the verb.

> Moral support *does lend* encouragement.
>
> High ideals *did lead* him to the nobler things of life.

Use the emphatic form only in the present and the past tenses of the active voice. The auxiliaries *do* and *does* before the present part of the verb form the present tense, and the auxiliary *did* before the present part of the verb forms the past tense.

In questions and in negative statements, *do, does,* and *did* are not used emphatically.

Exercise 1

Find the emphatic verb phrases and identify their tenses.

1. I did try my key in the lock.
2. She does love me.
3. Matthew and Claire do work well together.
4. He did think he had done the right thing.
5. Lucy does jog every afternoon.
6. Vernon did return the tapes.
7. I do see my mistake now.
8. The secretary did submit the report on time.
9. I did enjoy the first book, but I did not like the second.
10. You did receive the award this morning.
11. They did want you to know in advance.
12. My brother does play in the band.

Potential Form of the Indicative Mood

The potential form of the indicative mood is used to express permission, possibility, ability, necessity, or obligation.

PERMISSION:	You *may begin* the lecture, Robert.
POSSIBILITY:	Sheila *might return* tomorrow.
ABILITY:	My sister *can play* the violin.
NECESSITY:	You *must wind* this clock every night.
OBLIGATION:	We *should do* the work now.

The auxiliary verbs *may, might, can, could, must, should,* and *would* are used in the potential form.

Tenses of the Potential Form

The potential form is used in the present, the past, the present perfect, and the past perfect tenses, but not in the future tenses.

	ACTIVE VOICE
PRESENT TENSE:	We *must complete* the work.
PAST TENSE:	I *could* not *find* the paper.
PRESENT PERFECT TENSE:	He *might have broken* the chair.
PAST PERFECT TENSE:	You *should have packed* the lunch last night.

	PASSIVE VOICE
PRESENT TENSE:	All the work *must be completed.*
PAST TENSE:	The paper *could* not *be found.*
PRESENT PERFECT TENSE:	The chair *might have been broken.*
PAST PERFECT TENSE:	The lunch *should have been packed* last night.

Exercise 2

Identify the potential verb phrases and tell what form of expression they represent (permission, possibility, ability, necessity, or obligation).

1. Martin can swim faster than anyone in the state.
2. We should contribute to charity.
3. Rachel should have prepared her lesson.
4. Karl can speak German.
5. The campers might have lost their tent.
6. They could not find the trail.
7. You may borrow my guitar.
8. Tax forms must be filed by April 15.
9. You should have answered my question sooner.
10. Brad must get more outdoor exercise.
11. Oranges cannot grow in Alaska.
12. Tiffany may bring her friend along.

Outline for Special Forms of the Indicative

	PROGRESSIVE	EMPHATIC	POTENTIAL
USE:	Denotes action in progress	Lends emphasis to a statement	Expresses permission, possibility, ability, necessity, obligation
SIGN:	*ing* (present participle of the principal verb)	*Do, does,* or *did* used as auxiliaries	*May, can, must, might, could, should, would*
TENSE:	Present, past, future, present perfect, past perfect, future perfect	Present, past	Present, past, present perfect, past perfect
VOICE:	Active, passive	Active	Active, passive

Exercise 3

Name the special form, the tense, and the voice of each verb.

1. Too much sun does burn skin.
2. Gloria may have sent the package to your old address.
3. She did come to the party last night.
4. No one can disgrace me but myself.
5. The window must have been broken during the night.
6. Everyone did comment on his new hat.
7. Daniel should have combed his hair before they took the picture.
8. He has been wearing those yellow shoes every day.
9. Ron does work hard.
10. Lisa has been working at the hamburger stand.
11. Who could help her get a better job?
12. Randi is interviewing her tomorrow.
13. I do wash the dishes every night.
14. Their apartment is being painted.
15. The sharks are being fed.

Practice Power

▶ Write an imaginary dialogue in which you try to persuade another person—a parent, a friend, a coach—of your point of view. Use the emphatic and potential forms of the indicative mood in your sentences.

Imperative and Subjunctive Moods

Imperative Mood

Use the imperative mood to express a command in the second person. A mild command often takes the form of an entreaty or a request.

COMMAND: (you) *Present* arms!
ENTREATY: (you) *Have* pity on the man, my friends.
REQUEST: (you) *Close* the door quietly, Rose.

The present tense is the only tense in the imperative mood. The subject of a verb in the imperative mood is always in the second person, and it is usually not expressed.

Subjunctive Mood

The subjunctive mood generally expresses a wish or desire, an uncertainty, or a condition contrary to fact.

The subordinate conjunctions *if, as if, provided, though, lest, whether, unless,* and some of the potential auxiliaries are sometimes used to introduce a verb in the subjunctive mood. A subordinate conjunction or an auxiliary verb, however, is not always necessary when the verb is in the subjunctive mood.

WISH: Peace *be* to all! (no conjunction or auxiliary verb)

UNCERTAINTY: Whether that *be* true or not, we have not changed our plans. (with the subordinate conjunction *whether*)

CONTRARY TO FACT: If she *were* a queen, she could not be more gracious. (with the subordinate conjunction *if*)

382

In the subjunctive mood there are four tenses: the present, the past, the present perfect, and the past perfect. Study the subjunctive mood in the conjugations of the verbs *be* and *teach* on pages 397 and 400.

Exercise 1

Name the verbs in the imperative and the subjunctive moods. Explain what each verb expresses.

1. Take off your boots.
2. Long live the Cubs!
3. My sister would play the piano if she were here.
4. May she be happy in her new job!
5. Heaven help you!
6. Whether he be honest or not, we have to trust him.
7. We wish someone else were available.
8. Move to the rear of the elevator, please.
9. May the queen grant us this favor.
10. He looks as if he just swallowed a canary.

Practice Power

▶ **Supply the verb form called for in parentheses. All verbs are in the indicative mood except where indicated.**

1. The monks _____ books on sheepskin. (write—past tense, active voice)
2. The pizza _____ in a very short time. (consume—past tense, passive voice)
3. A modern bridge _____ over the lagoon. (build—present perfect tense, passive voice)
4. _____ of the fiendish monster. (beware—imperative mood, present tense, active voice)
5. Mount Rushmore in South Dakota _____ by many tourists. (visit—present tense, passive voice)
6. We _____ the bedroom as soon as the check comes. (redecorate—future tense, active voice)
7. Christopher Columbus _____ by Queen Isabella. (aid—past tense, passive voice)
8. They _____ many visitors this winter. (have—present perfect tense, active voice)

Agreement of Verb with Subject—*Part I*

Person and Number

The verb must always agree with its subject in person and number.

A verb may be in the first, second, or third person, and either singular or plural in number. What person and number it is depends upon the subject.

	SINGULAR NUMBER	PLURAL NUMBER
FIRST PERSON:	I draw.	Lanette and I draw. (we)
SECOND PERSON:	Keith, draw an apple. (you)	Students, draw an apple. (you)
THIRD PERSON:	Leah draws well. (she)	Henry and Jake draw well. (they)

Note that in the example, the verb keeps the same form except in the third person, singular number, when it ends in *s*. All verbs in the present tense take the *s* form in the third person, singular number.

The verb must agree with the subject even when the subject follows the verb, as in the case of a sentence beginning with the expletive *there*.

There *are* many *books* on the shelves.

One exception to agreement is the use of the forms *you are* and *you were*. These forms are used whether the subject is singular or plural.

Sara, *you are* a wonderful cook!
Children, *you are* not to play with matches.

Exercise 1

Give the person and number of each subject. Then select the correct form of the verb to complete each sentence.

1. There (is, are) twenty puppies in the kennel.
2. Mr. DiMartino (was, were) not home when I called.
3. In the garden (is, are) many bright flowers.
4. There (was, were) only one person in the car.
5. Morgan (give, gives) us moral support.
6. Native Americans (was, were) fine hunters.
7. Smooth roads (make, makes) driving easy.
8. You (is, are) a comical magician.
9. His friends (was, were) all amused.
10. The grocer (sell, sells) paper goods as well as food.
11. (Is, Are) you going to camp this summer?
12. (Was, Were) you on the honor roll this month?
13. Where (was, were) you this morning?
14. Why (is, are) crop rotation necessary?
15. There (is, are) large sulfur deposits in Texas and Louisiana.
16. *Silent Spring* (warn, warns) of the harmful effects of insecticides.
17. They (read, reads) the computer magazines every day.
18. The old chest (belong, belongs) to the museum.
19. The curators (think, thinks) the chest (contain, contains) ancient treasures.
20. She (worry, worries) about the consequences of her actions.

Doesn't and Don't

If the subject of a sentence is in the third person, *doesn't* is the correct form in the singular, and *don't* is the correct form in the plural.

> The coach *doesn't* want us for practice today.
> The clocks *don't* have the correct time.

In the first and second persons, the correct form is *don't,* whether the subject is singular or plural.

> I *don't* know whether alligators are in this swamp.
>
> We *don't* remember which path we took.
>
> Dave, *don't* mix those chemicals.
>
> Class, please *don't* forget to write the directions clearly.

Exercise 2

Select the correct form, *doesn't* or *don't*, to complete each sentence.

1. _____ it seem quiet since Franco went away?
2. Marsha _____ look very healthy.
3. Our plane _____ leave until after lunchtime.
4. _____ you understand the problem?
5. They _____ want to help push the car.
6. Julia _____ care whether she sees the play.
7. You _____ seem to notice the cold.
8. The sun _____ rise in the west.
9. The teacher _____ want Antonio to get hurt.
10. _____ he realize the value of close friends?
11. I _____ know who invented the submarine.
12. Michael _____ like tuna and tomato sandwiches.

Phrases and Parenthetical Expressions

A phrase or a parenthetical expression between the subject and the verb does not change the number of the verb. If the subject is singular, the verb must be singular; if plural, the verb must be plural.

> *One* of my sisters *goes* to college.

Exercise 3

Name the subject of each sentence and select the correct form of the verb to complete the sentence.

1. Several members of the team (practice, practices) here on Saturday mornings.
2. The delightful climate of the Hawaiian Islands (account, accounts) for the extensive tourist trade.
3. A stack of hot pancakes (was, were) placed on the table.
4. Jacqueline's description of her travels (was, were) thrilling.
5. This statue of Martin Luther King, Jr., together with its pedestal, (was, were) donated to the city.
6. Melanie, like her sisters, (is, are) very shy.
7. A shipment of oranges (is, are) expected soon.

8. The construction of new houses (seem, seems) shoddier than that of old ones.

9. The reference books, including a dictionary, (was, were) on the table.

10. The legends of Camelot (provide, provides) source material for the fiction and poetry of many generations.

11. The second game of the series (was, were) played in San Francisco.

12. Tuition, as well as the cost of books, (has, have) increased.

Practice Power

▶ **Complete each thought below. Make sure that the verb agrees with the subject. Use only action verbs in your sentences.**

1. The bus that passes my house . . .

2. My picture taken last year . . .

3. People living in France . . .

4. Books about science fiction . . .

5. Rob, as well as his friends, . . .

6. A meeting of foreign diplomats . . .

7. The sun shining through my window . . .

8. The redwood trees of California . . .

Agreement of Verb with Subject—*Part II*

Compound Subjects Connected by *And*

Compound subjects connected by *and* require a plural verb unless the subjects refer to the same person or thing or express a single idea.

> Ken and Cheryl *were* at the game.
>
> The writer and illustrator of this book *is* well known.

Exercise 1

Select the correct form of the verb. Give the reason for your choice.

1. Christine and Nancy (work, works) together.
2. The president and manager (was, were) not in her office.
3. (Was, Were) your father and mother at the meeting?
4. Ramona and her friend (is, are) expected soon.
5. Racquetball and soccer (is, are) fast-moving sports.
6. What (do, does) your parents and friends think about your haircut?
7. Just bread and water (seem, seems) a Spartan diet.
8. Oranges and limes (is, are) both citrus fruits.
9. My friend and classmate (write, writes) to me weekly.
10. Here (come, comes) the president and the treasurer together.
11. Purebred dogs and cats (is, are) registered.
12. His purpose and aim (is, are) to succeed.
13. The electricians and plumbers (agree, agrees) to strike in sympathy.
14. My dictionary and encyclopedia (is, are) on CD-ROMs.
15. Eggs and fruit (was, were) served.

Compound Subjects
Preceded by *Each* and *Every*

Two or more singular subjects connected by *and* but preceded by *each, every, many a,* or *no* require a singular verb.

> *Has* every pen and pencil been placed on the desk?

Exercise 2

Select the correct form of the verb. Give the reason for your choice.

1. Many a man and woman (buy, buys) foolish things at times.
2. Every aunt and uncle (was, were) at the family reunion.
3. Every town and borough (was, were) represented.
4. Many a cat and dog (has, have) tried to do that trick.
5. Every window and door in the house (was, were) blown open.
6. Almost every plate and glass (was, were) in the sink.
7. Each lion and tiger (is, are) dangerous when angry.
8. Many a firefighter and police officer (save, saves) lives.
9. Every house and store (was, were) covered with mud.
10. Many a puppet and beanbag (was, were) made by Cynthia.
11. Each day and hour (bring, brings) new trials.
12. Many a boy and girl (know, knows) how to play checkers.
13. Each senator and representative (was, were) present at the peace march.
14. No fortune and no position in life (make, makes) a person reconsider his or her goals.
15. Every nut and bolt (was, were) rusted tight.

Compound Subjects
Connected by *Or* or *Nor*

When compound subjects are connected by *or* or *nor,* the verb agrees with the subject closer to it.

> Neither the lion nor the <u>tiger</u> *is* hungry.
> Neither the lion nor the <u>tigers</u> *are* hungry.
> Neither he nor <u>I</u> *am* hungry.

Exercise 3

Select the correct form of the verb. Give the reason for your choice.

1. Neither math nor science (is, are) hard for me.
2. (Is, Are) either Anne or Eileen going?
3. Neither the letter nor the postcard (was, were) for me.
4. Lillian or her sister (is, are) going parachuting.
5. Neither the pilot nor the copilot (like, likes) to watch people jump from the plane.
6. Neither the horse nor the cows (was, were) warm enough during the blizzard.
7. Neither Dolores nor I (was, were) prepared for the test.
8. Either this cake or those candies (was, were) eaten by Claudia.
9. Either the vice president or her secretary (answer, answers) the angry questions.
10. Neither the tulips nor the daffodils (has, have) bloomed yet.
11. Neither I nor he (think, thinks) the woman is guilty.
12. Neither the trunk nor the box (has, have) arrived.
13. Either the door or the windows (was, were) not closed.
14. Neither wind nor waves (deter, deters) Rachel from swimming in the lake.
15. Neither the computer nor the printer (work, works) properly.

Practice Power

▶ Write a complete sentence for each of the compound subjects. In parentheses are the connecting word or words that should be used. Be sure to keep the verbs in the present tense.

1. cucumbers/radishes (either, or)
2. pen/pencil (each, and)
3. soccer/football (and)
4. airplane/space shuttle (and)
5. package/letters (neither, nor)
6. spaghetti/meatballs (and)
7. musician/artist (many a, and)
8. players/coach (either, or)

Agreement of Verb with Subject—*Part III*

Collective Nouns

A collective noun requires a singular verb if the idea expressed by the subject is thought of as a unit. A plural verb may be used if the idea expressed by the subject denotes separate individuals.

> The flock of sheep *was* seen on the mountainside. (unit)
> The flock of sheep *were* grazing. (sheep in the flock)

Exercise 1

Name the subject and select the correct form of the verb.

1. The choir (rehearse, rehearses) on Sunday evenings.
2. A group of whales (are, is) called a pod.
3. The committee (was, were) divided on the proposal to collect trash every ten days.
4. That team (display, displays) good spirit.
5. (Has, Have) the group submitted their reports?
6. The class (has, have) finished their projects.
7. The jury (has, have) reached a verdict.
8. The orchestra (offer, offers) a reward for the return of the violin.
9. (Has, Have) the crew sailed together before?
10. The drove of horses (was, were) sold to the farmer.

Distributive and Indefinite Pronouns

The distributive pronouns *each, either,* and *neither* and the indefinite pronouns *one, anyone, no one, anybody, nobody, everyone, everybody, someone,* and *somebody* are always singular and require singular verbs.

Each of the brothers *has* a new car.

Exercise 2

Name the subject of each sentence and give the correct present tense form of the verb in parentheses.

1. Somebody always (call) when I am asleep.
2. No one (want) to walk to the store.
3. Anyone who can think that way (frighten) me.
4. One of her favorite beverages, coffee, (come) from Brazil.
5. Neither of the men (want) to leave the game.
6. Each of the clowns (ride) a unicycle.
7. (Have) anyone taken my ticket?
8. (Be) either of your brothers going on the hike?
9. Everyone in the parade (carry) a banner.
10. Each of the bakers (wear) an apron.
11. Someone (keep) asking me your name.
12. Nobody except Margaret (know) what happened.
13. Neither of the recruiters (be) finding many interested students.
14. (Do) anyone help those refugees?
15. Everyone (like) to see the sun after weeks of rain.

Special Singular and Plural Nouns

Some nouns that are plural in form, but usually singular in meaning, require singular verbs. These include *aeronautics*, *athletics* (training), *civics*, *economics*, *mathematics*, *measles*, *molasses*, *mumps*, *news*, and *physics*.

Measles *is* a disease of the young.

Other nouns are usually considered plural and require plural verbs. These nouns include *ashes, clothes, eaves, glasses, goods, pincers, pliers, proceeds, scales, scissors, shears, suspenders, tongs, trousers,* and *tweezers.*

My scissors *have* been lost.

Exercise 3

Choose the correct verb form.

1. Athletics (develop, develops) the muscles.
2. Molasses (is, are) sweet and sticky.
3. His trousers (is, are) at the cleaners.
4. Measles (require, requires) careful treatment.
5. The ashes (is, are) still hot.
6. Tongs (is, are) used to remove the cinders.
7. Physics (is, are) a class with interesting experiments.
8. (Does, Do) these pliers belong to you?
9. The proceeds from the candle sale (was, were) enough to buy new instruments.
10. News (is, are) sometimes very upsetting.
11. The scales (was, were) weighted wrong.
12. Sarah's glasses (has, have) a small butterfly on them.
13. The eaves (is, are) sagging under the weight of the snow.
14. The goods (was, were) not delivered on time.
15. Civics (is, are) required in some high schools.

Exercise 4 REVIEW

Name the subject of each sentence and choose the correct verb form to complete the sentence.

1. (Doesn't, Don't) my brother drive his car well?

2. Each of the candidates (is, are) preparing for the campaign.

3. Today's news (bring, brings) joy to many people.

4. (Has, Have) everyone made a donation?

5. Everyone (was, were) happy when peace was declared.

6. Either Colleen or she (is, are) sure to be there.

7. Coal and iron (is, are) mined from the earth.

8. Measles (cause, causes) skin eruptions.

9. *The Adventures of Tom Sawyer* (is, are) very humorous.

10. Henry (doesn't, don't) like mushrooms.

11. Their home, as well as their possessions, (was, were) destroyed in the fire.

12. The band (is, are) marching into the stadium.

13. There (is, are) two motorboats on the river.

14. Several of my paintings (was, were) exhibited at the gallery.

15. My father and my brother (like, likes) fire trucks.

Putting It All Together

Choose a crime or heroic deed from the news or your history book and write an eyewitness account of the deed. First, describe the event using active voice whenever possible. Then rewrite your account using passive voice.

Present each description to the class. If you like, develop a character to go with each description. Invite your classmates to explain which account of events they prefer and why.

Chapter Challenge

Read this paragraph carefully and answer the questions.

¹"Look out!" screamed half a dozen voices as a boy old enough to know better dashed into the street from between two parked cars. ²What followed was a medley of screeching brakes, frightened screams, and confused shouts. ³The noise died to an awed hush as a doctor pushed his way through the crowd and knelt beside the injured lad. ⁴Was the boy beyond help? ⁵Luckily, he was not, for it is that same boy who is writing this story from a wheelchair, where he will spend several months repenting of one moment's folly. ⁶Why I did such a foolish thing I will never know! ⁷Sure, I was intent on catching the ball, but I should have stopped once I came to the street. ⁸I might have died if that doctor hadn't arrived so quickly. ⁹May I never forget this painful experience and the lesson it taught me!

1. What mood and tense is the first verb in this paragraph?
2. Is the verb *screamed* in the first sentence regular or irregular?
3. Is the verb *dashed* in the first sentence transitive or intransitive?
4. In the first sentence *parked* is a verb functioning as what other part of speech?
5. Name the three verbs in the third sentence.
6. In what mood and tense are these three verbs?
7. Name the linking verbs in the fifth sentence.
8. Find a progressive verb phrase in the fifth sentence.
9. In what tense is *will spend* in the fifth sentence?
10. What voice is *will know* in the sixth sentence? Give the principal parts of the verb *know.*
11. Name the potential verb phrase in the seventh sentence and give its tense and voice.
12. Name the potential verb phrase in the eighth sentence that expresses possibility. In what tense is it?
13. Name the verb in the ninth sentence that is in the subjunctive mood and explain what it expresses.
14. Give the principal parts of the verb *taught* in the ninth sentence.

Conjugation

Conjugation is the orderly arrangement of a verb according to voice, mood, tense, person, and number.

Conjugation of the Verb *Be*

	PRESENT	PAST	PAST PARTICIPLE
PRINCIPAL PARTS:	be	was	been

Indicative Mood

Singular	*Plural*
PRESENT TENSE	
I am	We are
You are	You are
He (she, it) is	They are
PAST TENSE	
I was	We were
You were	You were
He was	They were
FUTURE TENSE	
I shall be	We shall be
You will be	You will be
He will be	They will be
PRESENT PERFECT TENSE	
I have been	We have been
You have been	You have been
He has been	They have been
PAST PERFECT TENSE	
I had been	We had been
You had been	You had been
He had been	They had been
FUTURE PERFECT TENSE	
I shall have been	We shall have been
You will have been	You will have been
He will have been	They will have been

Subjunctive Mood

Singular	*Plural*

PRESENT TENSE

If I be	If we be
If you be	If you be
If he be	If they be

PAST TENSE

If I were	If we were
If you were	If you were
If he were	If they were

PRESENT PERFECT TENSE

If I have been	If we have been
If you have been	If you have been
If he have been	If they have been

PAST PERFECT TENSE

If I had been	If we had been
If you had been	If you had been
If he had been	If they had been

Imperative Mood

PRESENT TENSE

Be (be you)

INFINITIVES

PRESENT: To be

PERFECT: To have been

PARTICIPLES

PRESENT: Being

PAST: Been

PERFECT: Having been

Conjugation of the Verb *Teach*

	PRESENT	PAST	PAST PARTICIPLE
PRINCIPAL PARTS:	teach	taught	taught

Indicative Mood Active Voice

Singular | *Plural*

PRESENT TENSE

I teach	We teach
You teach	You teach
He teaches	They teach

PAST TENSE

I taught	We taught
You taught	You taught
He taught	They taught

FUTURE TENSE

I shall teach	We shall teach
You will teach	You will teach
He will teach	They will teach

PRESENT PERFECT TENSE

I have taught	We have taught
You have taught	You have taught
He has taught	They have taught

PAST PERFECT TENSE

I had taught	We had taught
You had taught	You had taught
He had taught	They had taught

FUTURE PERFECT TENSE

I shall have taught	We shall have taught
You will have taught	You will have taught
He will have taught	They will have taught

Indicative Mood Passive Voice

Singular   *Plural*

PRESENT TENSE

I am taught   We are taught
You are taught   You are taught
He is taught   They are taught

PAST TENSE

I was taught   We were taught
You were taught   You were taught
He was taught   They were taught

FUTURE TENSE

I shall be taught   We shall be taught
You will be taught   You will be taught
He will be taught   They will be taught

PRESENT PERFECT TENSE

I have been taught   We have been taught
You have been taught   You have been taught
He has been taught   They have been taught

PAST PERFECT TENSE

I had been taught   We had been taught
You had been taught   You had been taught
He had been taught   They had been taught

FUTURE PERFECT TENSE

I shall have been taught   We shall have been taught
You will have been taught   You will have been taught
He will have been taught   They will have been taught

Subjunctive Mood Active Voice

Singular   *Plural*

PRESENT TENSE
If I teach   If we teach
If you teach   If you teach
If he teach   If they teach

PAST TENSE
If I taught   If we taught
If you taught   If you taught
If he taught   If they taught

PRESENT PERFECT TENSE
If I have taught   If we have taught
If you have taught   If you have taught
If he have taught   If they have taught

PAST PERFECT TENSE
If I had taught   If we had taught
If you had taught   If you had taught
If he had taught   If they had taught

Subjunctive Mood Passive Voice

Singular   *Plural*

PRESENT TENSE
If I be taught   If we be taught
If you bc taught   If you be taught
If he be taught   If they be taught

PAST TENSE
If I were taught   If we were taught
If you were taught   If you were taught
If he were taught   If they were taught

PRESENT PERFECT TENSE
If I have been taught   If we have been taught
If you have been taught If you have been taught
If he have been taught   If they have been taught

PAST PERFECT TENSE
If I had been taught   If we had been taught
If you had been taught   If you had been taught
If he had been taught   If they had been taught

Imperative Mood

PRESENT TENSE

Active Voice

Teach (teach you)

Passive Voice

Be taught (be you taught)

INFINITIVES

PRESENT: To teach

To be taught

PERFECT: To have taught

To have been taught

PARTICIPLES

PRESENT: Teaching

Being taught

PAST: Taught

Taught

PERFECT: Having taught

Having been taught

Synopsis of a Verb

A synopsis is an abbreviated conjugation. It is made by giving the form for one person and number of each tense in a designated mood or moods.

Synopsis of the Verb *Teach*

(Indicative mood, third person, singular number)

	Active Voice	*Passive Voice*
PRESENT TENSE:	He teaches	He is taught
PAST TENSE:	He taught	He was taught
FUTURE TENSE:	He will teach	He will be taught
PRESENT PERFECT TENSE:	He has taught	He has been taught
PAST PERFECT TENSE:	He had taught	He had been taught
FUTURE PERFECT TENSE:	He will have taught	He will have been taught

15

VERBALS: PARTICIPLES, GERUNDS, INFINITIVES

Participles

Verb forms called verbals are used as other parts of speech. Three types of verbals—participles, gerunds, and infinitives—will be studied in this chapter.

A participle is a verb form that is used as an adjective. Participles often end in *ing* or *ed.*

> The children, *bearing* signs, marched through the park.
>
> Heavy rain was the forecast *announced* on the radio.

Bearing and *announced* are participles. Both words are derived from verbs and express action. *Bearing* has a direct object, *signs,* and *announced* is modified by the adverbial phrase *on the radio.* The participles are used as adjectives in that they modify nouns; *bearing* modifies *children,* and *announced* modifies *forecast.*

Properties of the Participle

A participle has the properties of a verb and an adjective.

PROPERTIES OF A VERB	PROPERTIES OF AN ADJECTIVE
It is derived from a verb.	It limits a noun or a pronoun.
It may take an object.	
It may be modified by an adverb or an adverbial phrase.	

About the Photograph

These students are doing double duty by organizing and playing in a football game after school. Did you know that words called verbals do double duty, too?

Forms of the Participle

A participle has voice and tense, but it does not have person and number.

	ACTIVE	PASSIVE
PRESENT:	seeing	being seen
PAST:	seen	seen
PERFECT:	having seen	having been seen

Position of the Participle

As an adjective, a participle may be placed after the noun or the pronoun it limits, or it may be used in an introductory phrase.

> Samuel Morse, *having invented* the electromagnetic telegraph, asked for monetary aid from Congress.

> *Having invented* the electromagnetic telegraph, Samuel Morse asked for monetary aid from Congress.

In both sentences, the participle *having invented* modifies *Morse.* In the first sentence, this participle follows the noun; in the second sentence, it is used in the introductory phrase.

Note that the participial phrase *having invented the electromagnetic telegraph* is a nonrestrictive phrase in both sample sentences. It is not a necessary part of the sentences and could be omitted. Participial phrases that are restrictive are essential to the meaning of a sentence. Commas set off nonrestrictive phrases but do not set off restrictive phrases.

> The man *asking for monetary aid from Congress* was Samuel Morse.

The participial phrase *asking for monetary aid from Congress* modifies the word *man* and limits it to a particular man. No commas are needed.

Exercise 1

Name each participle and tell which noun or pronoun it describes.

1. The rivers flowing into the Pacific Ocean have little inland transportation.
2. Cotton raised in Egypt has long, silky fibers.
3. The great oak, broken by the wind, fell to the ground.
4. A change made in the Constitution is called an amendment.
5. Congress cannot make laws prohibiting freedom of speech.
6. Fran gazed at the pictures hanging on the wall.
7. Did you hear the carolers singing in the street?
8. Finding themselves hopelessly lost in the dark, Tom and Thad decided to sleep in the woods until morning.
9. The lifeguard watched the children playing on the beach.
10. Jumping into the water, she caught the small boy as he fell in the waves.
11. His mother came running, calling his father to come, too.
12. David, waking during the night, found the cat at the door.
13. Realizing that the concert had already started, Fran dashed across the street.
14. Hillary watched her marbles rolling down the hill.
15. Noticing my sunburned face, Sergio gave me his hat.

Exercise 2

Complete each sentence with an appropriate thought.
Draw an arrow from the participle to the word it modifies.

1. Shouting joyfully, _____ .
2. Having discovered the hiding place, _____ .
3. _____ grown in California _____ .
4. _____ sitting on the bench _____ .
5. _____ being a very shy person, _____ .

Practice Power

▶ Compose five sentences that correctly use participial phrases.

The Correct Use of Participles

Tense of Participles

The present participle generally denotes action taking place at the same time as the verb.

> The chorus, *singing* the song, entered the hall. (present participle)

The perfect participle denotes action completed before the action of the verb.

> *Having finished* their work, the employees were dismissed. (perfect participle)

Dangling Participles

A participle does the work of a verb and an adjective. As an adjective, the participle modifies a noun or a pronoun. A dangling participle is one that modifies no other word in the sentence. Avoid writing sentences with dangling participles.

> *Walking* to school, the dog ran away.

In this sentence, *walking* does not modify any noun. Who is walking to school? It is not the dog. The participle *walking* must have a word that it limits. To correct a dangling participle, supply the missing noun or pronoun.

> Walking to school, *Becky* saw the dog run away.

Adding the noun *Becky* makes the meaning clear.

Exercise 1

Choose the correct tense of each participle to complete each sentence.

1. (Waving, Having waved) banners in front of the embassy for some time, the demonstrators moved on.
2. (Reading, Having read) the novel, Joan wrote a review of it for the school paper.
3. (Running, Having run) beside the car, the dog barked continuously.
4. Andrea spent three weeks (writing, having written) a paper about the Harlem Renaissance.
5. (Walking, Having walked) to school every morning, I see the sun rise.
6. (Eating, Having eaten) breakfast, Melinda packed a lunch to take with her.
7. (Feeding, Having fed) the fish, we watched them chase one another around the aquarium.

Exercise 2

The following sentences contain dangling participles. Rewrite them correctly.

1. Holding the child's hand, the elephant looked so big.
2. Having worked all morning, the job still was not finished.
3. Keeping my promise, the room was left in order.
4. Sitting on the porch, the storm passed.
5. Reading a book, the bus passed my stop.
6. Skipping down the street, the car arrived first.
7. Whistling loudly, the taxi sped away.
8. Folding one load of laundry, the dryer stopped.
9. Being suspended from school, Dad was very angry.
10. Opening the window, the robin flew away.

Practice Power

▶ Write two sentences for each verb below using the present participle form and the perfect participle form.

1. ride   2. swim   3. study

More Uses of Participles

Participial Adjectives

Not all words derived from verbs and ending in *ing* or *ed* are participles. Note the use of the word *running* in this sentence.

The *running* water wore away the stone.

Running is a descriptive word in the usual position of an adjective—before the noun. This participial form is one of the types of descriptive adjectives; it is called a participial adjective. A participial adjective

- describes a noun or pronoun.
- does not act as a verb.
- may not take an object.
- has the usual position of an adjective—before the noun or after a linking verb.

The Nominative Absolute

A participle may be used with a noun or a pronoun in an independent adverbial phrase to express the time, the condition, the cause, or the circumstances of the action expressed by the main verb in the sentence. The noun or the pronoun used in this absolute construction is in the nominative case, and the participle modifies it.

The game being over, the players left the field.

The sentence's introductory phrase is a nominative absolute. It expresses the circumstances of the players' leaving the field. The participle *being* modifies *game,* the noun in the nominative absolute.

The noun in a nominative absolute is not the subject of any verb. It is part of an independent adverbial phrase and is modified by the participle.

Compare these sentences.

Having thrown the rider, the bull dashed away.
The rider having been thrown, the bull dashed away.

In the first sentence the participle modifies *bull,* the subject. In the second sentence the participle *having been thrown* is part of the nominative absolute. The participle in this sentence modifies *rider,* the noun in the nominative absolute.

Exercise 1

Identify each participial adjective and the noun it modifies.

1. The neighbors watched the burning building with dismay.
2. An unopened letter lay on the desk.
3. Emmanuel's blazing eyes revealed his anger.
4. Mr. Mazzenga is a traveling sales representative.
5. The visiting professor had gone back to Detroit.
6. Experience is a trying teacher.
7. Drifting snow blocked the highway.
8. The doctor knelt over the injured calf.
9. Mom seems pleased with the news.
10. Running water is a luxury in many parts of the world.

Exercise 2

Write out the nominative absolute in each sentence. Identify the participle and the noun it modifies.

1. The lifeguard having jumped into the water, the child's mother came running.
2. The concert having started, the doors were closed.
3. The armistice having been signed, fighting ceased.
4. The parade approaching, the crowd cheered wildly.
5. The cars returned to the highway, the blizzard having finally ended.

Exercise 3 REVIEW

Name each participle and tell which noun it modifies.

1. Francis, whistling quietly, learned the tune.
2. We heard Jill singing in the next room.
3. Conquistadors having made the initial explorations, the Crown quickly claimed authority.
4. *Common Sense* is a pamphlet written by Thomas Paine during the American Revolution.
5. Urging separation from England, Paine captured the imagination of the colonial rebels.
6. The fire, spreading rapidly, caused great alarm.
7. We enjoyed a delicious Japanese meal, prepared by a trained chef.
8. Afflicted by allergies, Connie sneezed and sneezed.
9. The road leading to the lake has been washed away.
10. Ground having been broken, construction began immediately.

Complete each sentence with an appropriate participial phrase.

11. The house _____ began to deteriorate.
12. _____ , the guests departed.
13. The Jacksons own the sailboat _____ .
14. The baby _____ was not injured.
15. The doctor _____ asked some questions.
16. _____ , they set out for a day's ride.
17. _____ , the company made a generous offer.
18. New Orleans, _____ , controls much river trade.
19. _____ , the governor climbed onto the stage.
20. _____ , she left home.

Practice Power

▶ Use ten of the participles listed below in sentences of your own. Choose five to write as participial phrases and five to write as participial adjectives.

A. criticized	**E.** marked	**I.** having delivered
B. cruising	**F.** remembering	**J.** closing
C. discovered	**G.** rewriting	**K.** searching
D. having pretended	**H.** rewritten	**L.** imagining

LESSON 4

Gerunds

A gerund is a verb form ending in *ing* that is used as a noun.

Properties of the Gerund

A gerund has the properties of a verb and a noun. For this reason it is sometimes called a verbal noun.

PROPERTIES OF A VERB

It is derived from a verb.

It may take an object.

It may be modified by an adverb or an adverbial phrase.

PROPERTIES OF A NOUN

It is used as a noun.

Uses of the Gerund

As a noun, a gerund may be used as the subject or the object of a verb, as a subjective complement, as the object of a preposition, or as an appositive.

Traveling to distant places is a joy. (subject)

She enjoyed *skating* on the lake. (direct object)

His favorite pastime is *reading* biographies. (subjective complement)

He began by *speaking* to the jury. (object of preposition)

My appointed task, *washing* the car, kept me busy. (appositive)

Name the verb from which each gerund in the sentences above is derived, and point out the adverbial modifier or the object of each gerund.

Exercise 1

The gerunds in the following sentences are used as subjects. Identify the gerunds and name any direct objects or adverbial modifiers that follow them.

1. Sleeping in the park is forbidden.
2. Reading in the dark can hurt your eyes.
3. Playing baseball every afternoon keeps Jerri from doing homework.
4. Building sand castles is not my idea of a good time.
5. Watching the birth of the calf moved him to tears.
6. Finding dry firewood after the rain may be impossible.
7. Holding the sleeping child in one arm left her other arm free to open the door.
8. Riding a bicycle on the sidewalk is illegal in many places.
9. Jumping the boxes in the hallway caused Melanie to twist her ankle.
10. Driving during a rainstorm can be difficult.

Complete each sentence with an appropriate gerund used as a subject.

11. _____ is dangerous work.
12. _____ is fun for me.
13. _____ helps increase your vocabulary.
14. _____ is a good health habit.
15. _____ takes courage.

Exercise 2

The gerunds in the following sentences are used as direct objects. Identify the gerunds and name any direct objects or adverbial modifiers that follow them.

1. City ordinance forbids swimming in the lagoon.
2. Molly has just finished painting a picture of her canary.
3. Does Jeremy prefer taking the train?
4. Angie hates seeing violence on television.
5. The gardener has finished mowing the lawn.
6. Mr. Lavell stood waiting in the freezing rain.
7. The printer stopped printing.
8. Maura enjoys reading the newspaper.

Gerund Phrases

A gerund phrase consists of the gerund and its complements and modifiers. The entire gerund phrase acts as a noun.

Protecting the forests is the work of forest rangers.
Courtesy demands *answering an invitation promptly.*

Exercise 3

Complete each sentence with an appropriate gerund phrase used as a direct object.

1. Our opening exercises include _____ .
2. Do you enjoy _____ ?
3. Jessica proposed _____ .
4. We should avoid _____ .
5. Have they begun _____ ?

Exercise 4

The gerund phrases in the following sentences are used as subjective complements. Name each gerund phrase, and then rewrite the sentence substituting the gerund phrase for the subject and the subject for the gerund phrase.

1. An important industry in Australia is raising sheep.
2. Andrea's work is teaching reading.
3. My favorite kind of vacation is camping in the mountains.
4. The problem is finding the owner.
5. Jacob's duty is answering the telephone.

Complete each sentence with an appropriate gerund phrase used as a subjective complement.

6. The lifeguard's job is _____ .
7. The guide dog's duty was _____ .
8. Brian's greatest pleasure is _____ .
9. Kelly's goal is _____ .
10. Members of both clubs were _____ .

Exercise 5

The gerunds in the following sentences are used as objects of prepositions. Name the gerund and the preposition in each sentence. Give the verb from which the gerund is derived.

1. Do you have any objections to building the garage now?
2. She followed the directions for assembling the bike.
3. Don keeps in shape by running five miles every morning.
4. Tricia earned money for her vacation by mowing lawns.
5. He was commended for answering in a clear voice.
6. By pressing that button, you clear the screen.
7. Lauren's family was surprised by her taking the job.
8. By exercising daily, physical fitness can be maintained.
9. Leon got the job by calling the office every day.
10. The band prepared for the contest by practicing daily.

Complete each sentence with an appropriate gerund phrase used as the object of a preposition.

11. Do you find pleasure in _____ ?
12. What is the most effective way of _____ ?
13. Malik excels in _____ .
14. This will be a good reward for _____ .
15. Lisa got the party going by _____ .

Exercise 6

The gerunds in the following sentences are used as appositives. Name each gerund phrase used as an appositive, and tell which word it explains.

1. One of the major agricultural activities of the Midwest, raising corn, can rob the soil of its minerals.
2. Rachel's problem, learning the language, was difficult.
3. The programmer's task, creating a simple database, took longer than expected.
4. Ellen continues to pursue her lifelong ambition, becoming an acrobatic tightrope walker.
5. Their current activity, planting shrubs, may take hours.
6. Her favorite recreation, playing horseshoes, does not appeal to many people.

7. The third race, jumping the hurdles, is expected to be close.

8. The most important part of the lesson, making an outline, involves careful thought.

9. Eli likes his assignment, guarding the cupcakes.

10. The architects enjoyed their assignment, designing an inner-city police station.

Complete each sentence with an appropriate gerund phrase used as an appositive.

11. A thrilling winter sport, _____ , is enjoyed by our family.

12. My task, _____ , is always fun.

13. Debbie's hobby, _____ , occupies much of her time.

14. Marcus enjoys his daily exercise, _____ .

15. His summer job, _____ , gave him good experience.

Exercise 7   REVIEW

Name each gerund and tell how it is used in the sentence.

1. Ramona has considered taking a trip to Africa.

2. Raising the lid was a difficult task.

3. Irrigation is a means of converting desert land into fertile fields.

4. A common irrigation method is bringing water down from the mountains.

5. Tuan's task, directing traffic, was a challenge.

6. They enhanced their presentation by showing slides.

7. Exploring the attic is rainy day fun.

8. I remember writing that letter.

9. Wondering what you had done with it made me anxious.

10. You could help by returning the letter to me.

11. Saying those things was very unkind of me.

12. Joe's job, tracing unclaimed packages, is interesting.

13. Your singing the new song inspired everyone.

14. One of Manuel's favorite activities is snorkeling.

15. The latest trend, wearing two pairs of socks at one time, was stretching the shoes into odd shapes.

Exercise 8

Complete each sentence with an appropriate gerund phrase and tell how the gerund phrase is used.

1. Maureen jogs around the campus before _____ .
2. Windmills are used for _____ .
3. _____ requires special skill.
4. The students enjoyed _____ .
5. _____ is a fun and inexpensive form of recreation.
6. The clerk's job, _____ , was made easier by the new computer.
7. Paul tried _____ .
8. The process of _____ is taught by the career guidance counselor.
9. _____ can be fun.
10. _____ gives us a knowledge of our world.

Practice Power

▶ Locate three pictures in your social studies or science textbooks. Write a sentence for each picture, using a gerund phrase. Vary the use of the gerund phrase with each new sentence.

More About *ing* Words

Nouns and Pronouns Modifying Gerunds

A noun or a pronoun that modifies a gerund is usually in the possessive case.

> Cormack approves of *Wendy's* joining the club.
> Cormack approves of *our* joining the club.

Nouns Ending in *ing*

Many nouns end in *ing*. Some of these are formed from verbs and others are not. Do not mistake *ing* nouns for gerunds, participles, and other parts of speech.

> The *barking* of the dog aroused our attention.

Barking is a noun used as the subject of the verb *aroused*. It is modified by the article *the* and by an adjectival phrase, *of the dog*. An *ing* noun

- may not take an object.
- may not be modified by an adverb.
- is often preceded by the article *the* and followed by the preposition *of*.
- may have a plural form.

Recognizing Nouns, Gerunds, and Participles

Words ending in *ing* may be participles, participial adjectives, gerunds, *ing* nouns, or the progressive verb forms. Note the use of the word *singing* in these sentences:

> The *singing* of the birds was lovely. (*ing* noun)
> The boy *singing* the solo is my cousin. (participle)
> Claire takes *singing* lessons. (participial adjective)
> We enjoyed *singing* that song. (gerund)
> The choir has been *singing* for an hour.
>   (progressive verb form)

Exercise 1

Select the correct word to complete each sentence.

1. (Me, My) playing the French horn at midnight upsets my neighbors.
2. Joan would not approve (Bill, Bill's) attending the conference.
3. There is no doubt about (she, her) being the winner.
4. (Them, Their) being late worried us.
5. She was pleased by (him, his) returning her letter.
6. The (cat, cat's) purring pleased the baby.
7. There was some question about (Marilyn, Marilyn's) being able to pass the test.
8. (Duane, Duane's) making the team was cause for celebration.
9. Miles was afraid of the (company, company's) being robbed.
10. The coach noted (Darlene, Darlene's) jumping ability.

Exercise 2

Name the *ing* nouns and tell if each one is used as a subject, a direct object, or an object of a preposition.

1. We could hear the sighing of the wind in the trees.
2. He gave part of his earnings to charity.
3. The baby was awakened by the crashing of the waves.
4. We were frightened by the owl's screeching.
5. Have the Impressionist paintings gone on exhibit yet?
6. Confucius had many wise sayings.
7. The harvesting of the corn was hard work.
8. In all games, the feelings of the players must be remembered.
9. Scott's father had misgivings about his decision.
10. Our attention was attracted by the flashing of the lights on the sign.
11. The exercising of our freedoms requires good judgment.
12. Her timing was perfect.
13. Did Tim attend the meeting?
14. The writing of William Faulkner depicts life in the South.
15. The paying of the bills is a monthly ritual for my mother.

Exercise 3

Name the *ing* words and identify each as a participle, a participial adjective, a gerund, an *ing* noun, or a verb in the progressive form.

1. Tying garlic on a string around his neck didn't help his cold.
2. The school bell has been ringing every five minutes for the last hour.
3. Studying a foreign language helps us understand our own.
4. The neighborhood pranksters kept ringing our doorbell.
5. The girls took whatever was necessary for the camping trip.
6. Philip has a ringing in his ears.
7. Jacklyn was making a musical instrument as a science project.
8. Harold keeps losing his house keys.
9. We were watching a broken fragment of rainbow after the storm.
10. Jerome, listening intently to the radio headset, did not hear the approaching tornado.
11. The handbell ringing at the wrong pitch is that one.
12. Fearing a dead battery in the cold weather, he kept starting his car.
13. Her endearing personality does not excuse this behavior.
14. The ringing bells bothered people all over town.
15. The field being plowed, the farmer planted the seeds.

Practice Power

▶ **Choose one *ing* word. Then use that word in the following five ways in five different sentences.**

1. a participle
2. a participial adjective
3. a gerund
4. an *ing* noun
5. a verb in the progressive form

Infinitives

An infinitive is a verb form, usually preceded by *to*, that is used as a noun, an adjective, or an adverb.

> *To read* good books improves the mind.
>
> I have planned *to leave* early.

The infinitives *to read* and *to leave* are derived from verbs. *To read* has a direct object *books* and *to leave* is modified by the adverb *early.* Both infinitives are used as nouns, for the infinitive phrase *to read good books* is the subject of *improves* and the phrase *to leave early* is the direct object of *have planned.*

In the following sentences, the infinitives are used as an adjective and as adverbs.

> The florist has flowers *to sell.*
> (adjective—limits the noun *flowers*)
>
> The star sang *to please* the audience.
> (adverb—modifies the verb *sang*)
>
> I was pleased *to receive* your invitation.
> (adverb—modifies the adjective *pleased*)

Properties of the Infinitive

An infinitive has the properties of a verb and those of a noun, an adjective, or an adverb.

PROPERTIES OF A VERB	OTHER PROPERTIES
It is derived from a verb.	It may be used as a noun.
It may take an object.	It may limit a noun or
It may be modified by an	a pronoun.
adverb or an adverbial	It may modify a verb, an
phrase.	adjective, or an adverb.

Forms of the Infinitive

The infinitive is used in the present and the perfect tenses, active and passive voices.

	ACTIVE	PASSIVE
PRESENT:	to write	to be written
PERFECT:	to have written	to have been written

Uses of the Infinitive

In a sentence the infinitive may be used as a noun, an adjective, or an adverb. An infinitive phrase consists of the infinitive and its complements and modifiers.

> Juan likes *to write poetry.*
>
> *To paint beautifully* is Janet's dream.

Infinitives Used as Nouns

The infinitive is used as a noun when it does the work of a noun. It may be used as the subject or the object of a verb, as the object of a preposition, as a subjective complement, or as an appositive.

> *To win* was their only thought. (subject)
>
> I should like *to live* in Boston. (direct object)
>
> He was about *to write* the letter. (object of preposition)
>
> Bob's task is *to rake.* (subjective complement)
>
> She had one desire, *to win* the race. (appositive)

An infinitive is considered to be an appositive when it is used after the expletive *it.* An expletive is a word like *it* and *there* that is used to get a sentence started.

> It is a police officer's duty *to enforce the laws.*

In this sentence, the infinitive is in apposition with *it.* The infinitive phrase *to enforce the laws* is the logical, or real, subject. The infinitive phrase can replace the expletive *it.*

> *To enforce the laws* is a police officer's duty.

Exercise 1

The infinitives in the following sentences are used as subjects. Name the infinitive and the infinitive phrase in each sentence.

1. To refuse aid was out of the question.
2. To achieve honors requires much study.
3. To feed the hungry is a serious responsibility.
4. To find housing for poor people in the city is difficult.
5. To organize the assembly-line workers is Nora's job.
6. To speak in public requires skill.
7. To hope for success is not enough.
8. To practice daily requires discipline.
9. To study law is Luke's desire.
10. To cross the river on horseback took a long time.

Complete each sentence with an appropriate infinitive or infinitive phrase used as the subject.

11. _____ is an accomplishment.
12. _____ is a good feeling.
13. _____ can be dangerous.
14. _____ requires a lot of studying.
15. _____ makes me happy.

Exercise 2

The infinitives in the following sentences are used as direct objects. Name the infinitive and the infinitive phrase in each sentence.

1. Fiona tried to skate backward.
2. Ramón told me to give the dog a bath.
3. The drummer upstairs likes to practice at night.
4. Monica intends to sail from Canada to Mexico.
5. Have you decided to move to the country?
6. Nikki has been wanting to read that book.
7. Terri, try to be more careful.
8. We have planned to save coupons for free gifts.
9. Molly wanted to watch the meteor shower.
10. William wanted to study medicine.

Complete each sentence with an appropriate infinitive or infinitive phrase used as a direct object.

11. Jennifer intended _____ .
12. Joel promised _____ .
13. Do you want _____ ?
14. The water continued _____ .
15. We should try _____ .

Exercise 3

The infinitives in the following sentences are used as objects of prepositions. Name the infinitive and the infinitive phrase in each sentence. Give the preposition that introduces the infinitive phrase.

1. Linda wanted nothing but to preserve the peace.
2. The president is about to speak.
3. She had no choice but to change the flat tire.
4. Mark is about to open the mail.
5. Little was possible but to apologize.
6. Lydia is about to call the police.
7. Hank seemed about to cry.
8. No action can be taken but to suspend the students involved.
9. Olivia had no choice but to wait for the tow truck.
10. The concert is about to begin.

Complete each sentence with an appropriate infinitive or infinitive phrase used as the object of a preposition.

11. The astronauts had no choice but _____ .
12. About _____ , Conner behaved very politely.
13. The doctors had no other aim but _____ .
14. Bob has no motive except _____ .
15. I can think of no way to afford that bike except _____ .

Exercise 4

The infinitives in the following sentences are used as subjective complements. Name the infinitive and the infinitive phrase in each sentence.

1. Theresa's habit is to tip her head to the left when reading.
2. The job is to give everyone at least three choices.
3. Leo's task was to paint scenery for the play.
4. The main function of the safety patrol is to prevent accidents.
5. Her desire is to learn Spanish.
6. The goal of that group is to end racism.
7. The work of a prospector is to search for minerals.
8. The scout's mission was to find a safe pass through the mountains.
9. The worst fault is to be conscious of none.
10. Mary's decision was to sell her home.

Complete each sentence with an appropriate infinitive or infinitive phrase used as a subjective complement.

11. The governor's duty is _____ .
12. The joy of many parents is _____ .
13. A driver's responsibility is _____ .
14. The best plan is _____ .
15. Her most difficult problem was _____ .

Exercise 5

The infinitives in the following sentences are used as appositives. Name the infinitive and the infinitive phrase in each sentence. Tell what word the appositive explains.

1. David's job, to cut the grass, must come first.
2. Susan's plan, to organize a ski trip, succeeded.
3. The pilot's duty, to fly the plane safely, is a great responsibility.
4. Mom objected to Steve's proposal, to paint his room red with black stripes.
5. It is a smart thing to save some money.

Complete the following sentences with an appropriate infinitive or infinitive phrase used as an appositive.

6. Mr. Turner gave the final instructions, _____ .
7. Their desire _____ seemed funny to us.
8. The gardener's job, _____ , was nearly impossible.
9. My plan _____ will take only two weeks.
10. Margo's hope _____ failed.

Exercise 6

Identify the infinitives used as nouns, and tell their function in each sentence.

1. To reach the finish line at all was reward enough for Ted.
2. He tried to run at an even pace.
3. He seemed about to collapse at the halfway point.
4. Lauren's job was to pace him through the last three miles.
5. Karl's task, to bring water along, seemed simple enough.
6. To get water, however, was a problem.
7. The local water supply was about to go dry.
8. Lauren decided to find some juice.
9. We hope to see the finish line.
10. To run the race took four hours.
11. Ted refused to accept help.
12. His desire to finish kept him going.
13. Race officials promised to mail the results.
14. Will you try to run the race next year?
15. To be intent on winning is not the goal.

Complete each sentence with an appropriate infinitive or infinitive phrase. Give the use, or syntax, of the added word(s).

16. The parachutists dared _____ .
17. Would you like _____ ?
18. _____ was impossible.
19. _____ was her desire.
20. _____ required time.
21. That jet is about _____ .
22. It is a privilege _____ .
23. Ben plans _____ .
24. My little brother likes _____ .
25. Sometimes it is not enough _____ .

Infinitives Used as Adjectives and Adverbs

An infinitive is used as an adjective when it modifies a noun or a pronoun.

> This is a good place *to have* a picnic. (modifies *place*)
> Every citizen has the right *to vote.* (modifies *right*)

Infinitives are used as adverbs when they express the purpose, the cause, or the result of an action. An infinitive used as an adverb may modify a verb, an adjective, or an adverb.

> Rosa went *to see* the circus. (modifies the verb *went*)
> Abe was quick *to learn.* (modifies the adjective *quick*)
> We arrived too late *to gain* admission. (modifies the adverb *late*)

Exercise 7

Name the infinitives used as adjectives and the nouns they modify.

1. The lost kitten had no food to eat.
2. Marla is a person to be trusted.
3. An artist must have an ability to work with color.
4. Color blindness is the inability to distinguish colors.
5. Cherries to preserve are on sale here.

Exercise 8

Name the infinitives used as adverbs and the word each modifies. Tell whether the modified word is a verb, an adjective, or an adverb.

1. We eat to live.
2. The players are ready to start.
3. Marco came to feed his turtle.
4. That pitcher is used to hold orange juice.
5. The farmer went out to plant her crops.

Practice Power

▶ Write two sentences for each type of infinitive. Use information from your other subjects to help make your sentences interesting.

LESSON 7

The Correct Use of Infinitives

Tense of Infinitives

The present infinitive is used when the action expressed by the infinitive takes place at the same time as the action of the main verb or after the time expressed by the main verb. The perfect infinitive is used only when its action has been completed before the time of the main verb.

I like *to write* letters. (same time as main verb)

I had intended *to write* to you yesterday. (same time as main verb)

I shall come *to see* you. (after time of main verb; the seeing will take place after the coming)

She seems *to have succeeded* in her work. (action completed before time of main verb)

Both the present and the perfect infinitive may be used with the verb *ought.* The present infinitive indicates obligation or necessity; the perfect infinitive indicates that the action did not take place.

Joan ought *to call* immediately. (indicates duty or necessity)

Joan ought *to have called.* (indicates that she did not call)

Exercise 1

Choose the correct tense of each infinitive.

1. We are eager (to see, to have seen) your new home.
2. The train was scheduled (to leave, to have left) early in the morning.
3. I will be happy (to give, to have given) you the tour tomorrow.
4. Does Milton intend (to come, to have come) to the party?
5. That woman is said (to see, to have seen) every important city in Europe.
6. Did Lana mean (to do, to have done) that?
7. Ronny seems (to play, to have played) the piano every afternoon this week.
8. Gloria will be pleased (to receive, to have received) your letter.
9. Wanting (to meet, to have met) the principal, Ms. Liu requested an interview.
10. You ought (to finish, to have finished) yesterday.

Omission of the Infinitive Sign

The infinitive is used without *to,* often called the sign of the infinitive, in the following cases:

- after verbs of perception, such as *hear, see, behold, know, feel,* and so forth.

   We watched the great tree *fall.*
   The campers heard the bear *pass.*
   The doctor felt the patient *move.*

- after the verbs *let, dare, need, make, bid,* and so forth.

   The dean made the student *study.*
   The swimmers dared not *jump* into the shallow pool.
   You need not *go* to the library.

- frequently after the preposition *but* and the subordinate conjunction *than.*

   The lions did nothing but *roar* for food.
   It is more like him to write than *visit.*

Exercise 2

Identify the hidden infinitives.

1. Marshall saw the Hale-Bopp comet appear in the sky.
2. He dared not show his fear.
3. When will people see that comet blaze again?
4. The computer instructor's advice helped us fix the program.
5. Seeing the comet streaking through the sky made us feel small.
6. The commuters heard the whistle blow.
7. I felt something sting me.
8. The puppies did nothing but play all day.
9. Doug let her borrow his chemistry book.
10. We watched the astronomer look at it through a telescope.

Split Infinitives

A split infinitive occurs when a word or a group of words comes between *to* and the rest of the infinitive. Take care to avoid split infinitives.

AVOID: We hope *to* completely *weed* the garden today.

BETTER: We hope *to weed* the garden completely today.

Exercise 3

Tell where in the sentence the adverb at the left belongs.

not	1. Victor seemed to care very much.
already	2. The snow appears to have begun falling.
soon	3. They want you to announce the test date.
thoroughly	4. Denise seemed to enjoy the play.
not	5. Nat expected to see you today.
quickly	6. Don't expect to sweep the chimney.
justly	7. To speak of others is our duty.
smoothly	8. Sandra learned to land the plane.
eventually	9. Gail hopes to become a professional folksinger.
correctly	10. Bill planned to answer all the questions.

Exercise 4

Name each infinitive and its function: subject, direct object, object of preposition, appositive, adjective, or adverb.

1. Learn to ski properly.
2. To break your leg is not the goal.
3. Hallie tried to fit into my boots.
4. The idea, to have fun, got lost in the details.
5. To read silently by the fire is his greatest delight.
6. Lonnie was about to jump on the train when the police arrived.
7. David arrived too early to be admitted to the play.
8. Phoebe likes to read about the history of women.
9. The cold made Mike shiver.
10. To hurt your feelings was not my intention.
11. To see my relatives is the purpose of my visit.
12. Jessica went to the store to get milk.
13. Rebecca was almost to the finish line when she tripped.
14. Leroy wants to listen to his new compact disc player.
15. The farmer had baskets of green peppers to sell.

Putting It All Together

Here's a game to play using *ing* words. Write ten sentences using *ing* words. Vary your sentences to include at least one participle, one participial adjective, one gerund, one *ing* noun, and one progressive verb form. Copy each sentence onto a note card or sheet of paper. On the back, identify the use, or syntax, of the *ing* word.

Challenge a partner to identify the type of *ing* word used in each sentence. If your partner is correct, he or she keeps the card. If your partner is incorrect, you keep the card. The player with the most cards at the end of a round wins the game.

Chapter Challenge

Read this selection carefully and answer the questions that follow.

¹Standing in the raw winter wind had not been pleasant for the huge crowd gathered before the Capitol to view the inauguration of a new president. ²The prospect of witnessing so historic an event, however, compensated the waiting crowd for the many hours of discomfort.

³A sudden burst of applause announced that the proceedings were about to begin. ⁴A prayer having been offered, the president-elect stepped forward and, placing his hand upon the Bible, repeated in a firm voice the oath administered by the chief justice. ⁵In the inaugural address that followed, the president assured the people of his determination to labor untiringly to justify the confidence they had placed in him.

1. Name a participle in the first sentence.
2. What noun does the participle in the first sentence modify?
3. What part of speech is *waiting* in the second sentence?
4. Name the participles in the fourth sentence.
5. Why is the noun *prayer* in the fourth sentence in the nominative case?
6. What part of speech is *proceedings* in the third sentence?
7. Find a gerund in the first sentence.
8. How is the gerund in the first sentence used?
9. In what respects does the word *witnessing* in the second sentence resemble a verb?
10. What is the use, or syntax, of the word *witnessing* in the second sentence?
11. Find an infinitive in the third sentence.
12. Is the infinitive in the third sentence used as a noun, an adjective, or an adverb?
13. Find an infinitive in the fifth sentence that is used as an adjective and name the noun that it modifies.
14. What does the infinitive *to justify* in the last sentence modify?
15. Name an infinitive in the first sentence.
16. How is the infinitive in the first sentence used?

Classification of Adverbs

An adverb is a word that modifies a verb, an adjective, an adverb, a participle, a gerund, or an infinitive.

Sue walked *slowly*. (*Slowly* modifies the verb *walked*.)

Sue's gait was *very* slow. (*Very* modifies the adjective *slow*.)

Sue walked *too* slowly. (*Too* modifies the adverb *slowly*.)

Walking *slowly*, Sue sauntered down the street. (*Slowly* modifies the participle *walking*.)

The art of writing *well* is not acquired without effort. (*Well* modifies the gerund *writing*.)

Hugh, try to come *early*. (*Early* modifies the infinitive phrase *to come*.)

Classification According to Meaning

Adverbs of time answer the question *when* or *how often*. They include such adverbs as *again, before, early, frequently,* and *now*.

Adverbs of place answer the question *where*. These are adverbs of place: *above, away, below, down, forward, overhead,* and *upward*.

Adverbs of degree answer the question *how much* or *how little*. They include the following adverbs: *almost, barely, little, merely, quite, rather,* and *very*.

About the Photograph

Here's Sue walking slowly. How slowly does she walk? How often, when, and where does she walk? Adverbs can give you the answers.

ADVERBS

Adverbs of manner answer the question *how* or *in what manner. Easily, fervently, quickly,* and *thoroughly* are adverbs of manner.

Adverbs of affirmation and negation tell whether a fact is true or false. They include the adverbs *yes, no, indeed, never, doubtless,* and *not.*

Classification According to Use

Simple Adverbs

A simple adverb is an adverb used merely as a modifier.

Slowly the clouds moved across the blue sky.

Interrogative Adverbs

An interrogative adverb is an adverb used in asking questions. The interrogative adverbs are *how, when, where,* and *why.* They usually modify the verb.

Why is carbon monoxide dangerous?
Where is Yosemite National Park?
How can I identify this rock?

Exercise 1

Identify each italicized adverb according to time, place, degree, manner, affirmation, or negation.

1. Bill was *never* able to tell a story *quickly.*
2. He started *quite calmly.*
3. The lion had been seen running *away.*
4. *Hurriedly,* Ms. Little moved her children.
5. Walking *confidently* toward the lion, she talked *steadily* to it.
6. *Suddenly* the lion shook its head *very menacingly.*

7. She stood *still.*

8. The zookeeper strode *forward.*

9. The lion *slowly* lay *down.*

10. Now it is *back* at the zoo and will *doubtless* be more *securely* penned.

Exercise 2

Identify the adverbs in each sentence. Tell whether they are simple or interrogative adverbs.

1. The rusty car rolled forward slowly.

2. When did the car start to approach the corner?

3. It barely scraped Tom's car.

4. He quickly jumped out and started angrily shaking his fist.

5. He yelled loudly at the offending driver.

6. How long did he chase the empty car?

7. When did he realize his mistake?

8. The car kept rolling away from him.

9. The police finally stopped it.

10. Where will they take the old car?

Relative Adverbs

A relative adverb is a word that does the work of an adverb and a relative pronoun. The principal relative adverbs are *when, where,* and *why.*

Rick returned to the room *where* he had left his jacket.

Where explains the place of the action; hence it is an adverb. *Where* also does the work of a relative pronoun, for it joins the clause *where he had left his jacket* to the principal clause.

NOTE: A relative adverb usually follows a noun of time, place, or reason. The test of a relative adverb is that you may replace it with a prepositional phrase containing a relative pronoun.

Rick returned to the room *in which* he had left his jacket.

Adverbial Objectives

> **An adverbial objective is a noun that expresses time, distance, measure, weight, value, or direction and performs the function of an adverb.**

James has attended this school two *years*.

The word *years* is a noun. In this sentence, it indicates time, a function usually performed by an adverb, by telling how long James has attended school.

Because an adverbial objective resembles an adverb, it may modify a verb, an adjective, or an adverb. Because it is a noun, the adverbial objective may be modified by an adjective. In the sentence above, the adverbial objective *years* modifies the verb *has attended*, and it is modified by the adjective *two*.

Exercise 3

Identify the relative adverbs and tell whether they explain the reason for the action, its time, or its place.

1. San Antonio is the city where the battle of the Alamo was fought.
2. That is the reason why I like the story of Galileo.
3. This is the house where the author lived.
4. Winter is the time when the flowers sleep.
5. September is the month when autumn begins.
6. They drove past an orchard where many peach trees were in bloom.
7. There are moments when all wish to be alone.
8. We discovered a field where beautiful violets grow.
9. Paris is the place where we shall meet.
10. There are mornings when it is difficult to wake up.
11. I ran to the corner where the bus stop is.
12. Do you know the reason why the bus is late?
13. We do not know the hour when the bus will arrive.
14. I have no idea why we begin school so early.
15. This is the stop where I get off.

Exercise 4

Name the adverbial objectives and tell whether each expresses time, distance, measure, weight, value, or direction.

1. The meeting lasted three hours.
2. Moira spent a month in the hospital.
3. Brent waited all day for you.
4. This photograph costs fifty dollars.
5. Troy went home.
6. Each lane measures eight feet.
7. The Puccios live five kilometers from Venice.
8. My brother hopes to grow seven feet tall.
9. That package weighs eleven ounces.
10. The diving pool is four meters deep.

Complete the remaining five sentences with original adverbial objectives.

11. _____ my sister won the annual science fair award. (time)
12. Some people exercise _____ . (time)
13. The aircraft could carry _____ of food to the earthquake victims. (weight)
14. Mom used _____ of flour to make the cake. (measure)
15. The antelope journeyed _____ from its home. (distance)

Practice Power

▶ Choose a topic from another subject area such as math or science. Write five questions about the topic, using interrogative adverbs. Then answer your questions, using relative adverbs in your sentences.

Adverbs That Compare

Like adjectives, adverbs have three degrees of comparison: positive, comparative, and superlative.

Regular Comparison

The comparative degree of adverbs is formed by adding *-er* to the positive degree, and the superlative degree is formed by adding *-est* to the positive. The comparative degree of adverbs ending in *-ly* is generally formed by adding *more* or *less* to the positive degree, and the superlative degree is formed by adding *most* or *least* to the positive.

POSITIVE	COMPARATIVE	SUPERLATIVE
fast	faster	fastest
hastily	more hastily	most hastily

Irregular Comparison

Some adverbs are compared irregularly.

POSITIVE	COMPARATIVE	SUPERLATIVE
well	better	best
badly	worse	worst

Many adverbs denoting time and place *(here, now, then, when, where, again, always, down, above)* and adverbs denoting absoluteness or completeness *(perfect, eternally, never, universally)* cannot be compared.

Exercise 1

Name each adverb and its degree of comparison.

1. The editor examined the manuscript closely.
2. The editor should have examined the manuscript more closely.
3. This is the most closely examined manuscript any writer has ever written.
4. The judge listened most attentively.
5. Are you adequately prepared for this test?
6. Is your grandmother feeling better now?
7. The wind blew more strongly as we entered open water.
8. The physics award went to the one who most deserved it.
9. Bud ran faster than any other horse.
10. Time passed more slowly as the anticipation grew stronger.

Practice Power

▶ Use a different adverb to modify each of the adjectives listed below. Then use both words together in a sentence. Do not use the overworked adverb *very*.

Example: awkward

extremely awkward

Pam found herself in an *extremely awkward* situation.

1. sharp	**5.** sour	**9.** graceful
2. daring	**6.** strong	**10.** fierce
3. consistent	**7.** tall	**11.** boastful
4. beautiful	**8.** primitive	**12.** honest

The Correct Use of Adverbs

Distinguishing Between Adjectives and Adverbs

**Adjectives modify nouns and pronouns.
Adverbs modify verbs, adjectives, adverbs,
participles, gerunds, and infinitives.**

Adverbs and those adjectives that are used as complements are
often confused. In order to determine whether a modifier is a
complement or an adverb, study each sentence carefully and
ask yourself if the writer is trying to tell something about the
subject, the verb, or an adjective.

The candy tasted *good.* (candy *was* good; an adjective)

You may taste the candy *now.* (tells *when* you may taste;
an adverb)

Did the candy taste *exceptionally* good? (tells *how* good;
an adverb)

Words Used as Adjectives and Adverbs

An adjective describes or limits a noun or a pronoun. An
adverb modifies a verb, an adjective, or an adverb.

Marcia had the *highest* mark in the class. (adjective)

Of the three, John had tossed the football *highest.*
(adverb)

Exercise 1

Select the correct form of the word and tell whether the word is an adjective or an adverb.

1. Trish will return the book (prompt, promptly).
2. The bell sounds (harsh, harshly).
3. This chair seems (comfortable, comfortably).
4. The boxes fell (loud, loudly) to the floor.
5. These cherries taste (sweet, sweetly).

Identify each italicized word as an adjective or an adverb.

6. The band marched *first.*
7. Is this the *first* day of the carnival?
8. *Little* acorns grow into towering oaks.
9. The sick puppy plays *little.*
10. What do you mean by the *near* future?

Farther and *Further*

Farther refers to distance. *Further* denotes an addition. Both of these words may be used as adjectives and as adverbs.

> I live *farther* than you.
>
> I have nothing *further* to say.

Adverbs in Comparisons

Use *as . . . as* when making comparisons that denote equality between persons or things. Use *so . . . as* in negative comparisons that denote inequality between persons or things.

> Albert is *as* tall *as* Victor.
>
> I am not *so* old *as* you.

Equally as an Adverb

Equally means *as* when it modifies an adjective or an adverb. Practice using the correct forms *equally great, equally well,* and *equally good.* Never use *as* between *equally* and the adjective or adverb.

> The apples and the oranges are *equally* good.

Exercise 2

Select the correct word, *farther* or *further,* to complete each sentence.

1. Raise your hand if you need _____ instructions.
2. Denver is _____ west than Kansas City.
3. _____ research will be necessary.
4. Monica declared _____ discussion useless.
5. Kyle claimed he could throw the ball _____ than anyone.

Exercise 3

Select the correct word, *as* or *so,* to complete each sentence.

1. Cedric's bicycle is _____ good as mine.
2. San Francisco has _____ much fog as London.
3. Nanette is not _____ clever with her hands as Edie is.
4. At noon, the sky turned _____ dark as night.
5. That end of the pool is not _____ deep as this end.

Exercise 4

Select the correct adverb form.

1. Ava's parents are (equally pleased, equally as pleased).
2. We are (equally as qualified, equally qualified) for the job.
3. Jogging and swimming are (equally effective, equally as effective) exercises.
4. Sitting and standing seem (equally painful, equally as painful) to my back.
5. Woody and Max sing (equally as well, equally well).

Putting It All Together

Some playwrights specialize in writing dialogue that is quick, terse, and direct. Try writing dialogue that contains a variety of adverbs. Form an ensemble with three or four classmates. Have each ensemble member develop a character who speaks little and uses a certain kind of adverb, such as adverbs of time, place, degree, manner, affirmation, or negation. First improvise and then develop a scene in which the characters try to solve a problem. Then perform your scene for the class.

Chapter Challenge

Read the selection carefully and answer the questions.

¹The first astronauts had to be very brave. ²They ventured where none had ever been. ³Carefully trained in mind and body, they intrepidly began to explore parts of the universe previously seen only at a distance. ⁴As space activity pushes forward, inhabited Earth-orbiting stations that were once idly dreamed about are presently a reality. ⁵Even now, people with much less training than the early astronauts are able to travel out of Earth's atmosphere on space shuttles. ⁶How people will feel about living far from Earth is still a question.

1. Identify the adverb in the first sentence. Give its classification (time, place, degree, manner, affirmation, or negation).

2. Name the relative adverb in the second sentence. Name another adverb in that sentence and tell whether it modifies a verb, an adjective, or a participle.

3. What is the adverb of time in the third sentence?

4. Name the adverb in the third sentence that modifies a participle.

5. If you were going to add an adverb to the third sentence between the word *explore* and the word *parts,* would you choose *further* or *farther?* Why?

6. Name the adverb of manner in the fourth sentence.

7. What word does the adverb *even* modify in the fifth sentence? What part of speech is that word?

8. Name the other adverb in the fifth sentence that modifies an adjective.

9. Name an adverb of place in the sixth sentence.

10. Name the adverb of time in the sixth sentence.

PREPOSITIONS, CONJUNCTIONS, INTERJECTIONS

Prepositions

LESSON 1

A preposition is a word or a group of words placed before a noun, pronoun, phrase, or clause to show its relation to some other word.

Mohammed traveled *to* Detroit.

The most commonly used prepositions are listed here.

about	at	down	near	throughout
above	before	during	of	to
across	behind	except	off	toward
after	beside	for	on	under
against	between	from	over	until
among	beyond	in	past	up
around	by	into	through	with

Forms of Prepositions

The preposition may be a single word or a group of words used as one preposition.

A cry came *from* the woods.
Joan went fishing *in spite of* the cold weather.

Groups of words that are considered one preposition include the following:

because of	in addition to	in spite of
by means of	in front of	instead of
for the sake of	in regard to	on account of

About the Photograph

These boys' mural depicts the relationships between themselves and their community. In a similar way, prepositions and conjunctions show the relationships between words in a sentence.

The Object of a Preposition

The object of a preposition is a noun, a pronoun, or a group of words used as a noun. These groups of words might be a prepositional phrase, a gerund phrase, an infinitive phrase, or a noun clause. Study the examples below.

> We cannot succeed without more help from the *club*. (noun)
>
> Rosa gave the report to *him*. (pronoun)
>
> From *across the ocean* came the explorers. (prepositional phrase)
>
> Don't go without *asking Ben*. (gerund phrase)
>
> Annette had no choice but *to accompany them*. (infinitive phrase)
>
> We could see the parade from *where we stood*. (noun clause)

Exercise 1

Name each preposition and identify its object.

1. Which is the largest country in South America?
2. Louise led the girls across the field.
3. Phil gave a report on what the members had decided.
4. Barry put the cereal in the freezer.
5. The cat put her toy mouse under the sofa.
6. The sun set behind the lighthouse.
7. From what we have heard, the senator has been successful in her campaign.
8. John held the injured baby bird in his hand.
9. We took the train instead of taking the bus.
10. Helena rode the horse past the reviewing stand.

Practice Power

▶ Write a review of your favorite song or musical artist. Work at least five prepositions or prepositional word groups into your review. Use prepositions from the lists on page 445.

The Correct Use of Prepositions

Between and Among

When speaking of two persons, places, or things, use *between*. When speaking of more than two, use *among*.

> He divided the money *between* Helen and Joan.
> He divided the money *among* the four children.

Beside and Besides

Beside means "at the side of" or "next to." *Besides* means "in addition to."

> Carlo stood *beside* the barn.
> Pierre speaks French and Greek *besides* English.

In and Into

In denotes position within. *Into* denotes motion or change of position.

> The papers are *in* the desk drawer.
> The robin flew *into* its nest.

From and Off

From indicates the person from whom something is obtained. *Off* means "away from."

> We secured this paper *from* the vendor.
> The farmer hopped *off* the truck.

Behind

Use *behind* to indicate location at the rear of.

> The rooster is *behind* the barn.

Differ With and Differ From

Differ with denotes disagreement of opinion. *Differ from* denotes differences between persons or things.

> I *differ with* you about the scoring of the game.
> The ribbons *differ from* each other in color.

Different From

After the adjective *different,* use *from,* not *than.*

> The writing is *different from* his.

Need Of

Use *need of,* not *need for.*

> We shall have no further *need of* your help.

Within

Use *within,* not *inside of,* to indicate the time within which something will occur.

> I shall call for you *within* an hour.

Angry With and Angry At

Use *angry with* a person; use *angry at* a thing.

> I am *angry with* Sid.
> We were *angry at* the result.

At and To

At denotes presence in. *To* denotes motion toward.

> Jason was *at* the party.
> Jason walked *to* the gate.

Words Used as Adverbs and Prepositions

An adverb tells *how, when,* or *where.* A preposition shows the relationship between its object and some other word in the sentence.

> Have you ever visited Ottawa *before?* (adverb)
> Lee stood *before* the class. (preposition)

Exercise 1

Choose the correct preposition.

1. The four girls had a secret (between, among) themselves.
2. We planted ivy (beside, besides) the wall.
3. Margie's art project differs (with, from) Kate's.
4. The candidates filed (in, into) the press room.
5. We have no need (of, for) a car.
6. Irene was angry (with, at) the outcome of the election.
7. We shall be in the hall (inside of, within) an hour.
8. My sweater is different (than, from) yours.

Exercise 2

Identify each word in italics as a preposition or an adverb.

1. *Down* splashed the rain.
2. Inez piled the reports *on* my desk.
3. Sheila left the note *outside* your door.
4. Suddenly the door opened, and *in* rushed Michelle.
5. The gorilla stood *outside.*
6. Is that your hamster crawling *in* the dirt under the porch?
7. Jane is moving *away.*
8. The speaker proclaimed that the movement must carry *on.*

Practice Power

▶ With a partner, write fifteen to twenty prepositional phrases on a piece of paper. Compose a humorous short story using as many prepositional phrases as possible.

Conjunctions

A conjunction is a word used to connect words, phrases, or clauses in a sentence.

Washington *and* Oregon are western states. (connects words)

Pineapples grow in the Philippines *and* in Hawaii. (connects phrases)

Although we are tired, we are not discouraged. (connects clauses)

Kinds of Conjunctions

Coordinate Conjunctions

A coordinate conjunction connects words, phrases, or clauses of equal rank.

The most common coordinate conjunctions are *and, or, nor, but,* and *yet.*

Warren made one error, *but* André had a perfect score.

The adverbs *however, moreover, nevertheless, also, therefore,* and *consequently* are also used to link independent clauses.

He was exhausted; *therefore,* he went to sleep.

Correlative Conjunctions

Correlative conjunctions are coordinate conjunctions used in pairs.

Neither corn *nor* wheat is grown in this state.

Here are the most frequently used correlative conjunctions.

> both . . . and   neither . . . nor
> either . . . or   not only . . . but also

Subordinate Conjunctions

A subordinate conjunction is a conjunction that connects clauses of unequal rank.

> I will tell you *because* you ask me.

In this sentence there are two clauses. The first, *I will tell you,* is the principal, or independent, clause. It does not depend upon any other part of the sentence and forms a complete idea. The second clause, *because you ask me,* is a dependent clause answering the question *why* and modifying the verb *will tell.* The subordinate conjunction *because* joins the dependent or subordinate clause to the independent clause in the sentence.

The most common subordinate conjunctions are listed here.

> after   before   since   then   where
> although   for   so   unless   while
> as   if   than   until
> because   provided   that   when

Very often, groups of words are used as subordinate conjunctions. Learn these groups:

> as if   inasmuch as   so that
> as soon as   in order that   provided that

Exercise 1

Name the conjunctions and tell whether they connect words, phrases, or clauses.

1. Mexico, the United States, and Canada are in North America.
2. Shall I meet you in Sacramento or Reno?
3. They called us, but we did not hear them.
4. Ken won both academic and athletic awards.
5. Jay left clues under the apple tree and next to the house.

Exercise 2

Name the pair of correlative conjunctions in each sentence.

1. They traveled not only in Colombia but also in Brazil.
2. Alicia reads both history and science fiction.
3. Steven can play either the piano or the violin.
4. Both coal and iron ore are mined in Pennsylvania.
5. Not only did she sing, but she also danced.
6. Leonardo da Vinci was both an artist and a scientist.
7. Neither Linda nor I would agree to talk with him.
8. Colette is both an athlete and a scholar.
9. Either his smile is painted on or he is happy all the time.
10. Both mail and telephone service were disrupted during the revolution.

Exercise 3

Identify the principal clause, the subordinate clause, and the subordinate conjunction in each sentence.

1. If I knew how, I would install the new faucet.
2. Moving to Texas was a good decision, although we miss our old friends.
3. Inasmuch as he opposes violence, Nick turned off the TV.
4. Sylvia spoke only to Martha, as if I were invisible.
5. Since Minnesota is a border state, it has customs checkpoints along its northern boundary.
6. Lydia borrowed four dollars so that she could go bowling.
7. Julio sings better than I do.
8. Marco gave me his turtle because I promised to feed it.
9. Holly offered us a ride provided we would leave early.
10. Although this is a joyous event, some people are sad.

Practice Power

▶ Write three or four related sentences using a coordinate, a correlative, and a subordinate conjunction about the town, city, or state in which you live. The conjunctions may be used in any order.

LESSON 4

The Correct Use of Conjunctions and Prepositions

Prepositions are often carelessly used as conjunctions. The following prepositions and conjunctions require special study.

Without is a preposition and introduces a phrase. *Unless* is a conjunction and introduces a clause.

> Do not come *without your textbook.* (phrase)
> Do not come *unless you bring your textbook.* (clause)

Like is a preposition and introduces a phrase. *As* and *as if* are conjunctions and introduce clauses.

> John looks *like his father.* (phrase)
> John writes *as his father writes.* (clause)

Exercise 1

Select the correct word to complete each sentence.

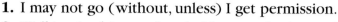

1. I may not go (without, unless) I get permission.
2. Walking in this weather (without, unless) wearing a hat is foolhardy.
3. William did that job (like, as if) he were used to the work.
4. Elena will be unhappy (without, unless) her friends around her.
5. Elena will be unhappy (without, unless) her friends are around her.
6. (Like, As) his father, David is very patient.
7. (Without, Unless) taking his keys, Phil stormed out of the house.
8. Theresa is walking in the rain (without, unless) her umbrella.
9. Sandy did (like, as) he was told.
10. Bianca looks very much (like, as) her brother.
11. Build this cabinet (like, as) these instructions direct.
12. (Without, Unless) you canceled the appointment, Veronica will arrive any moment.
13. We began (like, as) the sun was rising.
14. You will not finish this assignment (without, unless) you stop talking.
15. (Like, As) her sister, Fran wants to be a dancer.

Practice Power

▶ Write a short paragraph using *without* and *unless* and *like* and *as*. Make sure your usages are correct.

LESSON 5

Interjections

An interjection is a word that expresses some strong or sudden emotion.

Hurrah! Here comes the champion.

Ouch! I hurt my arm.

An interjection may express delight, disgust, contempt, pain, assent, joy, impatience, surprise, sorrow, wonder, or regret. It is generally set off from the rest of the sentence by an exclamation point. If the entire sentence is exclamatory, however, the interjection may be followed by a comma, and the exclamation point placed at the end of the sentence.

Ah, how beautifully that orchestra plays!

The most common interjections are listed here.

Ah	Good	Hush	Oh	Ugh
Beware	Hello	Listen	Ouch	What
Bravo	Hurrah	Lo	Shh	Wow

O and Oh

The interjection *O* is used before a noun in direct address and is not directly followed by an exclamation point. *Oh* expresses an emotion such as surprise, sorrow, or joy and is generally followed by an exclamation point. If the emotion continues throughout the sentence, however, *Oh* is followed by a comma, and the exclamation point is put at the end of the sentence.

O Marie! I wish I could go to the beach with you. (direct address)

Oh! The player was injured. (emotion does not continue)

Oh, how surprised I am! (emotion continues)

Exercise 1

Name the interjections and tell what emotion is expressed by each.

1. Alas! I am sorry to hear that.
2. Quiet! The librarian looks angry with us.
3. Oh, how the sun is shining!
4. Wait! I'm almost ready to go.
5. Congratulations! You earned highest honors.
6. O Liz! I missed having you around.
7. Hurrah! I passed the test.
8. Ouch! That pin prick hurt.
9. What! Is everybody leaving?
10. Beware! Few return from that cavern.

Exercise 2

Write an interjection from the list on page 455 to complete each sentence.

1. _____ ! It's good to see you.
2. _____ Laura! You are so lucky.
3. _____ ! You won.
4. _____ ! There's no talking during the movie.
5. _____ , so that's the answer!

Putting It All Together

Create the perfect hiding place by playing a round of Where Is It? One person begins the game by asking a classmate a simple question, such as *Where is the ball?* The classmate must answer with a prepositional phrase, such as *in the creek,* and another question, such as *How do I get there?* Appoint a student in the class to write down each answer.

After each student in the class has asked and answered a question, work together as a class to make a treasure map showing how to find the object.

Chapter Challenge

Read the selection carefully and answer the questions that follow.

[1]Less than a minute remained in the final Northern League basketball game of the season. [2]The contest had been an exciting, hard-fought battle between our Mayfair team and the Lincoln players. [3]Everything depended on what we did in the next few seconds, for Lincoln held a one-point lead. [4]In spite of close guarding, one of our players made a deft hook shot from under the basket. [5]Good! The spectators cheered loudly as two precious points put us in the lead. [6]Lincoln, now in possession of the ball, made a desperate attempt to score. [7]The ball, however, sailed harmlessly through the air and over the basket. [8]It fell into eager hands as a loud blast from a horn announced not only the end of the game but also a glorious victory for Mayfair.

1. Name the prepositions in the first sentence.

2. Find a coordinate conjunction in the second sentence, and tell what words it connects.

3. Is the group of words used as the object of the preposition *on* in the third sentence a phrase or a clause?

4. Name a subordinate conjunction in the third sentence.

5. Find a phrase that is used as the object of the preposition in the fourth sentence.

6. Identify a group of words used as a single preposition in the fourth sentence.

7. What part of speech is the first word in the fifth sentence?

8. Name the prepositions in the sixth sentence.

9. Name two phrases that are connected by a coordinate conjunction in the seventh sentence.

10. Name a correlative conjunction in the eighth sentence.

Phrases

A phrase is a group of related words used as a single part of speech.

Rugs *from Iran* are expensive.

Types of Phrases

A prepositional phrase is introduced by a preposition. Adjectival, adverbial, and noun phrases are types of prepositional phrases.

The boy *on stilts* is my brother. (adjectival phrase)

The club went *to the park* today. (adverbial phrase)

To the Airport was the sign they read. (noun phrase)

Adjectival prepositional phrases modify nouns or pronouns. Adverbial prepositional phrases modify verbs, adverbs, adjectives, participles, gerunds, or infinitives. Noun prepositional phrases may serve as the subject of the sentence, the direct object, the complement, the object of a preposition, or an appositive.

PHRASES, CLAUSES, SENTENCES

About the Photograph

It's hard to hop on just one foot in a footrace; it's also hard to express ourselves without phrases. Try to describe this picture without using any phrases. Can you do it?

A participial phrase is introduced by a participle.
An infinitive phrase is introduced by an infinitive.
A gerund phrase is introduced by a gerund.

The person *riding the bicycle* lives in my neighborhood.
  (participial phrase)
To succeed in life is our aim. (infinitive phrase)
Writing a poem is a pleasure. (gerund phrase)

Exercise 1

Identify the phrases as prepositional, participial, infinitive, or gerund. Then classify each phrase according to its part of speech in the sentence.

1. My grandparents live in a small village in the West.
2. Emilio works on a cattle ranch in Arizona.
3. Some commuters in San Francisco ride on cable cars.
4. To play professional baseball is Andy's real goal.
5. The sign read To the Mall.
6. The United States purchased Alaska from Russia.
7. Cotton is packed in bales and sent to mills.
8. The tunnel cuts through the mountains.
9. The landlord fixed the loose board on our back stairs.
10. Debby went into the test with great anxiety.
11. Walking to work provides me with good exercise.
12. Ellie likes to read poetry.
13. John, having explained the problem clearly, was questioned by the council.
14. Bananas are grown in Brazil and India.
15. In 1969, Neil Armstrong was the first person to walk on the moon.

Practice Power

▶ Write a description of the photograph on page 458. Circle the prepositional, participial, infinitive, and gerund phrases you used in your description.

Adjectival Clauses

A clause is a part of a sentence containing a subject and a predicate.

A principal clause expresses a complete thought. A subordinate clause does not express a complete thought and cannot stand alone.

Henry Ford, *who revolutionized the auto industry,* became immensely wealthy.

Henry Ford became immensely wealthy. (principal clause)

who revolutionized the auto industry (subordinate clause)

Subordinate clauses can be adjectival, adverbial, or noun clauses.

An adjectival clause is a subordinate clause used as an adjective.

What type of modifier describes the noun *person* in each of these sentences?

An *ambitious* person usually succeeds. (adjective)
A person *with ambition* usually succeeds. (adjectival phrase)
A person *who has ambition* usually succeeds. (adjectival clause)

In the first sentence, the adjective *ambitious* modifies the noun *person;* in the second sentence, *person* is modified by the adjectival phrase *with ambition;* in the third sentence, the modifier is a group of words, *who has ambition.* This group of words contains a subject and a predicate and is, therefore, a clause. Since the clause does the work of an adjective, it is an adjectival clause.

Some adjectival clauses are nonrestrictive; others are restrictive. A nonrestrictive clause is one that may be omitted from the sentence without changing its meaning. It is separated from the rest of the sentence by commas. A restrictive clause is one that is a necessary part of the sentence because it points out or identifies a particular person or object. No punctuation is required for restrictive clauses.

> The players, *who practice long hours,* will be rewarded. (nonrestrictive clause)

> The players *who practice long hours* will be rewarded. (restrictive clause)

Relative pronouns *(who, whom, whose, which, that)* or, sometimes, relative adverbs *(when, where, why)* introduce adjectival clauses.

Exercise 1

Identify the adjectival clauses and the noun or pronoun each modifies.

1. Wise is the person who keeps silent when ignorant.
2. Benjamin Franklin, who is credited with inventing lightning rods, was a printer as well as a political leader and inventor.
3. Pam is the person who taught us this technique.
4. That train, which leaves for New York in five minutes, is already full.
5. Philip is a man in whom I have great faith.
6. The idea that they could rest tomorrow gave the workers energy to finish the job today.
7. The girl who is last in line is the team captain.
8. The money that keeps our club going comes from projects like this.
9. Norway is a country where fjords abound.
10. The farm that provided our income is now deserted.

Exercise 2

Rewrite the following sentences, inserting an adjectival clause after the italicized word or words. Underline your adjectival clause, including the relative pronoun or relative adverb.

Example:

> We went to see the *play*.
> We went to see the play <u>that had the best review</u>.

1. The *Booster Club* held a pancake breakfast.
2. The *art* was displayed in the school library.
3. The antique *car* needed repair.
4. I bought a new computer *program*.
5. The *senator* was not reelected.
6. *Greg* signed out two books from the library.
7. The *pandas* were not interested in our funny faces.
8. *Jean* tried out for the Olympic team.
9. Frankenstein created a *monster*.
10. I remember the *day*.

Practice Power

▶ Look up the following in an encyclopedia or a dictionary and complete each thought by writing a sentence that contains an adjectival clause.

1. The Hoover Dam
2. The Gateway Arch
3. The Great Wall of China
4. Manhattan
5. Niagara Falls
6. The Fountain of Youth
7. Pyramids
8. Mount Rushmore

LESSON 3

Adverbial Clauses

An adverbial clause is a subordinate clause used as an adverb.

What type of modifier describes the verb *acted* in each of these sentences?

> Tina acted *courageously.* (adverb)
> Tina acted *with courage.* (adverbial phrase)
> Tina acted *as if she had courage.* (adverbial clause)

In the first sentence, the adverb *courageously* modifies the verb *acted;* in the second sentence, the adverbial phrase *with courage* modifies the verb *acted;* in the third sentence, the clause *as if she had courage* modifies the verb *acted.* Since this clause does the work of an adverb, it is an adverbial clause.

Adverbial clauses are usually introduced by subordinate conjunctions. These clauses may tell time, place, degree, manner, cause, or purpose.

In adverbial clauses of degree or comparison (those that answer the question *how much* or *how little),* there is often an omission of words.

> Peter jumped higher than he [jumped].
> I admire him more than [I admire] her.

Exercise 1

Identify each adverbial clause and the word or words it modifies.

1. Strike while the iron is hot.
2. Go when you are told.

3. We saw the Mounties when we were in Ottawa.
4. The plant flowered, for it received good care.
5. The rabbit ran faster than the turtle could.
6. She saved her money that she might attend college.
7. Judy ran as if she were late for dinner.
8. Pat is more devoted to skiing than to swimming.
9. The computer program worked although some of the commands were wrong.
10. Lynne invited me to the party because I tell great jokes.
11. The Saint Bernard played outside all day as if she did not notice the bitter cold.
12. I will get a loan if you need more money.

Exercise 2

Complete each of the following sentences with an adverbial clause and underline the subject and verb in the clause. The subordinate conjunctions are given.

1. Because _____ , the people panicked.
2. The zookeeper let us watch when _____ .
3. Since _____ , the Native Americans decided to fight for their land.
4. The Eastwood Eagles were winning the game until _____ .
5. While _____ , the mountain climbers scaled Mount Everest.
6. In order that _____ , April studies harder than ever.
7. You can learn to play the guitar if _____ .
8. So that _____ , the Puritans came to America.
9. Although _____ , we must still conserve our natural resources.
10. Pedro devoured the pie as if _____ .

Practice Power

▶ Write a short paragraph about how to operate your newly invented homework machine. Write sentences using the following subordinate conjunctions: *because, when, after, until, while.*

Noun Clauses

A noun clause is a subordinate clause used as a noun.

What is the subject of each of these sentences?

>Bryan's *defeat* was unfortunate. (noun)
>*That Bryan was defeated* was unfortunate. (noun clause)

In the first sentence, the noun *defeat* is the subject; in the second sentence, the clause *That Bryan was defeated* is the subject. Since this clause does the work of a noun, it is a noun clause. Noun clauses are usually introduced by the introductory words *how, whether, what, why,* and *that.*

Noun Clauses Used as Subjects

A noun clause may be used as the subject of a sentence. In sentences containing noun clauses, the entire sentence is considered the principal clause. The noun clause is the subordinate clause.

>That the polio vaccine benefits many persons has been proved. (principal clause)

>That the polio vaccine benefits many persons (noun clause used as subject)

Noun Clauses Used as Direct Objects

A noun clause may be used as the direct object.

> We know *that the polio vaccine benefits many persons.*

It is easy to recognize a subordinate clause, but it is important to remember that the entire sentence is the principal clause.

> We know that the polio vaccine benefits many persons. (principal clause)
>
> that the polio vaccine benefits many persons (noun clause used as the direct object)

Quotations, both direct and indirect, are considered noun clauses in such sentences as these:

> Jim said, *"I have finished my essay."* (direct quotation)
>
> Katrina asked *who painted the picture.* (indirect quotation)

Noun Clauses Used as Objects of Prepositions

A noun clause may be used as the object of a preposition.

> He spoke of *how the polio vaccine benefits many persons.*
>
> He spoke of how the polio vaccine benefits many persons. (principal clause)
>
> how the polio vaccine benefits many persons (noun clause used as the object of a preposition)

Exercise 1

Identify the noun clause used as the subject in each sentence.

1. That the magician was late for the party surprised me.
2. What we should do next was the question.
3. How to keep people entertained was an issue.
4. That they could entertain themselves soon became clear.
5. Whether they would pay attention to the magician was uncertain.
6. Why she did not call to explain her lateness disturbed us.
7. That she had lost the address and phone number did not occur to us.
8. How she finally found us is a mystery.
9. That our guests are enjoying her performance is obvious.
10. Whether they will ever want to leave is not certain.

Complete each of the remaining five sentences with an appropriate noun clause used as the subject.

11. _____ is my motto.
12. _____ was long remembered.
13. _____ was soon discovered.
14. _____ is an important piece of information.
15. _____ has always interested me.

Exercise 2

Identify the noun clause used as the direct object in each sentence.

1. Howard insisted that Andy eat the peas.
2. Janice wondered how he learned to water-ski.
3. Patrick Henry demanded that he be granted liberty.
4. Betsy announced that she would study women writers.
5. Appoint whoever is capable.
6. The bylaws state that all members must vote.
7. Have you heard when the boat will dock?
8. The textbook explains how kidneys purify the blood.
9. Can you explain how this machine operates?
10. I knew that I had finished that exercise.

Complete each of the remaining five sentences with an appropriate noun clause used as the direct object.

11. Earl did _____ .
12. Julie said, _____ .
13. I do not know _____ .
14. The newspaper announced _____ .
15. Senator Jackson declared _____ .

Exercise 3

Identify the noun clause used as the object of the preposition in each sentence.

1. The man addressed the crowd from where he stood.
2. Owen was surprised by what prize his project won.
3. Professor Candor angered every student by what he said about today's news.
4. The class is studying about how nuclear fission occurs.
5. Give the message to whoever arrives first.
6. The people were moved by what they saw in the film.
7. Did you hear about what Tiffany did on her vacation?
8. Lance cannot buy a car on what he earns.

Complete each of the remaining sentences with an appropriate noun clause used as the object of the preposition.

9. We could not see the stage from _____ .
10. Diego, work with _____ .
11. We should make use of _____ .
12. Megan is interested in _____ .

Practice Power

▶ **Use the following noun clauses in your own sentences. Use the noun clause as the part of speech in the parentheses.**

1. what you bought (direct object)
2. how Craig won (subject)
3. that you would come (subject)
4. whoever found the purse (object of the preposition)
5. that Jessica was elected (direct object)

More Noun Clauses

Noun Clauses Used as Complements

A noun clause may be used as a complement. Remember that the complement follows a linking verb and completes its meaning.

> The fact is *that the polio vaccine benefits many persons.*
>
> The fact is that the polio vaccine benefits many persons. (principal clause)
>
> that the polio vaccine benefits many persons (noun clause used as complement)

Noun Clauses Used as Appositives

A noun clause may be used as an appositive. An appositive clause explains or describes the noun or the pronoun that precedes it.

> The fact *that the polio vaccine benefits many persons* cannot be denied.

A noun clause is considered an appositive when it follows and explains the expletive *it.*

> It is a fact *that the polio vaccine benefits many persons.*

Do not confuse appositive clauses with adjectival clauses. An appositive clause is a noun clause and takes the place of a noun; an adjectival clause modifies a noun or a pronoun.

> The notice *that we would have a holiday* caused great joy. (appositive clause)
>
> The notice *that she posted* was read by everybody. (adjectival clause)

Exercise 1

Identify the noun clause used as the complement in each sentence.

1. My hope is that we finish this work soon.
2. The fact is that Nathan is not qualified for the position.
3. The question was how we could earn enough money to pay for the broken window.
4. The truth is that the person who made the decision did not have all the facts.
5. The rule is that no one may smoke in this room.

Complete each of the remaining five sentences with an appropriate noun clause used as the complement.

6. The greatest attribute of the team is _____ .
7. Jack's most admirable characteristic is _____ .
8. Her favorite saying is _____ .
9. The teacher's suggestion was _____ .
10. What Candice wondered was _____ .

Exercise 2

Identify the noun clause used as the appositive in each sentence.

1. It was a mystery how the duck got in among the chickens.
2. The fact that the class president gave such an enthusiastic speech was encouraging to everyone.
3. Janet told the truth, that she had not accepted a bribe.
4. He forgot his promise that he would take us for a boat ride.
5. The saying that many hands make light work is familiar.

Complete each of the remaining five sentences with an appropriate noun clause used as the appositive.

6. Have you heard the news _____ ?
7. It cannot be denied _____ .
8. It was Colette's hope _____ .
9. Do you believe the report _____ ?
10. Dan's dream, _____ , seemed a possible reality.

Exercise 3 REVIEW OF NOUN CLAUSES

In each sentence, identify the noun clause and its use.

1. Kyle's fear that the air conditioner would fall out the window seemed unreasonable.
2. How such a thing might happen was not clear to us.
3. The fact was that the air conditioner had not been securely installed.
4. That it shook loose and fell on the car stunned us.
5. Kyle showed us that the screws were in the wrong places.
6. The car owner was angry about how the accident had occurred.
7. That the man was not hurt did not change his complaint.
8. He told the police that people should be careful about how they install air conditioners.
9. The driver decided that we would not have to pay for damages.
10. He hopes that insurance will pay for the repair.
11. How we will pay for a new air conditioner is another question.
12. Kyle insists that he will install it this time.
13. He does not think that we should trust anyone else.
14. The police officer suggested that we use window fans instead.
15. The news that insurance would cover all damages delighted us.

Exercise 4 REVIEW OF CLAUSES

Name the clauses and identify each as an adjectival clause, an adverbial clause, or a noun clause.

1. Uneasy lies the head that wears the crown.
2. I was pleased when I heard the news.
3. Mr. Kunik, who visited us, promised me a ticket.
4. Lucy realized that she had made a mistake.
5. Bruce read a poem that Marietta had written.
6. The lawnmower, which was in the garage, needed repair.
7. Veronica was not home when we called.
8. The moon is visible because it reflects the sun's light.
9. It has one side that never faces the earth.
10. It is known that the moon's gravity is only a fraction of the earth's.
11. Kirsten practiced hard because she wanted to perform as well as she could.
12. The person who wrote that letter to the editor remained anonymous.
13. What we fail to understand is often what we need to do most.
14. That Sarah should pass the test is clear.
15. Baby William will not wander into the water if we stay on the grass.
16. Swim while the sun shines.
17. Can you tell me where the nurse's office is located?
18. Pablo proved in many ways that he was a good coach.
19. A barge is a flat vessel on which bulky materials are transported.
20. Do you know that they live in an old schoolhouse?

Practice Power

▶ **Use the following noun clauses in sentences of your own. Tell how each clause is used.**

1. that she was creative
2. how the team played the game
3. what she prized most
4. that the tourists arrived
5. that the flights were canceled

Sentences

A sentence is a group of words expressing a complete thought.

Hieroglyphics is the ancient picture writing of the Egyptians.

Essential Elements of a Sentence

No sentence is complete without a subject and a predicate.

The subject of a sentence names a person, a place, or a thing about which a statement is made. The predicate tells something about the subject.

The subject with all its modifiers is called the complete subject. The predicate with all its modifiers and complements is called the complete predicate.

COMPLETE SUBJECT	COMPLETE PREDICATE
People	expect good service.
Bert, [you]	write the letter.
The team trainers	watch over us.

Exercise 1

Tell which of the following groups of words are sentences.
Rewrite the sentence fragments as complete sentences.

1. Sitting on the floor.
2. Laughs heartily.
3. Stand.
4. Give it to me.
5. Knowledge is power.
6. The spectator who saw the boat race.
7. Riding a bicycle through the city streets.
8. Smooth seas make poor sailors.
9. Palaces beautifully constructed.
10. During the night the boat drifted out to sea.
11. Into the burning house.
12. Werner von Braun, who designed the first rocket.
13. Stood the guest speaker.
14. Beside the river stood a small cottage.
15. Where have you been?

Natural and Inverted Order in Sentences

Whenever the predicate verb follows the simple subject, a sentence is in the natural order. Whenever the verb or an auxiliary verb is placed before its subject, a sentence is in the inverted order.

    SUBJECT   **VERB**
Wildflowers bloom in the spring. (natural order)

    VERB   **SUBJECT**
In the spring bloom wildflowers. (inverted order)

Exercise 2

Copy each sentence and draw one line under the complete subject and two lines under the complete predicate.

1. Spanish conquistadors explored the New World.
2. A fierce storm blew across the lake last evening.
3. Around the field galloped the excited horses.
4. The *Titanic* struck an iceberg.
5. Competition in the computer industry is keen.
6. In Italy was born Pirandello, a famous writer.
7. Report at nine o'clock.
8. Mark Antony was defeated by Augustus at Actium.
9. Have you corrected all the errors in your essay?
10. Always be prompt.

Exercise 3

Identify the subject and the verb of each sentence. Tell whether the sentences are in the natural or the inverted order.

1. Have you read any books by the novelist Cynthia Voigt?
2. She has written many fine stories for young adults.
3. They should go to the studio immediately.
4. The swimmers rushed to the lake at the sound of the whistle.
5. Does the small village lie beyond the distant mountains?
6. Milk flowed like a white waterfall from the overturned truck.
7. From behind the bushes came the rampaging rhinoceros.
8. Is the planet with rings around it called Saturn?
9. In the corner of the cab's back seat slumped the tired passenger.
10. Ten thousand people marched for civil rights.
11. From around the corner sprang the hungry kitten.
12. During the night the sky turned an eerie green.
13. Tom will give his acceptance speech at nine o'clock.
14. Before the news could reach her parents, Susan called them.
15. Behind a loose board in the old mansion was hidden a bundle of hundred-dollar bills.

Division of Sentences According to Use

A declarative sentence states a fact. An interrogative sentence asks a question. An imperative sentence expresses a command. An exclamatory sentence expresses strong or sudden emotion.

The first man-made satellite was *Sputnik I.* (declarative)
Who was the first cosmonaut? (interrogative)
Read the history of space exploration. (imperative)
How interesting it is! (exclamatory)

Exercise 4

Classify each sentence according to use and tell what punctuation mark should end the sentence.

1. With her help we designed a river raft
2. What beautiful flowers these are
3. What is primogeniture
4. Who are the painters of the American Gothic school
5. What an important inventor Edison was
6. Beijing is one of the largest cities in the world
7. Bring the report to me at once
8. Betty was chosen secretary of the club
9. How was smallpox virtually eliminated
10. See the hydrofoil
11. Mail used to be delivered twice a day
12. Tokyo is the largest city in Japan

Practice Power

▶ Write an interesting sentence according to each set of directions.

1. an imperative sentence in inverted order
2. a declarative sentence in natural order
3. an interrogative sentence in inverted order
4. a declarative sentence in inverted order
5. an imperative sentence in natural order

Simple Sentences

According to form, sentences are divided into simple, compound, complex, and compound-complex sentences.

A simple sentence contains one subject and one predicate, either or both of which may be compound.

SUBJECT   PREDICATE
Leo Tolstoy <u>wrote</u> many fine novels.

If the subject of a sentence consists of more than one noun or pronoun, it is said to be a compound subject. If the predicate consists of more than one verb, it is said to be a compound predicate.

A sentence may have a compound subject, a compound predicate, or a compound subject and a compound predicate.

Spain and *Portugal* are the countries of the Iberian peninsula. (compound subject)

That line *owns* and *operates* ships in many waters. (compound predicate)

Toby and *Louise sing* and *dance.* (compound subject and compound predicate)

Exercise 1

Show that each sentence is simple by identifying its subject and predicate.

1. From the stage came the sound of the actor's voice.
2. Did Amanda and Louise invite you to the party?
3. Jill likes to swim and dive in the lake.
4. In October, the leaves change color and fall from the trees.
5. Terry and Roz are vegetarians.
6. Many people take vacations in the summer.
7. Singing and dancing, we celebrated the event.
8. Many varieties of fish are found in the aquarium.

Exercise 2

Complete each sentence by supplying a compound subject or compound predicate.

1. _____ and _____ are cities in the United States.
2. _____ , _____ , and _____ are playing together in the hay.
3. The sprinters and hurdlers on our team _____ and _____ every day.
4. _____ and _____ brought flowers home.
5. Juan and Judy either _____ a letter or _____ .
6. Darren _____ oranges and _____ them.
7. _____ and _____ hope to visit their cousins in Germany this summer.
8. The carpenter _____ and _____ the board.

Practice Power

▶ Write five simple sentences using the elements suggested below.

1. a compound subject and compound predicate in natural order
2. a compound subject in inverted order
3. a compound predicate in inverted order
4. a compound predicate in an interrogative sentence
5. a compound subject and compound predicate in an interrogative sentence

Compound Sentences

A compound sentence contains two or more independent clauses.

> The United States is a large country, and it is rich in natural resources.

This sentence contains two complete statements (simple sentences), which are connected by the conjunction *and*.

> The United States is a large country.
> It is rich in natural resources.

Exercise 1

Identify the subject and predicate of each independent clause in these compound sentences.

1. Class was dismissed and the students went home.
2. I cannot talk with you right now; I will explain later.
3. Henry expected to get an excellent grade on the test; nevertheless, he waited nervously.
4. I read *The Adventures of Tom Sawyer,* but I did not see the movie version.
5. The water had been shut off; yet no one could understand why.
6. I studied very hard for this test; moreover, I have always done well on science tests.
7. I wanted to go running, but the weather was just too cold.
8. Snow and ice covered the streets, and the car was buried in front of the building.
9. Carla did not paint the mural, nor did she carve the statue.
10. The students listened eagerly to the lunchtime announcements, but the principal did not dismiss school for the day.

Exercise 2

Combine each pair of simple sentences into one compound sentence.

1. A lake is a large body of standing water. A pond is a small body of standing water.
2. I watched. I did not see the man again.
3. Erin will read a poem or sing a song at the wedding. Joshua will play a new guitar composition.
4. The Mets and the Cubs play baseball in the National League. The Yankees and the White Sox play in the American League.
5. The man seemed to smile. He offered no help.
6. Anthracite is hard coal. Bituminous coal is soft coal.
7. Ichabod Crane was tall and lanky. His whole frame was loosely hung together.
8. Synonyms are words of similar meanings. Antonyms are words of opposite meanings.
9. Sun and wind sometimes burn skin. Water and harsh soaps can damage skin.
10. In the mountains, summer days are warm. Nights are cool.

Practice Power

▶ Choose one specific topic to write about. Write your sentences according to the suggestions below. Your sentences may be in any order.

1. a compound sentence with a compound subject in either clause
2. a compound sentence with a compound predicate in either clause
3. a simple sentence
4. a compound sentence
5. a simple sentence with any compound element

Complex and Compound-Complex Sentences

Complex Sentences

A complex sentence contains one principal clause and one or more subordinate clauses.

> Pennsylvania was settled by William Penn, who was the son of a wealthy English admiral.

> Pennsylvania was settled by William Penn (principal clause)

> who was the son of a wealthy English admiral. (subordinate clause)

Subordinate clauses may be adjectival, adverbial, or noun clauses, according to their use in the sentence.

Adjectival clauses are generally introduced by relative pronouns *(who, whom, whose, which, that)* or relative adverbs *(when, where, why)*. Adjectival clauses do the work of an adjective.

Adverbial clauses are generally introduced by subordinate conjunctions *(as, that, since, because, for, if, then, than, provided, unless, though, so, after, when, before, where, until, while)*. Adverbial clauses may tell time, place, degree, manner, cause, or purpose.

Noun clauses are generally introduced by the introductory words *how, whether, what, why,* and *that*. Noun clauses are used as nouns and may be subjects, direct objects, objects of prepositions, complements, or appositives.

Compound-Complex Sentences

A compound-complex sentence contains two or more principal clauses and one or more subordinate clauses.

Napoleon had an austere manner, but he was always kind to the soldiers who were under his charge.

Napoleon had an austere manner, (principal clause)
but (coordinate conjunction)
he was always kind to the soldiers (principal clause)
who were under his charge. (subordinate clause)

Napoleon had an austere manner, but he was always kind to the soldiers is a compound sentence connected by the coordinate conjunction *but. Who were under his charge* is an adjectival clause introduced by the relative pronoun *who.* A compound-complex sentence must contain two or more principal, or independent, clauses and one or more subordinate, or dependent, clauses.

Exercise 1

Indicate the principal clause and the subordinate clause in each sentence. Tell whether the subordinate clause is adverbial, adjectival, or noun.

1. I get excited when I see a rainbow in the sky.
2. Monte Cassino was a famous abbey that was destroyed during World War II.
3. Although Paris and Berlin had their charms, Debbie longed for home.
4. The dog came when she called him.
5. If you drive slowly, stay in the right lane.
6. We think that they are touring somewhere in Africa.
7. The compass indicates that we are moving north.
8. The seismograph is an instrument that records the direction, the intensity, and the duration of earthquakes.
9. Until you have lived through a tornado, you cannot fully comprehend its strength.
10. The woman who taught him to play the trumpet lives down the street.

Exercise 2

Complete the subordinate clauses and identify them as adjectival, adverbial, or noun clauses.

1. That _____ was no surprise to me.
2. Since _____ , the United States had been involved in a space race.
3. A monument now stands here because _____ .
4. Suzie's cello teacher, who _____ , encourages her to practice.
5. Diane arranged the flowers that _____ .
6. Lester was talking about what _____ .
7. I always respond when _____ .
8. London, which _____ , is on the bank of the River Thames.
9. Molly admires people who _____ .
10. If _____ , I will not wait for you.

Exercise **3**

Make one complex sentence from each of the following groups of simple sentences. Identify the introductory word of any subordinate clause.

1. Watch where you walk. Rusty nails are sticking out of the boards.
2. Leo Tolstoy was a Russian author. He wrote *War and Peace.*
3. President Monroe was concerned about the influence of European powers on countries in the Western Hemisphere. He issued the Monroe Doctrine.
4. The ancient Egyptians made paper from the papyrus plant. This plant grew along the banks of the Nile.
5. I studied the lesson. The lesson was assigned yesterday.
6. I looked up the river. I saw a beautiful boat sailing. The boat was sailing toward me. The boat was sailing swiftly.
7. Jim plowed the land. He planted the seeds. The seeds were for corn.
8. The plant drooped. It had not been watered in two weeks. It would have died. Tina watered it.
9. The waves washed a broken rowboat up onto the beach. The rowboat had been tied to a dock before the storm.
10. The sun was shining brightly. It melted the snow.

Exercise 4

Identify each of the following sentences as simple, compound, complex, or compound-complex.

1. Dolley Madison, the wife of President James Madison, was a Quaker.
2. She first married John Todd, who was also a Quaker.
3. Her marriage to John lasted a short three years.
4. Dolley had two sons, but one died the same year as her husband [died].
5. In 1794, Dolley married James Madison.
6. Because her husband was not a Quaker, Dolley was rejected by the Society of Friends, and she could no longer attend Quaker meetings.
7. Dolley, who excited everyone with her style and charm, served as White House hostess for sixteen years.
8. Because Thomas Jefferson was a widower, Dolley assumed the role of First Lady during his administration.
9. Dolley was the first to serve ice cream in the White House.
10. When the British invaded Washington in 1814, Dolley fled the city.
11. She took with her many important documents, and she saved a famous portrait of George Washington.
12. Dolley was anxious to return to the White House after it had been burned.
13. She wanted to resume her entertaining, but the restoration progressed slowly.
14. President Madison left office before the White House was ready to be occupied, but James Monroe was able to enjoy its new beauty.

Putting It All Together

Sometimes facts are complex. For example, the grocer down the street might be hostile on some occasions and kind on others. In describing him, you might say, *Mr. Smith, who chases us out of his store, donated money to our baseball team.*

Think of some other opposite facts about people, places, or things. Then write sentences containing both facts. Use principal clauses to describe the more important facts and subordinate clauses to describe those that are less important.

Chapter Challenge

Read this selection carefully and answer the questions that follow.

[1]What are the factors that determine the occupations of those who live in certain localities? [2]To answer this question, consider carefully the physical features of the region. [3]If the climate, soil, and rainfall favor the raising of crops, the people turn to farming. [4]The fact that they live near the sea moves others to make fishing their work. [5]Inhabitants of districts having rich mineral deposits find employment in the mines. [6]In thickly populated areas many workers are available, and raw materials are easily transported. [7]If power resources are sufficient, manufacturing becomes important in such sections. [8]Since the other occupations are similarly controlled by natural environment, we see that an individual's choice of a life's work is limited greatly by the area in which he or she lives.

1. Name two adjectival clauses in the first sentence.

2. What kind of phrase is *to answer this question* in the second sentence?

3. Name the subordinate clause in the third sentence. Is it adjectival or adverbial?

4. Name the adverbial phrase in the fourth sentence.

5. What kind of a clause is *that they live near the sea* in the fourth sentence? Give the syntax, or use, of this clause.

6. Is the fifth sentence in the natural or the inverted order?

7. What kind of phrase is *having rich mineral deposits* in the fifth sentence?

8. Find a compound sentence in the paragraph.

9. Name a prepositional phrase in the seventh sentence.

10. Find an adverbial clause in the seventh sentence.

11. Is the phrase *of a life's work* in the last sentence adjectival or adverbial?

CHAPTER

19

PUNCTUATION AND CAPITALIZATION

488

Periods and Commas

The purpose of punctuation is to make clear the meaning of what is written. In speaking, the inflection of a person's voice helps to convey his or her message to a listener. In writing, different kinds of punctuation marks—the period, comma, semicolon, colon, exclamation point, question mark, quotation marks, apostrophe, hyphen, and dash—are used to clarify ideas for the reader. In this chapter, you will learn the basic rules for punctuation and capitalization.

The Period

Use a period

- at the end of a declarative or an imperative sentence.

  The Parthenon is an ancient Greek temple.
  Come here, Margarita.

- after an abbreviation and an initial.

  D.D.S.   James A. Longnose

The Comma

Use a comma

- to separate words or groups of words used in a series.

  Some berries were red, unripe, and bitter.
  Mike visited the museum, the park, and city hall.

About the Photograph

Do you have a message to convey? Remember, correct punctuation helps to make your ideas crystal clear.

- to separate independent elements and words of direct address.

> Yes, it is flying toward the river.
> Paul, can you see that plane?

- to set off a short direct quotation and the parts of a divided quotation, unless a question mark or an exclamation point is required.

> "I shall be glad to come," answered Linda.
> "Someday," said Leo, "I'll be a doctor."
> "Have you ever read *Call of the Wild?*" asked Sue.

- to set off the parts of dates, addresses, or geographical names.

> The earthquake struck San Francisco, California, on April 18, 1906.

- to separate nonrestrictive phrases and clauses from the rest of the sentence.

> The boat, crowded with people, sailed away.
> Brian, who has been to Boston, returned last night.

NOTE: A nonrestrictive phrase or clause is one that may be omitted from a sentence without changing the meaning. Some phrases and clauses are necessary to the meaning of a sentence and cannot be omitted. They are called restrictive phrases or clauses and are not separated by commas.

> The whale that was beached drew much attention.

- after long introductory phrases and clauses, and when needed to make the meaning clear.

> Seated in the midst of a group of enthusiastic spectators, Michael clapped and cheered.
> If you had stopped, Vince would have followed.

- to set off an appositive that is not part of a proper name or that is not restrictive.

> Julius Caesar, a Roman politician and dictator, was a brilliant general.
> William the Conqueror became king of England in 1066.

- to set off a parenthetical expression; that is, a word or a group of words inserted in the sentence as a comment or an explanatory remark, and one that is not necessary to the thought of the sentence.

> You are, indeed, an industrious worker.
> Copernicus was, without a doubt, an intelligent man.

- to separate the clauses of a compound sentence connected by the conjunctions *and, but, or, nor,* and *yet.* If the clauses are short and closely connected, the comma may be omitted.

> Your team won two games, but ours won three.
> The door opened and he entered quietly.

- after the salutation in a social letter and after the complimentary close in all letters.

> Dear Maureen,
> Dear Mrs. Thanopoulous,
> Sincerely yours,

Exercise 1

Give the reason each period is used and the rule that explains why each comma is used.

1. Manuel bought a hamburger, but Ollie wanted tuna salad.
2. If the soccer game is over, we can give Tim a ride home.
3. Dad told us about Elizabeth Cady Stanton, a woman who fought for women's right to vote.
4. Marjorie, we were told, excels in all of her classes.
5. "Come and see my new canoe," said Nick.
6. On August 25, 1998, our team won the league championship.
7. Yes, I know that running in the hall is against the rules.
8. Cynthia, please turn off the lights.
9. The firefighters, who climb ladders often, helped Gwen retrieve the ball from the roof.
10. My dreams, however odd they seem to you, give me hope.

Exercise 2

Punctuate each sentence correctly.

1. It is time to sleep children
2. Answer all questions truthfully completely and courteously
3. Frank parked his car a green station wagon in front of the gym
4. Italy surrendered on September 8 1943 but Germany did not give up until May 8 1945
5. Come over Greg and see my new skates
6. The setting for example should be carefully arranged
7. Although Philip and Bill are no longer roommates they correspond regularly
8. If you had called Cecilia would have told you where I was
9. Sharon Kim's friend made David angry
10. We moved from Harrisburg Pennsylvania to Memphis Tennessee

Practice Power

▶ The following excerpt is taken from *Pilgrim at Tinker Creek* by Annie Dillard. Ms. Dillard has made excellent use of commas in this selection, but none appear below. Rewrite the paragraph, inserting commas and periods where you feel they are appropriate.

When the muskrat went under the bridge I moved so I could face downstream comfortably He reappeared and I had a good look at him He was eight inches long in the body and another six in the tail Muskrat tails are black and scaled flattened not horizontally like beavers' tails but vertically like a belt stood on edge In the winter muskrats' tails sometimes freeze solid and the animals chew off the frozen parts up to about an inch of the body. . . .

Other Types of Punctuation

The Semicolon

Use a semicolon

- to separate the clauses of a compound sentence when they are not separated by a coordinate conjunction.

  Gary did not go to the football game; he went on a hike instead.

- to separate the clauses of a compound sentence that are connected by such words as *nevertheless, moreover, therefore, then,* and *thus.*

  She was a good worker; therefore, her name was added to the list.

- before *as* and *namely* when these words introduce an example or an illustration.

  In the body there are two kinds of blood cells; namely, the red cells and the white cells.

- to separate the members of a series when a comma alone would not separate them clearly.

  I am a farmer. For me democracy means the freedom to plant and harvest my own crops; to sell them or to use them to feed my cattle; and to use the earth, the sun, and the rain for the well-being of all people.

The Colon

Use a colon

- after the salutation of a business letter.

    Dear Ms. Grayes: Gentlemen: Dear Mr. Reed:

- before a list or enumeration of items.

    They ordered the following: a desk, a chair, a bookcase, and a table.

- before a long direct quotation.

    The author wrote: "I have traveled a great distance and I am tired; I will go no farther until I am rested."

The Exclamation Point

Use an exclamation point

- after an exclamatory sentence.

    What a magnificent scene lay before us!

- after an exclamatory word, phrase, or clause.

    "Silence!" called the speaker.

The Question Mark

Use a question mark at the end of every question.

    Where is my camera?

Quotation Marks

Use quotation marks

- before and after every direct quotation and every part of a divided quotation.

    "Then you shall have it!" said the king.
    "I would rather be right," said Henry Clay, "than be president."

NOTE: Sometimes a quotation includes another quotation. Such an included quotation is known as a quotation within a quotation and is marked with single quotation marks.

    "When the crowd screamed, 'Watch out for the car!' I froze," confessed Neil.

- to enclose titles of stories, poems, magazine articles, newspaper articles, TV shows, and radio programs.

    The best poetry recitation on the program was Kilmer's "Trees."

NOTE: Titles of books, magazines, movies, works of art, plays, and newspapers are printed in italics. In typing or handwriting, italics are indicated by underlining.

    The Call of the Wild is an exciting book.
    <u>The Call of the Wild</u> is an exciting book.

The Apostrophe

Use an apostrophe

- to show possession.

    Men's shoes are on sale.

- with *s* to show the plural of letters when the omission of the apostrophe would lead to confusion.

    i's   *t*'s   *a*'s

- to show the omission of a letter, letters, or figures.

    didn't   I'll   class of '99

The Hyphen

Use a hyphen

- to divide a word at the end of a line whenever one or more syllables are carried to the next line.

   My grandfather, who lives in California, will be visiting in July.

- in compound numbers from twenty-one to ninety-nine.

   She is twenty-five years old.

- to separate the parts of some compound words.

   self-respect   son-in-law

The Dash

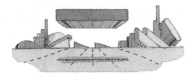

Use a dash to indicate a sudden change of thought.

   I suddenly turned—I am still surprised at my action—and left the room.

Exercise 1

Insert semicolons and commas where they are needed.

1. The subway car seemed filled to capacity nevertheless four more people squeezed into it.
2. Leave the arrangements to me I'll take care of them.
3. The school newspaper has four reporters namely Scott Ellen Dan and Audrey.
4. To write a paragraph select and limit the subject build a vocabulary make an outline and follow the outline to write beginning middle and ending sentences.
5. I know how to play the guitar however my finger is broken.

Exercise 2

Insert colons, exclamation points, question marks, and quotation marks where they are needed.

1. We will take these things with us on the camping trip a tent, sleeping bags, and food for two days.
2. Who ate my tangerine asked Madeline.

3. I did cried Karin.
4. Why do you think she did that
5. My, am I hungry
6. When looking to the future, consider these words Know what roads lie before you and make an intelligent choice. Don't be fooled by how narrow or how wide the path. If it leads to your goal, take it.
7. Maya Angelou wrote the poem On the Pulse of the Morning.
8. Patrick Henry said, If this be treason, make the most of it.
9. What a thrilling play she wrote
10. Did Carmen promise to take us to the zoo

Exercise 3

Practice using quotation marks by writing dialogue between two persons. Keep the following points in mind:

- Each time you introduce a different speaker, you must indent the first line.
- When your reader knows who is saying the next line, the speaker does not need mentioning.
- Vary your quotations by naming the speaker first, last, or in the middle of the dialogue (divided quotation).

Review the example below and then write four lines of dialogue for each situation.

Example: butcher to customer

"How much ham would you like?" asked the butcher.

Mrs. Robb answered, "Just slice me one pound, but give me a pound and a half of Swiss cheese, please."

"Anything else?" (speaker not mentioned)

"Not right now, thank you," said Mrs. Robb. "I'll make do with this." (divided quotation)

1. driving instructor to new driver
2. coach to team member
3. teacher to student
4. baby-sitter to young child

Practice Power

▶ **Indicate the correct punctuation.**

1. Make your *w*s more plainly
2. Did John buy twenty five acres of land
3. When you play play hard when you study study hard
4. James laughed and said Ill stay home
5. Dante an Italian poet wrote many famous poems
6. Ouch I cut my finger
7. What is her name her age and her address
8. Oh what a beautiful baby exclaimed the woman in the blue coat
9. The library is open three days this week Monday Wednesday and Saturday
10. Jean asked Do you know who wrote that note
11. We hoped we were always hoping that the outcome would be different
12. Yes I will attend the party
13. A mouse cried Marsha
14. Good morning Susan called the doorkeeper
15. When Lil said You are wrong I decided to reconsider said Peter
16. It was early when we arrived the shops were not open
17. The work had to be done Anne was elected to do it
18. Percy Shelley an English poet wrote the following poems Mont Blanc Ode to Liberty and To a Skylark
19. Garys mother in law is very ill
20. The letter was mailed from Lima Peru

Capital Letters

Use a capital letter for

- the first word in a sentence.

    Tall trees shaded the park.

- the first word of every line of most poetry.

    The day is ending,
    The moon is bending
    Over a star-studded sky
    Sprinkling silver
    Where the pathways lie.

- the first word of a direct quotation.

    Jane cried, "Come quickly!"

- proper nouns and proper adjectives. These include particular persons or groups of persons, months of the year, days of the week, holidays, religious denominations, political parties, institutions, buildings, cities, states, and streets.

    Joseph, French, March, Tuesday, Veterans Day, Mormon, Democrats, Republican party, Empire State Building, Tokyo, North Carolina, Broadway Avenue

- titles of honor and respect when preceding the name.

    Judge O'Hara   Queen Elizabeth

Do not capitalize any title not followed by a proper noun unless it is used in direct address as a substitute for the name.

    The judge has entered the courtroom.
    Not guilty, Your Honor.

- *north, east, south,* and *west* when they refer to sections of a country.

    He comes from the West.

- all names referring to a deity, the Bible or parts of the Bible, and all other sacred books.

    The Koran is the collection of the sacred writings of Muhammad.

- the principal words in the titles of books, plays, poems, and pictures.

    Adventures of Huckleberry Finn

- the pronoun *I* and the interjection *O.*

    O Mr. Barbera! I see the meteor.

- abbreviations when capitals would be used if the words were written in full.

    Gen.   St.

Do not capitalize

- the seasons of the year.

    fall
    winter

- the articles *a, an, the,* conjunctions, or prepositions in titles, unless they are the first words.

    Life on the Mississippi   *The Time of Your Life*

- the names of studies, unless they are derived from proper nouns.

    history   geography   English

- the words *high school, college,* and *university,* unless they are parts of the names of particular institutions.

> My brother goes to high school in Dayton.
> My sister is a senior at the University of
> Southern California.

- the word *god* or *gods* when referring to mythology.

> Who was the king of the gods?

Exercise 1

Choose the phrase that contains the correct capitalization.

1. **a.** heading northeast
   b. heading Northeast
2. **a.** in the autumn
   b. in the Autumn
3. **a.** Elementary School
   b. Weber Junior High
4. **a.** June graduation
   b. june Graduation
5. **a.** President of the Company
   b. President Johnson

6. **a.** "the Raven"
   b. "The Raven"
7. **a.** I'm enjoying math.
   b. I'm enjoying Math.
8. **a.** Mars, God of War
   b. Mars, god of war
9. **a.** living in the South
   b. living in the south
10. **a.** Kingston road
    b. Kingston Road

Putting It All Together

The playwright William Shakespeare used line breaks, punctuation, and capitalization as a way to insert acting directions in his plays. Modern punctuation does the same.

Copy a passage from a story or poem you admire. Then read it aloud, using punctuation as a performance guide. If you wish, mark up your copy to provide yourself with additional performance notes. Capitalize words that deserve extra emphasis, and add underlines, dashes, or other marks to help yourself remember how to perform the passage.

Chapter Challenge

Copy and divide the following two selections into sentences. Use the necessary capital letters and insert the proper punctuation marks.

1. my father as i said was greatly delighted if my teacher had compared me to william shakespeare or had exclaimed he is a genius he could not have felt better he called me into the living room and with a beaming smile said

   there is no need for me to tell you i was pleased when your teacher said henry is a good student but even more he is a person of integrity who is respected by his peers i am not going to diminish the praise youve been given by rewarding you materially as you are aware the best reward for being true to the moral values in which you believe is a clear conscience

2. a merry christmas uncle god save you cried a cheerful voice it was the voice of scrooges nephew who came upon him so quickly that this was the first intimation he had of his approach

   bah said scrooge humbug

   he had so heated himself with rapid walking in the fog and frost this nephew of scrooges that he was all in a glow his face was ruddy and handsome his eyes sparkled and his breath smoked again

   christmas a humbug uncle said scrooges nephew you dont mean that i am sure

   i do said scrooge merry christmas what right have you to be merry if i could work my will every idiot who goes about with merry christmas on his lips should be boiled with his own pudding and buried with a stake of holly through his breast

   —from *A Christmas Carol,* by Charles Dickens

CHAPTER

20

MODEL DIAGRAMS

504

Model Diagrams

Diagrams show in a graphic manner the relationships that exist among the various words that make up a sentence. As you have seen, there are simple, compound, and complex sentences. Since sentences of all types may contain modifiers, no one form of diagram will serve for every kind of sentence. The diagrams given here are those that should help you in your work. When asked to diagram a sentence, look here for a sentence of the same kind and see how the diagram is made.

Diagraming sentences serves a double purpose. First, it makes it easier for you to understand the complete meaning of every sentence you read. Second, it helps you to write effectively and to avoid the use of faulty sentences. If you keep these purposes in mind, diagraming will improve your English. It should not become merely a mechanical exercise, but instead should help you to read more intelligently and to write more correctly.

Simple Sentences

Nominative Case

Subject: Into the fort stumbled the exhausted *messenger.*

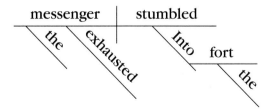

Subjective Complement: Five seventh-grade girls are the new *cheerleaders.*

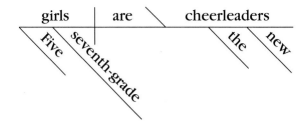

Appositive: Basil, the *soldier,* was the father of Gabriel.

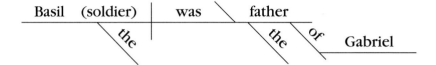

Direct Address: *Jeb,* be our guide on this journey.

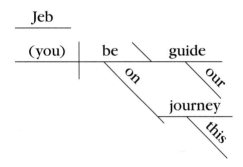

Exclamation: *Action!* The play needs action.

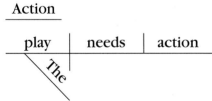

Absolute: The football *game* having ended, the spectators jumped to their feet.

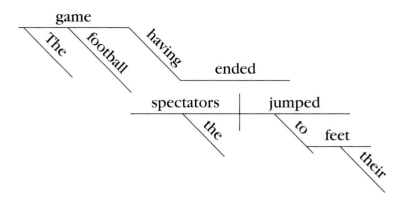

Objective Case

Direct Object: Squirrels collect *nuts.*

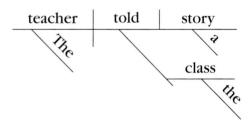

Indirect Object: The teacher told the *class* a story.

Appositive: We visited Tokyo, the *capital* of Japan.

MODEL DIAGRAMS

Object of a Preposition: Washington performed his duties with great *courage.*

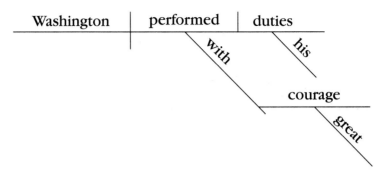

Adverbial Objective: This *morning* the ground was covered with frost.

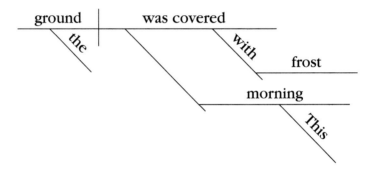

Objective Complement: The committee appointed Joseph *secretary.*

Compound Predicate: Rebecca *gathered* books and *read* them.

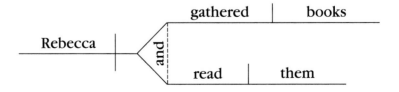

Compound Sentences

The tourists visited Independence Hall and they saw the Liberty Bell.

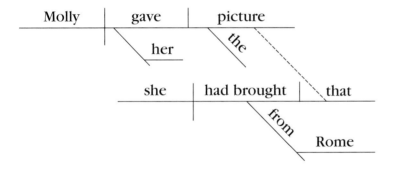

Complex Sentences

Adjectival Clauses

Molly gave her the picture *that she had brought from Rome.*

This is the boy *whose horse won the prize.*

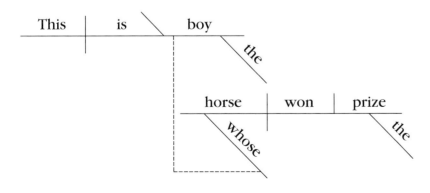

Adverbial Clauses

Connie came *because you sent for her.*

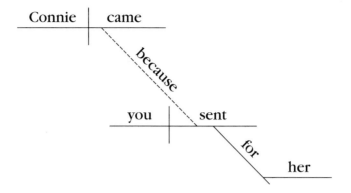

When snow falls, the town presents a beautiful picture.

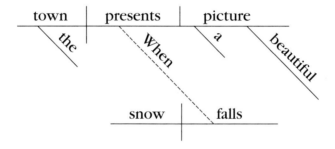

Noun Clauses

Subject: *That the ocean is large* is evident.

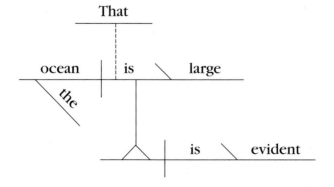

510

Subjective Complement: My hope is *that we finish the work soon.*

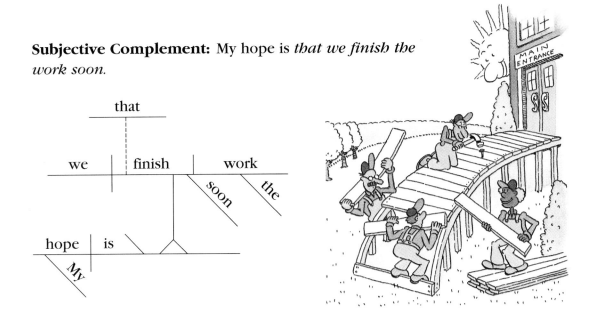

Direct Object: He realized *that he had made a mistake.*

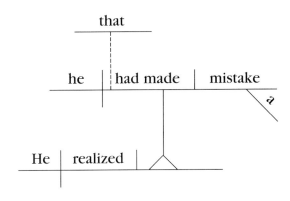

Object of a Preposition: The hikers could see the town from *where they had camped.*

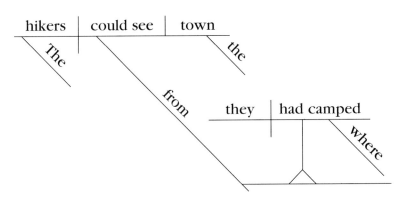

Appositive: The fact *that he was honest* could not be denied.

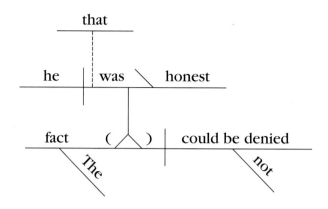

Infinitives

Subject: *To win* was their only thought.

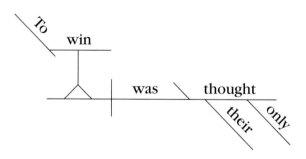

Subjective Complement: The boy's aim was *to rescue* his dog.

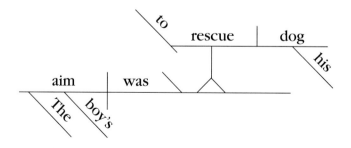

Object: I like *to see* good movies.

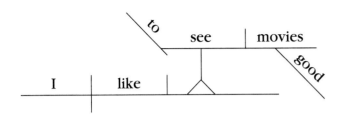

Object of a Preposition: He was about *to write* the letter.

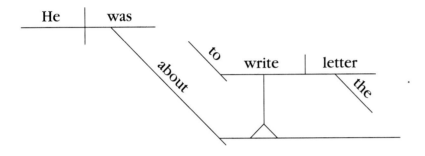

Appositive: It is the duty of a police officer *to enforce* the laws.

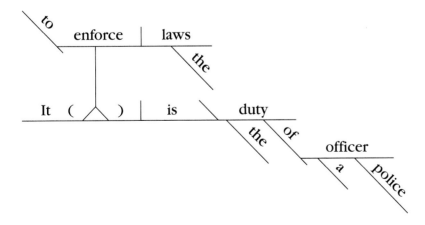

Adjective: They have many opportunities *to visit* the planetarium.

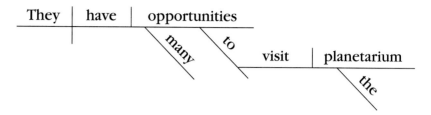

Adverb: Chrissy went *to buy* a new car.

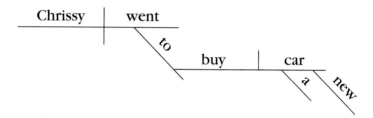

They were anxious *to return*.

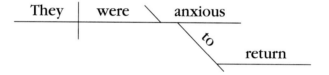

The king is powerful enough *to gather* an army.

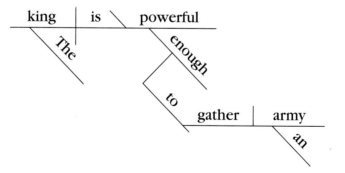

Subject: Whom do you expect *to govern* the country for the next four years?

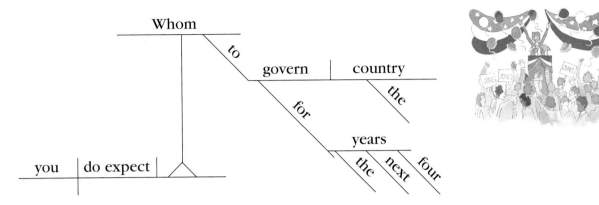

Participles

The protesters, *bearing signs,* marched into the square.

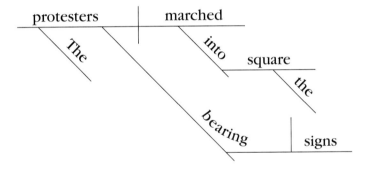

Shouting joyfully, they marched around the football field.

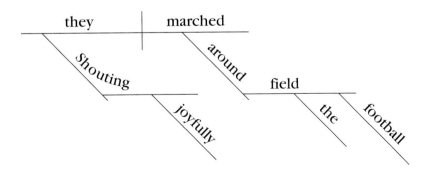

Participial Adjective

The *running* water wore away the stone.

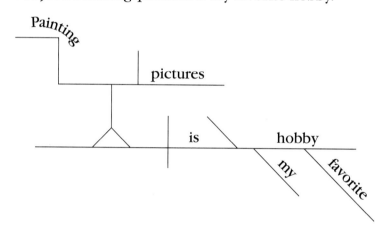

Gerunds

Subject: *Painting* pictures is my favorite hobby.

Direct Object: I remember *writing* that letter.

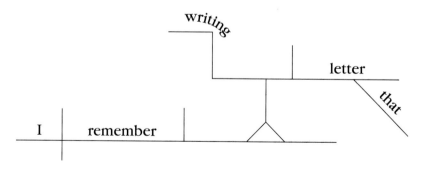

Object of a Preposition: Windmills are used for *pumping* water.

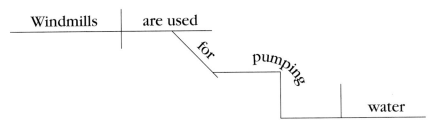

Subjective Complement: My favorite pastime is *reading* biographies.

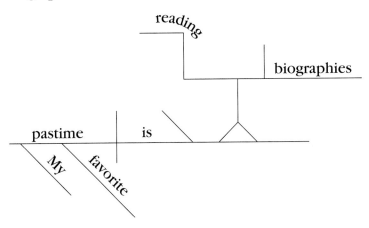

Grammar and Writing Handbook

Grammar

ADJECTIVES

An adjective describes or limits a noun or a pronoun. Adjectives may be divided into two general classes: descriptive adjectives and limiting adjectives.

Adjectival Clauses

An adjectival clause is a subordinate clause used as an adjective.

The storyteller told us a story *that was fascinating*.

Common Adjectives

A common adjective expresses the ordinary qualities of a noun or a pronoun.

tall ship   *majestic* mountains

Comparison of Adjectives

Comparison is the change that adjectives undergo to express different degrees of quality, quantity, or value. Most adjectives have three degrees of comparison.

The positive degree denotes quality.
> Green Lake is *deep.*

The comparative degree denotes quality in a greater or a lesser degree and is used when two are compared.
> Is Green Lake *deeper* than Fox Lake?

The superlative degree denotes quality in the greatest or the least degree and is used when more than two are compared.
> Green Lake is the *deepest* lake in our state.

Demonstrative Adjectives

A demonstrative adjective points out a definite person, place, or thing *(this, that, these, those).*

Descriptive Adjectives

A descriptive adjective describes a noun or a pronoun. The two types of descriptive adjectives are proper adjectives and common adjectives.

> The *French* student told us about France. (proper)
> The *frisky* puppy would not come near us. (common)

Interrogative Adjectives

An interrogative adjective is used in asking a question *(which, what, whose).*

Limiting Adjectives

A limiting adjective either points out an object or denotes number.

The articles *the, an,* and *a* show whether a noun is used definitely or indefinitely. *The* is the definite article. *An* and *a* are indefinite articles.

A numeral adjective denotes exact number. It may refer to the number of things or to the place of an item in a sequence.

A pronominal adjective may also be used as a pronoun. Words such as *this, his, each, several,* and *what* may be used either as pronouns or adjectives.

Participial Adjectives

A participial adjective is descriptive, does not act as a verb, may not take an object, and has the position of an adjective before a noun or after a linking verb.

Creeping vines covered the trellis.

Possessive Adjectives

The possessives that modify nouns are called possessive adjectives.

Pronominal Adjectives

Pronominal adjectives are usually divided into five classes.

A demonstrative adjective points out a definite person, place, or thing *(this, that, these, those).*

A possessive adjective denotes ownership *(my, our, your, his, her, its, their).*

A distributive adjective refers to each person, place, or thing separately *(each, every, either, neither)*.

An indefinite adjective points out no particular person, place, or thing *(any, all, another, both, few, many, much, etc.)*.

An interrogative adjective is used in asking a question *(which, what, whose, who, whom)*.

Proper Adjectives

A proper adjective is formed from a proper noun.

Brazilian merchant   *Swiss* tour guide

ADVERBS

An adverb modifies a verb, an adjective, an adverb, a participle, a gerund, or an infinitive.

Adverbs of time answer the question *when* or *how often.*
   The chorus *frequently* sings for us.

Adverbs of place answer the question *where.*
   Harvey walked *forward* to the edge of the stage.

Adverbs of manner answer the question *how* or *in what manner.*
   Abraham Lincoln spoke *truthfully.*

Adverbs of degree answer the question *how much* or *how little.*
   Today is a *very* windy day.

Adverbs of affirmation or negation tell whether a statement is true or false.
   Yes, we will go with you.

Adverbial Clauses

An adverbial clause is a subordinate clause used as an adverb. Adverbial clauses are usually introduced by subordinate conjunctions. These clauses may tell time, place, degree, manner, cause, or purpose.

You may go to the dance *when your room is clean.*

Adverbial Objectives

An adverbial objective is a noun that expresses time, distance, measure, weight, value, or direction and performs the function of an adverb.

Treshon earned six *dollars* baby-sitting.
This class session will take two *hours.*

Comparison of Adverbs

Adverbs, like adjectives, have three degrees of comparison: positive, comparative, and superlative.

Interrogative Adverbs

An interrogative adverb is used in asking questions. The interrogative adverbs are *how, when, where,* and *why.* They usually modify the verb.

When will the bus arrive?
How will I know when you are ready?

Relative Adverbs

A relative adverb does the work of an adverb and a relative pronoun. The principal relative adverbs are *when, where,* and *why.*

March is the month *when* the robins return.
The alderman wondered *why* the meeting was adjourned.

Simple Adverbs

A simple adverb is used merely as a modifier.

Carl Lewis ran *quickly.*

ANTECEDENTS

The word to which a pronoun refers is its antecedent.

Laurie wants us to follow her.

APPOSITIVES

An appositive is a word or group of words that renames a noun, pronoun, or word group.

Mr. Hiller, *our biology teacher,* is absent today.

ARTICLES

Articles are limiting adjectives: *the, a,* and *an.*

CASE

How a noun or pronoun is used in a sentence tells the case.

Nominative Case

A noun used in direct address is in the nominative case.
Sylvia, it's time to practice your saxophone.

If a nominative case noun has an appositive, the noun in apposition is also in the nominative case.
The small monkeys, *marmosets,* are at the zoo.

A noun used independently to express strong emotion is in the nominative case.
Lucky *guy!* You just won first prize.

A noun before a participle in an independent phrase (nominative case absolute) is in the nominative case.

The *parade* having passed by, everyone went home.

A noun or pronoun used as the subject of a verb is in the nominative case.

The *campfire* glowed in the night.
I will sweep the floors.

A noun or pronoun used as a subjective complement is in the nominative case.

He became the *president* of our club.
The chairperson of our committee is *she.*

Objective Case

A noun in apposition that explains a direct object, an indirect object, or an object of a preposition is in the objective case.

The team met with their coach, *John Dominguez.*

A noun or pronoun used as the direct object of a verb is in the objective case.

The delivery person brought a *package.*
Our neighbors invited *me* to join them.

A noun or pronoun used as the indirect object of a verb is in the objective case.

Salomon showed *Lupe* the latest dance.
Vince sent *her* a dozen roses.

A noun or pronoun used as the object of a preposition is in the objective case.

Tracy rode her bike around the *town.*
Claire knew the roses were from *him.*

A noun used as an adverbial objective is in the objective case.

The rescue squad hiked ten *miles.*

A noun used as an objective complement is in the objective case.

The city elected Mr. Daley *mayor.*

A noun used as a cognate object is in the objective case.

The ballet corps danced my favorite *dance.*

Possessive Case

A noun that expresses possession, ownership, or connection is in the possessive case.

To form the singular possessive, add *'s* to the singular form of the noun.

judge   judge's decision

To form the plural possessive of nouns ending in *s,* add the apostrophe only.

musicians   musicians' instruments

To form the possessive plural of nouns that do not end in *s,* add *'s.*

children   children's

Proper names ending in *s* usually form the possessive case by adding *'s.*

Mr. Sarkis's restaurant

In compound nouns the *'s* is added to the end of the word.

brother-in-law's stereo system

If two or more nouns are used together to indicate separate ownership, the *'s* is used after each noun.

We enjoyed reading Erin's and Masashi's stories.

If two or more nouns are used together to indicate joint ownership, the *'s* is used after the last noun only.

We are sleeping over at Don and Judith's home.

CLAUSES

A clause is a part of a sentence containing a subject and a predicate.

A principal, or independent, clause is one that expresses a complete thought.

A subordinate, or dependent, clause is one that does not express a complete thought and cannot stand alone.

Adjectival Clauses

An adjectival clause is a subordinate clause used as an adjective.

The storyteller told us a story *that was fascinating.*

Adverbial Clauses

An adverbial clause is a subordinate clause used as an adverb. Adverbial clauses are usually introduced by subordinate conjunctions. These clauses may tell time, place, degree, manner, cause, or purpose.

You may go to the dance *when your room is clean.*

Noun Clauses

A noun clause is a subordinate clause used as a noun.

That Mary would visit is Grandmother's wish.

COGNATE OBJECTS

A cognate object is a noun that repeats the meaning of and closely resembles the verb of which it is the object.

The fans cheered a *cheer* that could be heard all over town.

CONJUNCTIONS

A conjunction is a word used to connect words, phrases, or clauses in a sentence.

Coordinate Conjunctions

A coordinate conjunction connects words, phrases, or clauses of equal rank. The most common coordinate conjunctions are *and, or, nor, but,* and *yet.*

Correlative Conjunctions

Correlative conjunctions are coordinate conjunctions used in pairs. The most frequently used correlative conjunctions are *neither/nor, either/or, not only/but also,* and *both/and.*

Subordinate Conjunctions

A subordinate conjunction connects clauses of unequal rank. Some common subordinate conjunctions are *after, as soon as, before, because, in order that, unless,* and *so that.*

DIRECT OBJECTS

The receiver of the action of the verb is the direct object.

The direct object of a verb may be determined by placing *whom* or *what* after the verb.
The coach chose *Ken* to play.
The eighth graders planned a *dance*.

GENDER

Gender of a noun is that quality by which sex is distinguished. There are three genders: masculine, feminine, and neuter.

GERUNDS

A gerund is a verb form ending in *ing* that has the properties of a verb and a noun and is used as a noun.

Studying takes patience.

Gerund Phrases

A gerund phrase consists of the gerund and its complements and modifiers.

The lifeguard's job is *watching the swimmers.*

INDIRECT OBJECTS

The object to whom or for whom something is done is called the indirect object.

The prepositions *to* or *for* can usually be placed before the indirect object without changing the meaning of the sentence.
The flight attendant gave *the passengers* a snack.

INFINITIVES

An infinitive is a verb form, usually preceded by *to*, that has the properties of a verb and the properties of a noun, an adjective, or an adverb. An infinitive does the work of a noun, an adjective, or an adverb.

To eat ice cream is Kaitlyn's greatest pleasure. (noun)
Kaitlyn has ice cream *to eat.* (adjective)

Infinitive Phrases

An infinitive phrase consists of the infinitive and its complements and modifiers.

Split Infinitives

A split infinitive occurs when a word or a group of words comes between *to* and the rest of the infinitive. Try to avoid split infinitives.

Avoid: Sonja learned to smoothly skate on the ice.
Better: Sonja learned to skate smoothly on the ice.

INTERJECTIONS

An interjection expresses some strong or sudden emotion.

Hooray! I'm going to be in the play.

MOODS

Mood or mode is the attribute or quality of a verb that denotes the manner in which the action, the being, or the state of being is expressed.

Imperative Mood

The imperative mood is used to express a command in the second person. A mild command often takes the form of an entreaty or a request. The subject of the verb is often not expressed and is understood to be *you.*

Fly this plane to London.

Indicative Mood

The indicative mood is used to state a fact, to deny a fact, or to ask a question.

This airplane *flies* nonstop to London.

The progressive form of the indicative mood denotes an action as going on or in progress.

This airplane *is flying* nonstop to London.

The emphatic form of the indicative mood gives emphasis to the verb.

This airplane *does fly* nonstop to London.

The potential form of the indicative mood is used to express permission, possibility, ability, necessity, or obligation by using the auxiliary verbs *may, might, can, could, must, should,* and *would.*

This airplane *might fly* nonstop to London.

Subjunctive Mood

The subjunctive mood generally expresses a wish or desire, an uncertainty, or a condition contrary to fact. The subordinate conjunctions *if, as if, provided, though, lest, whether, unless,* and some potential auxiliaries sometimes introduce a verb in the subjunctive mood.

If the airplane *were flying* nonstop to London, I'd be on it.

NOUNS

A noun is a name word. The qualities of a noun are case, gender, number, and person.

Case is that quality of a noun that shows its relation to some other word or words in the sentence. There are three cases: nominative, possessive, and objective.

Gender is that quality of a noun by which sex is distinguished. There are three genders: masculine, feminine, and neuter.

Number is the quality of a noun that denotes whether it refers to one person, place, or thing (singular number) or more than one (plural number).

Person is the quality of a noun through which the speaker (first person), the one spoken to (second person), or the one spoken about (third person) is indicated.

Abstract Nouns

An abstract noun expresses a quality, a condition, or an action apart from any object or thing.

beauty   truthfulness   behavior

Collective Nouns

A collective noun denotes a group of persons, animals, or things considered as one.

team   herd   bunch

Common Nouns

A common noun names any one of a class of persons, places, or things.

readers   province   star

Concrete Nouns

A concrete noun names a person, a place, or a thing that can be seen or touched.

Most nouns are concrete nouns.

   mayor   valley   compact disc

Gender of Nouns

Gender is that quality of a noun by which sex is distinguished. There are three genders: masculine, feminine, and neuter.

The masculine gender denotes the male sex.

   brother   nephew

The feminine gender denotes the female sex.

   niece   queen

The neuter gender denotes things that have no sex.

   hair   house

Some nouns may be taken as either masculine or feminine.

   child   doctor   manager

Some nouns in certain occupations are now used for both genders.

   firefighter   mail carrier   actor

Noun Clauses

A noun clause is a subordinate clause used as a noun.

That Mary would visit is Grandmother's wish.

Proper Nouns

A proper noun names a particular person, place, or thing.

   Michael Jordan   Isle of Man   World Trade Center

NUMBER

Number is the quality of a noun or a pronoun that denotes whether it refers to one person or thing (singular number) or more than one (plural number).

PARTICIPLES

A participle is a word that does the twofold work of a verb and an adjective, and it limits a noun or a pronoun.

The waves *battering* the shore capsized our small boat.

A participle has voice and tense but it does not have person and number.

Dangling Participles

A dangling participle modifies no other word in the sentence.

Incorrect: Reading a book, the bus passed my stop.
Correct: Reading a book, I missed my bus.

Nominative Absolutes

In a nominative absolute, the participle and the noun it modifies are in an adverbial phrase independent of the rest of the sentence.

The tickets being so expensive, we decided not to go.

Participial Phrases

A participial phrase is introduced by a participle.

The person *riding the bike* lives near me.

PERSON

Person is that quality of a noun or a pronoun through which the speaker, the one spoken to, or the one spoken about is indicated.

First person denotes the speaker.
Second person denotes the one spoken to.
Third person denotes the one spoken about.

PHRASES

A phrase is a group of related words used as a single part of speech.

Gerund Phrases

A gerund phrase is introduced by a gerund.

Cory enjoys *riding his trail bike.*

Infinitive Phrases

An infinitive phrase is introduced by an infinitive.

To succeed in life is Joan's aim.

Participial Phrases

A participial phrase is introduced by a participle.

The person *riding the bike* lives near me.

Prepositional Phrases

A prepositional phrase is introduced by a preposition. The phrase may be an adjectival, an adverbial, or a noun phrase.

PREDICATES

The predicate tells something about the subject.

Our team *won.*

Complete Predicate

The complete predicate is the predicate with all its modifiers and objects or complements.

The horses from Kentucky *jump all the hurdles well.*

Compound Predicate

If the predicate consists of more than one verb, it is said to be a compound predicate.

Our team *played* and *won.*

PREPOSITIONS

A preposition is a word or a group of words placed before a noun, pronoun, phrase, or clause to show its relation to some other word.

Objects of a Preposition

The object of a preposition is a noun, a pronoun, or a group of words used as a noun.

Janna put the check into an *envelope* in spite of her *suspicion*.

Prepositional Phrases

A prepositional phrase is introduced by a preposition. The phrase may be an adjectival, an adverbial, or a noun phrase.

Most insects feed *on plants*. (adverbial)

PRONOMINALS

A pronominal is a pronoun that can also be used as an adjective. The common pronominals are possessive, interrogative, demonstrative, indefinite, and distributive.

PRONOUNS

A pronoun is a word used in place of a noun.

Compound Relative Pronouns

A compound relative pronoun is formed by adding *ever* or *soever* to *who, whom, which,* and *what.*

The commission honors *whoever* is deserving.

Demonstrative Pronouns

A demonstrative pronoun points out a definite person, place, or thing. The demonstrative pronouns are *this, that, these,* and *those.*

This and *these* denote objects that are near. *That* and *those* denote distant objects.

Are *these* your glasses?

That was an entertaining movie.

Distributive Pronouns

A distributive pronoun refers to each person, place, or thing separately. The distributive pronouns are *each, either,* and *neither.* The distributive pronouns are always singular and require singular verbs.

Each of us is expected to do his or her best work.

Indefinite Pronouns

An indefinite pronoun points out no particular person, place, or thing.

all   both   few   several   some

Intensive Pronouns

An intensive pronoun is used to emphasize a preceding noun or pronoun.

You *yourself* will be first in line.

Interrogative Pronouns

An interrogative pronoun is used in asking a question. The interrogative pronouns are *who, whom, whose, which,* and *what.* They are used in both direct and indirect questions.

Whom did you see at the beach?
Dad asked *what* we wanted for dinner.

Personal Pronouns

A personal pronoun denotes by its form the speaker, the person spoken to, or the person or the thing spoken about. Pronouns change form to denote case and number.

First person pronouns (the speaker) are *I, mine, me, we, ours,* and *us.*

Second person pronouns (the person spoken to) are *you* and *yours.*

Third person pronouns (the person, the place, or the thing spoken about) are *he, she, it, his, hers, its, him, her, they, theirs,* and *them.*

Compound Personal Pronouns

Compound personal pronouns are made by adding *self* or *selves* to certain forms of the personal pronouns.

myself   ourselves
himself   themselves

A compound personal pronoun must agree with its antecedent in person, number, and gender.

Thomas bought *himself* a new baseball.
The kayaking travelers tired *themselves.*

Compound personal pronouns are used as intensive or reflexive pronouns.

He *himself* went to the play. (intensive pronoun)
Cheryl knelt *herself* down. (reflexive pronoun)

Possessive Pronouns

A possessive pronoun denotes possession or ownership by the speaker, the person spoken to, or the person, place, or thing spoken about.

The possessive pronouns *mine, ours, yours, his, hers, its,* and *theirs* are sometimes called independent possessives.
Mine is untied.

The possessive pronouns *my, our, your, his, her, its,* and *their* modify nouns and are called possessive adjectives.
My shoe is untied.

Reflexive Pronouns

A reflexive pronoun is used as an object referring to and denoting the same person or thing as the subject.

You might cut *yourself* with a sharp knife.

Relative Pronouns

A relative pronoun does the work of a conjunction. A relative pronoun joins a subordinate clause to the antecedent in the principal clause.

Who, whom, and *whose* refer to persons.
> The speaker *who* talked for an hour is my boss.

Which refers to animals and things.
> The moon, *which* is full tonight, is covered by clouds.

That refers to persons, places, or things.
> The oak tree *that* stands in the meadow is very old.

What refers to things.
> Everyone knows *what* a hammer is.

SENTENCES

A sentence is a group of words expressing a complete thought. No sentence is complete without a subject and a predicate.

> Incomplete thought: beside the river
> Complete thought: The woman stood beside the river.

Complex Sentences

A complex sentence contains one principal clause and one or more subordinate clauses.

> A person who has ambition usually succeeds.

Compound Sentences

A compound sentence contains two or more independent clauses.

> We often sail the boat, but we never leave the harbor.

Compound-Complex Sentences

A compound-complex sentence contains two or more principal clauses and one or more subordinate clauses.

If you go home, I will go with you; however, June will stay here.

Declarative Sentences

A declarative sentence states a fact.

The river flows through the valley.

Exclamatory Sentences

An exclamatory sentence expresses strong or sudden emotion.

The river is so beautiful!

Imperative Sentences

An imperative sentence expresses a command.

Tell me where the river flows.

Interrogative Sentences

An interrogative sentence asks a question.

Where does the river flow?

Inverted Order in Sentences

Whenever the verb or an auxiliary verb is placed before its subject, a sentence is in the inverted order.

Around the corner came Sue's brother.

Natural Order in Sentences

Whenever the predicate verb follows the simple subject, a sentence is in the natural order.

Sue's brother came around the corner.

Simple Sentences

A simple sentence contains one subject and one predicate, either or both of which may be compound.

Our bicycle and our car have flat tires.

SUBJECTIVE COMPLEMENTS

A subjective complement completes the meaning of a subject after a linking verb and renames the subject.

Rita is my *neighbor.*
These apples are *sweet.*

SUBJECTS

The subject of a sentence names a person, place, or thing about which a statement is made.

Our *team* won.

Complete Subjects

The complete subject is the subject with all its modifiers.

The sleek horses from Kentucky jump hurdles well.

Compound Subjects

If the subject of a sentence consists of more than one noun or pronoun, it is said to be a compound subject.

Kukla and *Ollie* were puppets on early television.

TENSES

Tense is the quality of a verb that denotes the time of the action, the being, or the state of being.

Compound Tenses

Present perfect tense signifies action, being, or state of being completed or perfected in present time.

Billy *has thrown* the ball to the batter.

Past perfect tense signifies action, being, or state of being completed or perfected before some definite past time.

Billy *had thrown* the ball after time out was called.

Future perfect tense signifies action, being, or state of being that will be completed or perfected before some specified time in the future.

After the next pitch, Billy *will have thrown* the ball forty-two times.

Simple Tenses

Present tense signifies action, being, or state of being in present time.

The sisters *study* Latin.

Past tense signifies action, being, or state of being in past time.

The sisters *studied* Latin last year.

Future tense signifies action, being, or state of being in future time.

The sisters *will study* Latin next year.

In the passive voice the tense is shown by the auxiliary verb.

My report *is written.* (present tense)
My report *was written* last night. (past tense)
My report *will be written* in time for class. (future tense)

VERBALS

A verbal is a word derived from a verb and functioning as another part of speech. Three types of verbals are participles, gerunds, and infinitives.

VERBS

A verb is a word used to express action, being, or state of being.

Auxiliary Verbs

A verb used with the principal verb to form its voice, mood, and tense is called an auxiliary verb.

Cognate Verbs

A cognate verb is a verb whose object repeats the meaning implied by the verb itself.

Mother *washes* the *wash* on Mondays.

Intransitive Verbs

An intransitive verb has no receiver of its action.

The question *whom* or *what* after the verb will receive no answer because there is no receiver.

The street lights *glow* warmly.

Irregular Verbs

An irregular verb does not form its past and its past participle by adding *d* or *ed* to the present form.

Linking Verbs

A linking verb couples, or links, the subject with a noun, a pronoun, or an adjective.

The verb *be* in its various forms is the most common linking verb. Other verbs that may be used as linking verbs are *appear, become, continue, feel, grow, look, remain, seem, smell, sound,* and *taste.*

Principal Parts

The principal parts of the verb are the present, the past, and the past participle, because all other forms of the verb are determined from these.

Regular Verbs

A regular verb forms its past and its past participle by adding *d* or *ed* to the present form.

Transitive Verbs

A transitive verb expresses an action that passes from a doer to a receiver.

To determine the receiver of the action, ask the question *whom* or *what* after the verb.

Mr. Hale *discovered* the new comet with his telescope.

VOICE

Voice is the quality of a verb that shows whether the subject is the doer or the receiver of the action.

In the active voice the subject is the doer of the action.

The kitten *chased* the string.

In the passive voice the subject is the receiver of the action. Only transitive verbs are used in the passive voice.

The string *was chased* by the kitten.

WRITING

CAPITALIZATION AND PUNCTUATION

Apostrophes

Use an apostrophe to show possession.

The ostrich's egg is huge.

Use an apostrophe with *s* to show the plural of letters when the absence of the apostrophe would lead to confusion.

t's   *i*'s

Use an apostrophe to show the omission of a letter, letters, or figures.

I'll (I will)   Class of '99 (1999)

Capital Letters

Capitalize the first word in a sentence.

Capitalize the first word of every line of most poetry.

Capitalize the first word of a direct quotation.

Capitalize proper nouns and proper adjectives.

Capitalize titles of honor and respect when preceding the name.

Capitalize *north, south, east,* and *west* when they refer to sections of the country.

Capitalize all names referring to a deity, the Bible or parts of the Bible, and all other sacred books.

Capitalize the principal words in the titles of books, plays, poems, and works of art.

Capitalize the pronoun *I* and the interjection *O.*

Capitalize abbreviations when capitals would be used if the words were written in full.

Do not capitalize the seasons of the year.

Do not capitalize the articles, conjunctions, or prepositions in titles, unless they are the first words.

Do not capitalize the names of studies, unless they are derived from proper nouns.

Do not capitalize the words *high school, college,* and *university,* unless they are parts of the names of particular institutions.

Do not capitalize the word *god* or *gods* when referring to mythology.

Colons

Use a colon after the salutation of a business letter.

Dear Ms. Lee:

Use a colon before a list or enumeration of items.

Bring the following school supplies: pencils, erasers, pens, paper, and notebook.

Use a colon before a long direct quotation.

Commas

Use a comma to separate words or groups of words in a series.

Use a comma to set off parts of dates, addresses, and geographical names.

Use a comma to separate independent elements and words of direct address.

Use a comma after the salutation in a social letter and after the complimentary close in all letters.

Use a comma to set off an appositive that is not part of the noun or is not restrictive.

Use a comma to set off short direct quotations and the parts of a divided quotation unless a question mark or an exclamation point is required.

Use a comma to separate nonrestrictive phrases and clauses from the rest of the sentence.

Use a comma after long introductory phrases and clauses, and when it is needed to make the meaning clear.

Use a comma to set off a parenthetical expression; that is, a word or a group of words inserted in the sentence as a comment or an explanatory remark that is not necessary to the thought of the sentence.

Use a comma to separate the clauses of a compound sentence connected by the conjunctions *and, but, or, nor,* and *yet.* If the clauses are short and closely connected, the comma may be omitted.

Dashes

Use a dash to indicate a sudden change of thought.

Mr. Malarkey is odd—in a nice sort of way.

Exclamation Points

Use an exclamation point at the end of an exclamatory sentence or after an exclamatory word, phrase, or clause.

Hyphens

Use a hyphen to divide a word at the end of a line whenever one or more syllables are carried to the next line.

Many facts can be found on the Internet if you know where to look.

Use a hyphen in compound numbers and to separate the parts of some compound words.

twenty-one   self-respect   mother-in-law

Periods

Use a period at the end of a declarative or an imperative sentence. Use a period after an abbreviation and an initial.

Question Marks

Use a question mark at the end of a question.

Quotation Marks

Use quotation marks before and after every direct quotation and every part of a divided quotation.

Philip said, "There is going to be an election."
"Philip," Harry asked, "when will the election be held?"

Use quotation marks to enclose titles of stories, poems, magazine articles, newspaper articles, television shows, and radio programs.

Semicolons

Use a semicolon to separate the independent clauses of a compound sentence when they are not separated by a coordinate conjunction.

The sand was firm and not too wet; it was perfect for building sand castles.

Use a semicolon to separate the independent clauses of a compound sentence that are connected by such words as *nevertheless, moreover, therefore, then,* and *thus.*

Use a semicolon before *as* and *namely* when these words introduce an example or an illustration.

The city provides two kinds of services; namely, snow removal and garbage pickup.

Use a semicolon to separate the members of a series when a comma alone would not separate them clearly.

For dinner we prepared stuffed grape leaves, a Greek dish; chili, a Texas dish; and éclairs, a French pastry.

Index

Steps in THE WRITING PROCESS are set in capitals for easy reference.

Index

Index

Index

Acknowledgments

11–17 Excerpt from *Anastasia's Album* by Hugh Brewster. Copyright © 1996, Hyperion/Madison Press Books.

177 "Dreams," from *Collected Poems* by Langston Hughes. Copyright © 1994 by the Estate of Langston Hughes. Reprinted by permission of Alfred A. Knopf, Inc.

178 "All the World's a Stage," from *As You Like It* by William Shakespeare. Copyright © 1952 by Encyclopaedia Britannica, Inc. Published by The Great Books of the Western World.

179 "Southbound on the Freeway" by May Swenson. Reprinted with the permission of Simon & Schuster Books for Young Readers, an imprint of Simon & Schuster Children's Publishing Division from *The Complete Poems to Solve* by May Swenson. Copyright © 1963 by May Swenson.

182 "The Sea-Gull" from *Verses From 1929 On* by Ogden Nash; first appeared in *Harper's Bazaar*. By permission of Little, Brown and Company.

182 "The Toaster," from *Laughing Time: Collected Nonsense* by William Jay Smith. Copyright © 1990 by William Jay Smith. Reprinted by permission of Farrar, Straus & Giroux, Inc.

183 "The Garden Hose" by Beatrice Janosco. Reprinted by permission.

186–87 "Hungry Mungry" from *Where the Sidewalk Ends: The Poems and Drawings of Shel Silverstein*. Copyright © 1974 by Evil Eye Music, Inc. Reprinted by permission of HarperCollins Publishers, Inc.

189–90 "Foul Shot" by Edwin A. Hoey. Copyright © 1962 by Field Publications. Published by *Read Magazine*.

191 "Hark! Hark!" from *The Tempest* by William Shakespeare is in the public domain.

192 "Cheers" from *It Doesn't Always Have to Rhyme* by Eve Merriam. Copyright © 1964, 1992 by Eve Merriam. By permission of Marian Reiner.

192–93 "Jabberwocky," by Lewis Carroll from *The Complete Illustrated Works of Lewis Carroll*. Copyright © 1982. Published by Chancellor Press.

242–43 "When Dawn Comes to the City" from *Selected Poems of Claude McKay*. Copyright © 1981 by Twayne Publishers, a division of G. K. Hall & Co., Boston.

244 "Football," from *Walt Mason, His Book* by Walt Mason. Copyright © 1916 by Barse & Hopkins. Used by permission of Grosset & Dunlap, Inc., a division of Penguin Putnam Inc.

245 "Some People," from *Poems* by Rachel Field. Copyright © 1957 by Macmillan Publishing Company. Reprinted with permission of Simon & Schuster Books for Young Readers, an imprint of Simon & Schuster Children's Publishing Division.

246 "Swift Things Are Beautiful," from *Away Goes Sally* by Elizabeth Coatsworth. Copyright © 1934 by Macmillan Publishing Company; copyright renewed © 1962 by Elizabeth Coatsworth Beston. Reprinted with the permission of Simon & Schuster.

247 From "Mediterranean Beach, Day After Storm" in *Selected Poems 1923-1975* by Robert Penn Warren. Copyright © 1966 by the author. Published by Random House, Inc.

280 Sample entry from *Readers' Guide to Periodical Literature*, November 1997, Volume 97, page 832. Copyright © 1997 by The H. W. Wilson Company. Material reproduced with permission of the publisher.

492 Excerpt from *Pilgrim at Tinker Creek* by Annie Dillard. Copyright © 1974 by Annie Dillard. Reprinted by permission of HarperCollins Publishers, Inc.

All attempts possible have been made to contact author and publisher for cited works in this book.

Art & Photography

Cover Paul E. Rendel, *Soaring in the Rockies*. Used by permission of Paul E. Rendel, Pittsburgh, PA.

8–9 Umberto Boccioni, *Dynamism of A Cyclist*. Scala/Art Resource, NY.

11–14, 17 Beinecke Rare Book and Manuscript Library, Yale University.

261 Rockwell Kent, from *Moby Dick* by Herman Melville. Cassell & Co., Ltd., 1930.

286–87 Abraham Ortelius, *Map of the Pacific, Theatrum Orbis Terrarum*. The Huntington Library, Art Collections and Botanical Gardens, San Marino, CA/SuperStock.

Photographs: Adobe Image Library, 68, 402. **CLEO Photography,** 172, 340. **Digital Stock,** 356. **PhotoDisc, Inc.,** 3(T), 4(T), 21, 32, 36, 38, 41, 43(B), 44(T), 46(B), 53, 55, 70, 75, 78, 96, 102, 107, 113, 120, 122, 124, 136, 137(B), 144, 147(B), 149, 151, 152(B), 157, 159, 161, 165, 168, 176, 190(B), 200, 210, 211, 212, 230, 232, 234, 236, 242, 244, 245, 246, 247, 258, 260, 267, 277, 278, 288, 310, 313, 326, 336, 337, 345, 346, 363, 372, 388, 399, 401, 404, 407, 408, 412, 415, 419, 420, 422, 423, 425, 432, 439, 442, 444, 448, 449, 458, 463, 465(T), 475, 476, 477, 484, 504, 509(T), 510, 511(B), 512, 515(B), 516. **Skjold Photographs,** 488.

Illustrations: Mary Lynn Blasutta, 3(B), 6(BR), 45, 79(BR), 83, 110, 128, 146, 154(T), 187, 289, 292, 311, 334, 342, 349, 427(T), 441, 446(T), 451. **Susan Blubaugh,** 46(T), 517(B). **Nan Brooks,** 79(TL), 291. **Ted Carr,** 2(M), 4(MR), 6(BL), 117, 129, 223, 227, 233, 235, 240(TL), 298(B), 299(T), 304, 308, 316, 324, 329, 426, 452, 460, 462(T). **Ralph Creasman,** 7(T), 39, 49(B), 71, 103, 135, 147(T), 155, 173, 191, 213, 237, 263, 290(B), 293, 378, 379, 393, 414, 450, 452, 465(B), 485. **David A. Cunningham,** 5(T), 63, 160, 162, 169, 240(BL), 275, 299(B), 314, 370, 406, 445, 462(B), 492, 508, 509(B). **Pat Dypold,** 4(ML), 44(B), 174, 262, 270, 272, 273, 317, 318, 319, 437(T), 454(L), 467, 478. **Kerry Gavin,** 131. **Jean Cassels Helmer,** 2, 7(B), 72, 73, 89, 125, 177, 192, 328, 350, 358, 437(B), 446(B), 447, 507. **Cynthia Hoffman,** 1(T), 34, 42, 54, 85, 87, 100, 106, 123, 150, 152(T), 153, 216, 251(R), 390. **Paul Hoffman,** 181, 243, 371. **Mary Jones,** 6(M), 7(M), 61, 80, 81, 91, 115, 133, 163, 201, 302, 351, 360, 384, 391, 416, 490, 501, 502. **G. Brian Karas,** 5(M), 183, 239, 281, 343, 353, 418, 429, 471(T), 474, 479. **Carl Kock,** 1(B), 5(BL), 40, 43(T), 47, 48, 49(T), 50, 51, 56, 59, 66, 79(TR), 84, 92, 93, 97, 98, 111, 126, 130, 148, 154(M,B), 156, 158, 164, 175, 178, 182, 184(B), 189, 190(T), 195, 198, 203, 221, 222, 224, 241, 248, 249, 251(L), 256, 264, 269, 276(B), 279, 290(T), 295, 298(T), 300, 303, 305, 306, 307, 315, 323, 325, 327, 330, 331, 335, 344, 352, 357, 359, 361, 364, 366, 368, 369, 373, 376, 377, 381, 383, 385, 386, 387, 389, 394, 403, 405, 409, 417, 421, 427(B), 428, 430, 436, 438, 440, 454(T), 455, 456, 459, 464, 470, 471(B), 480, 481, 483, 489, 491, 493, 494, 495, 496, 497, 498, 499, 500, 505, 506, 513, 517(T). **Laura Lydecker,** 461. **Eileen Mueller Neill,** 3(M), 184(T), 217, 220, 294, 296, 348, 354, 362, 374, 375, 410, 411, 468, 469. **Robert Post,** 22, 515(T). **Publishers Resource Group,** 10, 11–19 (border art), 23, 14?, 205, 268, 276(T). **Phil Renaud,** 1(M), 44(M), 52, 60, 185, 207, 332. **William Seabright,** 4(B), 322. **Slug Signorino,** 5(BR), 57, 79(BL), 109, 137(T), 179, 180, 188, 250, 271, 380, 435, 47? 511(T). **Carl Whiting,** 6(T), 400, 424, 466, 473.